The Debt Threat

D0306401

The Debt Threat

The Dangers of High Real Interest Rates for the World Economy

TIM CONGDON

Basil Blackwell

British Library Cataloguing in Publication Data

Congdon, Tim
    The debt threat: the dangers of high
    real interest rates for the world economy.
    1. Economic conditions. Effects of high
    interest rates
    I. Title
    332.8'2

    ISBN 0–631–15953–3
    ISBN 0–631–15954–1 Pbk

Library of Congress Cataloging in Publication Data

Congdon, Tim.
    The debt threat: the dangers of high real interest rates for the
world economy/Tim Congdon.
    p. cm.
    Bibliography: p.
    ISBN 0–631–15953–3. ISBN 0–631–15954–1 (pbk.):
    1. Debt. 2. Interest rates. I. Title.
HG3701.C596 1988
336.3'435—dc19   88–5037

Typeset in 10 on 12pt Times
by Cambrian Typesetters, Frimley, Surrey.
Printed in Great Britain by
T J Press Ltd, Padstow, Cornwall

Contents

CONTENTS

Foreword

The themes of this book are a response to the events of the 1980s. The ideas themselves are not new, although they are presented here in a new and perhaps unexpected way. My hope is that the book will bring more attention to the problems created by high real interest rates. Its aim is to encourage governments in all countries to choose policies, particularly fiscal and tax policies, which will keep real interest rates at moderate levels. (It should be noted that this is emphatically *not* a recommendation that interest rates be held down artificially by arbitrary official restrictions.) Because the intention is mainly to influence the public debate about economic issues it has been written at a fairly popular level. I will be disappointed if regular readers of, say, *The Financial Times* and *The Wall Street Journal* find anything which is technical, obscure, and difficult to understand.

But I also hope that academic economists will find the book of interest. It needs to be said that, although business magazines and newspapers have provided me with much of my material (as will be clear from the list of sources), the key ideas were originated in academic circles. Perhaps the starting-point of modern discussion about the growth of debt was a paper by the American economist Professor Evesey Domar in 1944, which recognized the vital importance of the relationship between interest rates and growth rates. More specifically, it argued that – with the low interest rates of 2 or 3 per cent then prevailing – reasonably high economic growth would prevent the American national debt becoming too burdensome. This was all that economists had to know about debt for most of the post-war period, since real interest rates were much beneath growth rates – in both developed and developing countries – in the 1950s, 1960s, and 1970s. But in 1981 real dollar interest rates rose abruptly to levels way above sustainable economic growth rates. In October 1982, at a conference in Tokyo organized by the Bank of Japan, Professor Albert Ando gave a seminal paper which highlighted the dangers for American fiscal policy of the changed situation. The runaway growth of American public debt soon became a talking-point among economists in Britain, not least because some commentators began flirting with Reagan-style tax cuts and recommended them to the Chancellor of the Exchequer, Mr Nigel Lawson, in 1984.

My interest in public debt began in the mid-1970s, when I was anxious about the implications of very large UK budget deficits for inflation and the stability of financial markets. I wrote several articles about debt interest and 'crowding out' (see page 84 for an explanation of this term) in *The Times* in 1975 and 1976. The Ando paper and the British debate about supply-side economics gave a new stimulus. In 1984 I had a weekly column in *The Times* business section. In a number of articles, I developed the argument that high real interest rates greatly increased the risk that fiscal reflation would lead to an explosive increase in public debt. It was a particularly persuasive criticism of the then-fashionable recommendation of large tax cuts and a higher budget deficit. This drew me on to an analysis of the long-run conditions for sustainability in fiscal policy, which reinforced my awareness of the pivotal importance of the relationship between interest rates and the growth rate of borrowers' income. In particular, I realized that – when interest rates are much above the growth rate of incomes – borrowers can slide into a debt trap where the accumulation of interest charges results in unsustainable debt growth.

In 1983 and 1984 I was also watching the debt problems of the Third World closely, since the possibility of outright default or repudiation seemed quite serious. It was soon clear that the developing countries' financial difficulties were another example of the debt trap. The relationship between the interest rates on their external debt and the growth rates of their exports was critical to their long-run solvency, just as that between the interest rate on domestic debt and the growth rate of national income was fundamental to the outlook for American public debt. The point was the focus of a paper given by the Brazilian economist Mario Simonsen to a conference arranged by the Institute for International Economics in Washington in September 1984.

Much recent stockbroker research in the USA has been concerned with the rapid growth in consumer debt and in the ratio of all non-financial debt to national income (known, more briefly, as the debt/income ratio and discussed in the Introduction). I worked in the London stockbroking firm of L. Messel & Co. in the early 1980s, where this kind of research frequently appeared on my desk. It was natural, since I was thinking about the public debt problem in the USA and the external debt problem in the Third World at the same time, to apply the debt trap idea to an explanation of the behaviour of the American debt/income ratio. As far as I am aware, the importance of the relationship between interest rates and the growth rate of the US economy to the behaviour of private debt has had little academic attention. It is this omission – and a more widespread failure to see the interdependence of the world's contemporary debt problems – which provides part of the justification for writing *The Debt Threat*. There is (I believe) no other book which so single-mindedly identifies high real interest rates as the culprit for the dilemmas of debt control which confront the world's economic policy-makers today.

In late 1986 I submitted evidence on 'High real interest rates and the debt crisis' to an inquiry on international credit and capital markets being carried out by the Treasury and Civil Service Committee of the House of Commons. The evidence emphasized that the apparently separate issues of rising American public debt, unmanageable sovereign debt in the Third World, and growing private debt in the USA were all interconnected, and pointed an accusatory finger at high real interest rates. This book is essentially an expansion of that evidence.

Most of the book was completed in August 1987. Much has happened since then and several of the facts, and some of the judgements, are now out-of-date. However, I decided not to revise the text, since it would be impossible for such a topical book to be fully up-to-the-minute. Once one set of revisions was finished (which might take two months), the world would have moved on and another set of revisions would be necessary.

I have had help from many people in preparing this book. I would like to acknowledge the comments of David Hale, Christopher Huhne, Richard O'Brien, John Porter, and Martin Wolf who read some or all of earlier drafts. I would also like to thank Andrew Dean of the OECD in Paris for alerting me to some of the OECD's excellent research on public debt issues; Hector Luisi of the Inter-American Development Bank for letting me see some of the IDB's estimates of resources flows to and from Latin America; and Dr Allen Sinai and his team for statistics on the ratio of non-financial debt to gross national product in the USA. Of course, none of the above are necessarily in agreement with the arguments presented here and responsibility for remaining errors lies solely with the author. Shearson Lehman kindly gave me enough leisure in the summers of 1986 and 1987 to write the book, and I would like to thank them as well. Finally, I would like to thank René Olivieri of Basil Blackwell for his encouragement and understanding, and my secretary, Miss Grace Graham, for helping so cheerfully with some of the chores which are inevitable in a work of this kind.

Tim Congdon

Introduction:
the Central Argument

I

This book is self-consciously and deliberately alarmist. But it is best to begin by stating the limits of its ambition. Its purpose is not to predict the end of the world, the breakdown of Western civilization or even the disintegration of the international financial system. Its aim is instead to highlight a problem which began six or seven years ago, is still deteriorating and, unless something is done, will soon cause many books to be written on the impending disintegration of the international financial system, the imminent breakdown of Western civilization and countless other horrors.

The problem is the explosive growth of debt in all its forms in most of the developed nations and the overwhelming majority of developing countries. Of course, the existence of debt and the tendency for debt to grow through time are not new. Evidence of legally enforceable debt contracts in ancient Egypt and Assyria has been found by archaeologists. A banking system, which we tend to regard as modern man's method of registering and settling debts, operated in an advanced form two millennia ago in Ptolemaic Egypt. It arranged the payment of taxes by farmers, cleared private debts and had numerous branches subordinate to a central state bank. Sometimes, perhaps to ensure that due respect was paid to temporal as well as spiritual obligations, these branches were located next to temples.[1]

Indeed, some economists have argued that the growth of financial systems and the accompanying increase in debt contribute to material progress. When industrialists can borrow on well-developed capital markets, they can assemble the resources to create large companies and exploit economies of scale; when businesses have ready access to a flexible banking system, they can use short-term loan facilities to tide them over temporary interruptions to cash flow, enabling them to plan their long-term investments with confidence. Professor Goldsmith of

Yale University, who has studied the historical patterns of financial evolution in many countries, believes that improvements in productivity and living standards are related to a long-run trend for financial business to increase more rapidly than national output. He has suggested that the 'existence of clearly different paths of financial development is doubtful. The evidence now available is more in favour of the hypothesis that there exists only one major path of financial development.' On that path both financial assets and debt rise faster than national income.[2]

Adam Smith, the founder of modern economics, appreciated the benefit that efficient banking organizations could bring to an economy. In a neglected passage in *The Wealth of Nations*, written in the early 1770s, he mentioned reports that

> the trade of the City of Glasgow doubled in about fifteen years after the first erection of the banks there; and that the trade of Scotland has more than quadrupled since the first erection of the two public banks at Edinburgh . . . . Whether the trade, either of Scotland in general, or of the city of Glasgow in particular, has really increased in this proportion, during so short a period, I do not pretend to know . . . . That the trade and industry of Scotland, however, have increased very considerably during this period, and that the banks have contributed a good deal to this increase, cannot be doubted.[3]

The experience of mid-eighteenth-century Scotland suggests that it may not have been altogether accidental that Ptolemaic Egypt was one of the most prosperous societies of antiquity.

Why, then, should there be such concern about the rapid increase in debt in recent years? Why have banks, including some of the largest and most reputable in the world, been criticized as the prime culprits for a debt crisis which is said to have impoverished whole continents? Why is it necessary to write a book warning about processes which, in some historical contexts, appear to have been largely benign? The answer is that a sharp distinction needs to be drawn between increases in debt which are sustainable and increases in debt which are unsustainable. Increases in debt are unsustainable when the borrower, sooner or later, will find himself unable to repay the lender in full. One of the most obvious characteristics of debt is that once it begins to run out of control the loss of control becomes self-feeding. Retribution for omissions in the proper management of debt can therefore be disproportionate to the initial sins of commission. Perhaps the most telling illustration of this point is the collapse in economic activity in the USA after the Great Crash of 1929. As a nation can owe nothing to itself, there is something absurd in the idea of banks and factories closing down because its citizens cannot pay their debts to each other. But that was the tragedy the USA experienced in the Depression of the early 1930s. Between 1930 and 1933 9,000 banks closed their doors, while industrial production fell by 40 per cent and unemployment increased to almost 25 per cent of the labour force.

The causes of the Great Crash and the Depression remain a matter for dispute. But one aspect of the American economy in those years was without precedent: a sudden and massive rise in the ratio of debt to national income. As companies and individuals found themselves unable to service this debt, they could not repay their bank loans. Banks had to suspend operations, causing a general contraction in credit and intensifying the slump in demand and output.

In order to pin down more precisely the meaning of an unsustainable increase in debt we shall use the concept of the ratio of debt to national income extensively. Debt in this context includes all borrowings by non-financial institutions where there is an obligation to repay at least principal. In practice, most debt also has an interest element and – as we shall see – it is this element which is almost invariably the troublemaker. Equity liabilities to shareholders are not part of the definition because it is recognized that their value may fall to nil without infringing any contractual understanding, while debt owed by financial institutions is not included because these institutions have a financial assets on the other side of the balance sheet and their net debt should therefore be very small. The debt/income ratio under consideration here is a macro concept, but in our discussion of its dynamics we shall frequently resort to micro illustrations.

A particular debt/income ratio is clearly sustainable if borrowers and lenders are well informed about their respective circumstances and borrowers are servicing their debts, with respect both to principal and interest, on time. If a certain ratio has been established for many years and debt is growing in line with rising income there is no need for anxiety about the increase in debt. Indeed, a gradual creep upwards in the ratio of debt to income is not necessarily dangerous. As societies advance, standards of education and literacy improve, company accounts become more detailed and commercial information of all kinds flows more freely and in greater quantity. These trends ease the appraisal of borrowers' creditworthiness and so debt/income ratios may rise without causing trouble.

However, improvements in credit appraisal do not permit the debt/income ratio to increase indefinitely. Most lenders want to have the assurance that their loans are backed not merely by the personal guarantee or the 'name' of the borrower but by solid physical things of recognized value. They want debt to be secured against tangible assets.

If a company's debt is growing because it is investing in buildings, plant and equipment, or if an individual's debt is growing because he has taken out a mortgage to buy a house, the new debts are evidently matched by such assets. In these circumstances there should not be a problem of unsustainability.

But there would be a problem if the debt/income ratio was rising and new debt lacked adequate collateral in the form of tangible assets. When debt is similar in value to, or somewhat exceeds, a nation's tangible assets, further increases in debt should not proceed more rapidly than increases in national income. Here is a powerful and general constraint on the incurral of debt.

Ideas developed by Goldsmith in his work on financial evolution give further insight into the question of unsustainability and allow some formalization of the discussion. He proposed the notion of a financial interrelations ratio (FIR), which is the quotient of financial assets and tangible assets.[4] (For example, if a nation has $1,000m of tangible assets and $1,250m of financial assets, its FIR has a value of 1.25.) It is not the same as the debt/income ratio, but it is related because financial assets must either be claims on tangible assets or be matched by debt. If the FIR exceeds unity, there must be some debt unmatched by tangible assets. As we have explained that there are limits to debt incurral without tangible collateral, there must also be an upper bound to the FIR.

That is exactly what Goldsmith discovered in his examination of the evidence from 20 countries for the last 300 years. In the most primitive societies, without strong rule of law or trust between citizens, the FIR may be very low, taking a value in an extreme case of only 0.1. As economies become richer and more mature, the FIR increases steadily – along 'the one major path of financial development' identified by Goldsmith – and in advanced industrial societies reaches a value of between 1 and 1¼. It then levels off. Very few countries have ever had FIRs in excess of 1¾ and, with one exception (Switzerland), the FIR has not been above 1½ on a continuous basis in any country. The highest FIR found by Goldsmith was 2.7 in Great Britain in 1939, but this appears to have been a freak due to the undervaluation of tangible assets in the depressed conditions of the 1930s. It seems, therefore, that the need to provide adequate collateral has in the past imposed a formidable obstacle to the expansion of debt.[5]

One further aspect of financial development should be mentioned. Although ratios of financial to tangible assets, and of debt to national income, do rise in the course of economic advance, they do so slowly. It is most unusual for debt to increase 2 or 3 per cent a year faster than national income in the long run. An increase of 2 or 3 per cent a year may not sound much, but because of compound interest 2 per cent maintained for a century would cause the debt/income ratio to rise seven times. A rise of 3 per cent a year would result in a 19-fold increase. It sounds inherently implausible that debt growth on this scale could be managed successfully. There is, in fact, no example in Goldsmith's work of a country which increased its FIR by almost 20 times in the 100 years to 1978. The FIR is not the same thing as the debt/income ratio, but we have suggested that the two concepts are related. If the FIR has never increased 20 times in a century, we can be reasonably certain that the debt/income ratio has never done so either.

We may conclude from our discussion that a nation's debt/income ratio can rise over time, but only up to the point at which debt is a finite proportion of the value of tangible assets and only by at most 1 or 2 per cent a year in the long run. If either or both of these conditions are broken, the growth in debt is unsustainable. These conditions are demanding. It is probably not an exaggeration to say that, for an advanced industrial country which already has a financial interrelations ratio greater than unity, the growth rate of debt has to be restricted over the medium term to the growth rate of national income. If it is much faster, debt problems are likely to emerge. The purpose of the coming chapters is to describe and analyse the various forms that these problems may take.

II

But, before we can examine the many different varieties of debt problem, we need to ask whether there are any general determinants of the growth of debt. Perhaps because debt enables the borrower – at least for a time – to enjoy something for nothing, the subject invites moral homilies. David Hume, the eighteenth-century Scottish philosopher, not known for making extravagant judgements, considered government borrowing not just practically unwise but a sign of human inadequacy. In his view, 'there is a strange supineness, from long custom, creeped into all ranks of men, with regard to public debts, not unlike what divines so vehemently complain of with regard to their religious doctrines.' In the end, whenever a 'government has mortgaged all its revenues, . . . it necessarily sinks into a state of languor, inactivity and impotence.'[6] There may be much good sense in these remarks, but unfortunately they do not give analytical leverage on the questions at issue. The growth rate of debt varies through time and there is no simple way of relating these variations to changes in the degree of man's 'strange supineness'. In fact, the countless moral diatribes on this subject over the centuries contribute little to understanding because the follies of human nature cannot be measured in a way readily amenable to economic reasoning. We have to be more scientific.

A natural approach is to consider the effect of interest rates on the growth of debt. The common-sense assumption is that the higher are interest rates, the slower will be the increase in debt. It seems obvious that the more expensive it is to have the use of borrowed money, the less people will want to borrow. In practice, the relationship between interest rates and debt is more complicated and paradoxical.

Strange as the thought may seem on first acquaintance, many debts are very old. The British national debt exemplifies the point in an extreme, but not misleading, way. As the British government has not repudiated any of its obligations since the Exchequer Stop of 1672, part of today's national debt is over 300 years old. Britain may be exceptional because of its long history of political stability and internal peace, but even a nation like Turkey – which has been dismembered out of recognition over the same 300-year period – can legitimately tell its creditors that it is servicing debts incurred by the Ottoman Empire. The debts may have been rescheduled and partially dishonoured on many occasions, but at least a small fraction of the original debt survives. Old debts are like old soldiers: they never die, but only fade away.

In general, and disturbing though it may be to common sense, relatively few debts are altogether extinguished at the first repayment date. Most debts are repaid, then renewed, and subsequently repaid and renewed many times. As this exercise becomes a pointless chore in some instances, the borrower may decide to issue perpetual debt with no specific repayment date envisaged. Indeed, the British government counts among its financial obligations some gilt-edged securities which are known in financial markets as 'irredeemable'. This is not – as might be thought – an open affront to its creditors, who are perfectly happy as long as they receive regular and punctual interest payments.

The purpose of emphasizing the longevity of debt is to show that the behaviour of debt in total depends more on what is happening to old debt than on decisions about new debt. It may be that the higher are interest rates, the less new debt is incurred. But the effect of higher interest rates on old debt is quite different. If a borrower has a loan with variable interest rates, an increase in interest rates implies an increase in interest charges. The higher interest charges will by themselves cause an *acceleration* in the growth of debt. Even with a fixed-rate loan, an increase in interest rates can result in faster debt growth. The reason is that, when the loan matures, the borrower faces the choice of renewal or repayment. If for some reason he opts for renewal, the growth of his debt will in future be quicker than it would have been at the previous lower level of interest rates. The message seems to be that the relationship between interest rates and debt growth is ambiguous. A rise in interest rates discourages the incurral of new debt, but it may cause old debt to expand more rapidly. The net effect on the growth of debt totals is uncertain.

In the previous section we suggested that debt growth is unsustainable in an advanced industrial nation when the debt/income ratio is rising at more than 1 or 2 per cent a year. The next step is therefore to introduce the debt/income ratio into our discussion of interest rates and debt growth. The pivot of our discussion – indeed, the centrepiece of the argument of this book – is the relationship between the interest rate and the growth rate of income.

To understand its significance we may outline a simple example. Suppose that a borrower is facing an interest rate above the growth rate of his income. Unless he makes an effort to service his loan, either by repaying some principal or meeting interest payments as they fall due, the loan increases every year by the addition of interest charges. If there is no debt servicing whatever, the growth rate of the debt is the interest rate. It follows that, because the interest rate is above the growth rate of income, debt increase faster than income and the debt/income ratio rises.

This is an extremely important and powerful result. As we shall see in coming chapters when we survey the evidence from many countries, it is the changed relationship between interest rates and income growth which is the root cause of the debt explosion of recent years. In the 1970s interest rates were beneath the growth rate of incomes and debt/ income ratios tended to fall; in the 1980s interest rates have been above the growth rate of incomes and debt/income ratios have, with few exceptions, increased.

The idea may benefit from some elaboration. It is clear that in the absence of debt servicing the debt/income ratio increases when the rate of interest is above the growth rate of a borrower's income. This outcome is not certain, however, if there is some debt servicing. If the borrower sets aside part of his income to pay a proportion of the interest, the debt/income ratio could rise, fall or remain stable. It depends on the size of the debt servicing. Obviously, if the borrower pays all the interest and his income is growing, the debt/income ratio must decline. (The details are discussed in a mathematical appendix.)

The only way that a borrower can make a debt service payment is to keep his expenditure on items other than interest lower than his income. In other words, he has to run a 'budget surplus'. (Note that this is not a traditional surplus concept, but one exclusive of interest.)[7] We have put the phrase 'budget surplus' in quotation marks here, because it seems a little peculiar to use it about an individual. But the line of reasoning we have developed in the last few pages is valid for any economic agent. It applies to companies, governments and countries as well as persons. When applied to governments, the words 'budget surplus' are, of course, altogether appropriate. But the term is sometimes serviceable in other contexts.

So far we have talked about the dynamics of the debt/income ratio of a particular borrower, but we said earlier that most attention would be focused on the debt/income ratio of a nation. How do we extend the argument to the national level? Let us leave the question of external debt to one side for the time being. Then, as a heuristic trick, we can divide a nation into the two categories of debtors and creditors. In practice, most economic agents have both debts and financial assets, but it simplifies exposition to regard debtors and creditors as quite separate. Evidently, if no one runs a budget surplus and interest rates are on average above the growth rate of national income, the liabilities of the debtors to the creditors must be increasing faster than national income and the debt/income must be rising. To the extent that debtors achieve budget surpluses, a brake is imposed on the increase in the debt/income ratio. But if they have budget deficits an extra twist is added to the spiral in the debt/income ratio. The broad conclusion is that debts will grow very rapidly in relation to national income when interest rates are in excess of the growth rate of income and when debtors are unable to live within their means.

The argument has the same structure if it is applied to external debt but, instead of thinking in terms of a 'budget surplus', we have to talk about the current account of the balance of payments. The increase in a country's external debt is driven, like an individual's, by two components – the addition of interest to the existing debt and the incurral of new debt. If there is exact balance on the non-interest transactions between the debtor country and its creditors, its external debt will grow faster than national income when the interest rate on the debt is above the growth rate of national income. An extra dimension is introduced by the possibility that the debt is expressed in terms of a foreign currency, as an adjustment then needs to be made for changes in the exchange rate. But the underlying logic of the problem is the same. A major influence on the ratio of external debt to income is again the relationship between interest rates and the growth rate.

Enough has been said to demonstrate that the dynamics of debt are conditioned by the relationship between the rate of interest and the rate of growth of borrowers' income. There is a frightening implication of this central theme. We have shown that, when the interest rate exceeds the growth rate of a borrower's income and the borrower fails to run a budget surplus, his debt/income ratio increases. Is there any limit to this tendency? The answer is that, as long as the two conditions relating to the interest rate/income growth mix and his budgetary position remain as assumed, there is no limit at all. The debt/income ratio increases indefinitely.

The borrower can soon find himself in a sad predicament. If he makes no effort to service his debt, interest is added to his old debts in the first year. In the second year, because his debt is larger, his interest payments are heavier. If he again does nothing about debt servicing, a large interest payment is added to his debt. In the third year, because his debt is larger again, his interest payments are even heavier than in the second year, and so on. The root of the trouble is that interest is charged not only on the loan principal but on the accumulating interest which is annexed to it over time. In due course, particularly in a world where nominal interest rates are 10 per cent or more, interest on the interest exceeds interest on the principal.

At first sight, this may seem improbable, not to say bizarre. But let us examine the consequences of 10 per cent interest rates more carefully. A little dexterity with a pocket calculator shows that a loan doubles after 7.27 years of 10 per cent interest rates. In other words, by that stage accumulated interest equals the principal and interest on the interest must equal interest on the principal. It is also clear that in subsequent years interest on the interest must exceed interest on the principal. Eventually the annual interest payment will become as large as the initial loan. In fact, this happens after slightly more than 24 years.

This tendency of interest charges to acquire a life of their own, to become a Frankenstein's monster no longer connected to the borrower's original purpose, is the cause of what we shall call 'the debt trap'. The debt trap is a situation in which, because interest rates exceed the growth of a borrower's income, his debt/income ratio is rising explosively. It is the compounding of interest which makes it so difficult to escape. While the levels of interest rates and income growth remain unfavourable, the only way a borrower can keep his debt position manageable is to cut his non-interest expenditure so that it is lower than his income. If he neglects to take austerity measures now, the debt/income ratio is higher in future. The austerity measures which then become required will be more costly and disagreeable because they have been postponed.

It is obviously very unfortunate to become enmeshed in the debt trap. The borrower's plight and the inevitability with which it worsens are so unsubtle and so ghastly that there seems to be a puzzle that anyone could be snared in this way. But, as we shall see, in the last few years the debt trap's many victims have included not only improvident individuals but also governments and countries.

It is not only the borrowers' behaviour that has to be explained. There is also a need to identify and rationalize the lenders' motives. When a borrower's debt/income ratio has risen to intolerable levels and he is evidently unable to service the debt meaningfully any more, the lender has to write off part of the debt. The loss falls on him as well as the borrower. Why is the lender so misguided as to keep on extending credit when the borrower's position is increasingly and manifestly untenable? Why does he not call a halt, refuse more money and restore a semblance of common sense? Why does he pretend that the realities of the borrower's inability to pay have not overwhelmed the fictions contained in the legal documents?

To understand how easy it is for both borrowers and lenders to enter the debt trap and then to remain its prisoners, we should recall our discussion of the sustainability of debt growth. We found that a rising debt/income ratio was not always a sympton of unsustainability. On the contrary, it is sometimes an associate of or even a motive force behind economic improvement. Equally critical is the constraint that the value of debts should not exceed that of tangible assets. When lenders extend credit, they take a view based not only on borrowers' potential for income growth, but also on the assets acting as collateral.

Indeed, banks have traditionally relied on asset backing to protect themselves against borrowers who fail to comply with the terms of loan agreements. Their practice is to ascertain the value of borrowers' assets and to restrict their lending to a proportion of that value. The ratio varies widely depending on the quality and saleability of the assets and on an assessment of each individual borrower's ability to generate cash, but it is typically 60 to 80 per cent of asset value. If a borrower's debt/income ratio is rising because of the burden of interest charges, the bank may nevertheless be well placed to ensure eventual repayment.

It has two layers of protection. First, there is the margin between the loan itself and the value of the assets. Secondly, and in the last 30 years of much greater importance, there is the tendency for asset values to increase. Banks feel particularly safe in an environment of constantly rising property prices, because property is the most common form of collateral for loans. It has the great merit that if a borrower decides to flee from his bank manager (by catching a plane to the Bahamas, emigrating to Costa Rica or something similar) he cannot physically detach the land from its soil or the bricks and mortar from their foundations and take them with him.

If a borrower makes no contribution to servicing his loans, but the assets which constitute his collateral are increasing in value in line with interest rates, his bankers may be perfectly content. They may not care even if his debt/income ratio is rising and, hence, his ability to service the debt from current receipts is deteriorating. As long as the collateral is ample cover for the loan, they should not lose any money. Their complacency about slippage in the borrower's debt/income position may be reinforced if they believe that the dip in his income or the strain of high interest rates on his debt-servicing capacity are temporary.

In fact, we see here why much of banking is merely the mechanical addition of interest to old loan principals and why bankers find nothing strange in the idea that loans do not need actually to be repaid. There may seem to be a wide gap between the conventional understanding of financial prudence and the actual forms of banking practice. But there is nothing sinister or alarming about this gap in a tranquil, prosperous world where asset values are increasing steadily over the years and providing bankers with ever better security. If bank managers have lived through a long period of appreciating asset values, they are likely to take a relaxed view of a rise in borrowers' debt/income ratios over a two- or three-year period. They have probably been through similar episodes of cyclical anxiety in the past, but in the end borrowers' circumstances have tended always to revive enough to stabilize or improve debt/income ratios. The banks have in any case, through such phases of short-term worry, had ample collateral to prevent them incurring serious loan losses.

But bankers cannot take the appreciation of asset values and recoveries from interruptions to their borrowers' cash flow for granted. They are not predestined and inevitable. In a lucid account of the antecedents to the banking failures of the early 1930s, Keynes remarked that banks allow for some fluctuation in asset values through the fixing of a 'margin' of collateral, but proceeded to ask

> . . . consider what happens when the downward change in the money value of assets within a brief period of time *exceeds* the amount of the conventional "margin" over a large part of the assets against which money has been borrowed. The horrible possibilities to the banks are immediately obvious. Fortunately, this is a very rare, indeed a unique event. For it had never occurred in the modern history of the world prior to the year 1931.

He concluded, correctly as we know in retrospect, that

> Modern capitalism is faced . . . with the choice between finding some way to increase money values towards their former figure, or seeing widespread insolvencies and defaults and the collapse of a large part of the financial structure; after which we should all start again . . . but having suffered a period of waste and disturbance and social injustice, and a general rearrangement of private fortunes and the ownership of wealth. Individually many of us would be "ruined", even though collectively we were much as before.[8]

The message here is that banks are unwise to tolerate deterioration in their borrowers' capacity to service debt when asset values have been falling and seem likely to continue falling until the safety margin on their collateral is altogether eliminated. But these matters are very subjective. It is one of banks' prime functions to finance their customers through short, finite periods of unsatisfactory cash flow, and such periods may often coincide with transient weakness in the property market, share prices and other asset values. As Keynes realized, most bankers – by the age they assume executive responsibilities – have seen many borrowers pass through every phase of financial sickness, only to be restored eventually to robust health. So 'lifelong practices . . . make them the most romantic and the least realistic of men'. Indeed, 'it is so much their stock-in-trade that their position should not be questioned, that they do not even question it themselves until it is too late'.[9]

Of course, he was exaggerating. But the exaggeration is instructive in helping us to understand why bankers – and financial institutions in general – are prepared not to call in loans when standard criteria of creditworthiness appear to have been violated. In particular, it gives us an explanation for banks' willingness to keep on adding interest to loans and to cause borrowers' debt/income ratios to increase when the probability of repayment is diminishing and appears to be rather slight.

The subjectivity of any loan assessment in the private sector is largely attributable, therefore, to the problems of valuing the assets which are supposed to constitute collateral. The difficulties are in one sense much less and in another much greater with public sector debt. They are less in that the government, almost by definition, is the most creditworthy borrower within any political unit. As the government can in principle extract taxes at will, its ultimate ability to pay – at least in terms of its own domestic currency – is much stronger than any other institution's. The difficulties are greater, however, because in practice there are constraints on the size of the government's debt in real terms and there is much uncertainty about the point at which these constraints become binding. The constraints are imposed because the taxes required to service the debt become so heavy that they undermine incentives and effort, reducing national income and destroying part of the tax base. To offset the loss of the tax base the government must again raise tax rates, but this further undermines incentives and erodes the tax base. The process is unstable and can culminate in confiscation, confrontation between citizens and the tax authorities, and ultimate ungovernability. The struggle for resources between government and governed charac- teristically takes the form of a rising price level, with the citizens subject to an effective 'inflation tax' as their money balances fall in real value.

Perhaps here is to be sought the motive for Hume's tirade on government borrowing and his rhetoric on its termination in 'a state of languor, inactivity and impotence'. Indeed, he went further, warning that the temptation to redirect funds earmarked for debt interest into current expenditure was ever-present and irresistible. It would lead to the 'natural death of public credit: for to this period it tends as naturally as an animal to dissolution'. He even talked about 'the violent death of public credit' when defeat in war extinguished a government's debt liability.[10] This may sound far-fetched, but even as recent and sophisticated a society as France in the 1930s was fractured and weakened by the obligation on taxpayers to meet the bondholders' claims. 'There can be no doubt that the huge French debt was the major cause of the political confusion and the industrial lethargy which hung like a pall over France for the five or six years before 1939.'[11]

The maximum feasible ratio of government debt to national income depends, then, on how far the community is prepared to tolerate high taxation. But tax tolerance is not easy to measure. In contrast with private sector debt, where the adequacy of loan collateral can be quantified, there is no simple formula for judging when government debt has become excessive. Moreover, its domestic creditors cannot readily call in the loans, sell the collateral and so limit their losses, because governments are more powerful than private citizens and can simply refuse to comply. In any case, most internal debts take the form of bonds with a specified maturity date. The government's foreign creditors may be able to take these steps, but – as we shall see in chapter 5 – the subject of sovereign debt default is extremely problematic.

III

Before we complete our central argument and relate it to the present debt problem, it may be helpful to recapitulate the main points so far. We have seen that, although a tendency for financial activities to grow faster than the economy as a whole is an aspect of economic development, this process seems to stop when a society has reached the level of industrial and financial sophistication we associate with the advanced Western countries. If the debt/income ratio in such a country starts to rise at more than 2 per cent a year, the situation is unsustainable and must eventually be halted. We have also suggested that the key determinant of the dynamics of the debt/income ratio is the relationship between interest rates and the rate of increase in national income. If interest rates are above the rate at which incomes are growing, borrowers can be caught in the debt trap, with interest charges cumulating explosively and wrecking their financial position beyond repair. Finally, we have recognized that creditors may fail to check the runaway growth in debt, from which they as well debtors must lose, not because of weakness of will or technical incompetence but because there are genuine problems in assessing when debt has become impossible to service.

In the discussion so far we have referred to the two key variables as 'the interest rate' and 'the growth rate of borrowers' income'. We could equally well talk in terms of the 'the real interest rate' and 'the growth rate in borrower's real income', where the nominal magnitudes are both adjusted by the inflation rate. At the national level the growth in real income is, of course, the same as the growth of output or gross domestic product (GDP).[12]

The reason for this shift in terminology is that it makes it easier to connect our ideas to the debt problem of today. Just as an increase in nominal interest rates caused trouble in our examples if it resulted in them being higher than the growth rate in nominal incomes, so an increase in real interest rates should cause trouble in any economy if real interest rates come to exceed the growth rate in real incomes. In most economies the underlying growth rate of output is fairly stable over long periods spanning several business cycles. It follows that large changes in real interest rates are likely to have profound repercussions on the behaviour of debt and on a nation's debt/income ratio. This point is critical because, at the beginning of the 1980s, a substantial and abrupt change in real interest rates occurred in the USA, which not only has the world's largest economy but is also able to affect business conditions in many other countries strongly. The extent of the change is indicated in table 1.

Real interest rates are measured here by the excess of prime rates over the change in the producer price index for finished goods. This measurement, like any other, is to some extent arbitrary. Ideally we want to compare how much a representative borrower has to pay for a loan with the increase in price level of all goods and services. However, the notion of a representative borrower is rather elusive as every borrower has his own special characteristics and prime rate – which is charged by US banks to their most creditworthy customers – seems the most sensible to use in this context. Other price indices – such as the deflator for gross national product (GNP) or the consumer price index – have advantages and disadvantages compared with the producer price index. But, if we measured real interest rates with, say, the commercial paper rate and the GNP deflator, we would identify the same underlying trends and tell more or less the same story. An important extra dimension is added, however, if we compare one of the bellwether interest rates with the price index of a selected group of products or products at different stages of processing. As we shall see later, in the

Table 1   The move to high real interest rates in the USA in the early 1980s

	Increase in US Producer prices, finished goods (%)	Prime rate charged by banks (%)	Implied real interest rate (%)
Average of five-year periods:			
1951–5	1.7	3.0	1.3
1956–60	1.9	4.2	2.3
1961–5	0.4	4.5	4.1
1966–70	2.9	6.7	3.7
1971–5	8.3	7.5	−0.7
1976–80	9.6	10.1	0.5
1980–5	3.6	13.3	9.4
Annual series:			
1971	3.1	5.7	2.5
1972	3.1	5.3	2.1
1973	9.1	8.0	−1.0
1974	15.3	10.8	−3.9
1975	10.8	7.9	−2.6
1976	4.4	6.8	2.3
1977	11.2	6.8	−3.9
1978	7.8	9.1	1.2
1979	11.1	12.7	1.4
1980	13.5	15.3	1.6
1981	9.2	18.9	8.9
1982	4.0	14.9	10.4
1983	1.6	10.8	10.0
1984	2.1	12.0	9.7
1985	0.9	9.9	8.9
1986	−1.4	8.3	9.8

Implied real rate is obtained from the formula

$$\text{real rate } (\%) \;=\; \left(\frac{\text{prime rate } (\%) + 100}{\text{increase in prices } (\%) + 100} - 1 \right) \times 100$$

There are some problems with rounding.

Source: *Economic Report of the President* (Washington: US Government Printing Office, 1986), tables B–61 and B–68

1980s commodity prices have not been keeping pace with the price of finished goods and services. This is the main reason that the financial plight of commodity-exporting debtor nations in the Third World has been more serious than that of most debtors in the American economy and that, within the USA, commodity producers have been in worst straits than other sectors.

Table 1 shows that, over most of the post-war period, real interest rates have been under 5 per cent. In the 1950s and 1960s they varied a little from one five-year period to the next and sometimes fluctuated considerably from year to year. Although the annual data are not given before 1971, it should be mentioned that the real interest rate changed by 10 per cent between 1951, when it was −6.3 per cent, and 1952, when it was 3.6 per cent. This sizeable swing was exceptional, reflecting the blip in inflation which was a by-product of the Korean War. Over the whole period there was a fair degree of stability in real interest rates at low or moderate levels.

The situation changed radically between 1979 and 1981, with the establishment of real interest rates of almost 10 per cent. The contrast with the late 1970s, when real interest rates were negligible, is stark; the suddenness and the extent of the change, a virtual 10 per cent upward shift in two years, has no precedent in the post-war period except for the Korean War episode; and, unlike that episode, it has not been quickly reversed. In the early and mid-1980s real interest rates in the USA averaged about 10 per cent, clearly the highest level over a sustained period since the war. Indeed, although occasional one- or two-year aberrations with real interest rates of 10 per cent or so can be found throughout American history, there is no previous example of such high real interest rates maintained over a quinquennium – except, ominously, in the early 1930s.

Has the change in interest rates in the early 1980s been reflected in the behaviour of the American debt/income ratio? Our argument has been that the debt/income ratio should tend to increase if real interest rates are above the growth rate of real incomes. As the growth rate of the US economy in the early and mid-1980s has been about 2 per cent, much less than the 10 per cent real interest rate, the debt/income ratio should have risen sharply. That is precisely what has happened. Over the 40 years to 1980 the debt/income ratio was impressively – indeed, remarkably – stable. It had a value of 1.35 – 1.45 in the late 1940s but tended to fall. In 1952 it stood at 1.27, but then crept upwards to 1.43 in late 1964. It hovered between 1.3 and 1.4 for the next 15 years and was just under 1.4 at the end of 1981. Since then it has risen significantly year by year. The details, and the conspicuousness of the change in trend after 1981, are shown in table 2 and figure 1. Strong emphasis

Table 2 The debt/income ratio in the USA: stability for 30 years to 1981 and the abrupt increase since then

	Debt owed by domestic non-financial sectors ($b)	GNP at annual rates ($b)	Debt/income ratio
1952	461.1	364.0	1.267
1953	489.3	368.2	1.329
1954	515.0	381.2	1.351
1955	551.1	416.9	1.322
1956	577.1	438.3	1.318
1957	604.0	450.9	1.340
1958	641.9	474.2	1.354
1959	692.9	502.4	1.379
1960	727.3	513.0	1.418
1961	770.3	551.5	1.397
1962	822.7	582.8	1.412
1963	878.9	622.1	1.413
1964	942.4	660.6	1.427
1965	1,011.6	732.0	1.382
1966	1,078.2	790.9	1.363
1967	1,155.8	837.1	1.381
1968	1,251.5	917.4	1.364
1969	1,340.1	983.5	1.363
1970	1,432.0	1,030.9	1.389
1971	1,568.2	1,127.3	1.391
1972	1,725.9	1,263.5	1.366
1973	1,910.8	1,413.3	1.352
1974	2,082.7	1,516.8	1.373
1975	2,267.0	1,678.2	1.352
1976	2,510.2	1,843.7	1.362
1977	2,828.9	2,062.4	1.372
1978	3,195.6	2,367.6	1.350
1979	3,581.5	2,591.5	1.382
1980	3,925.8	2,848.6	1.378
1981	4,301.2	3,114.4	1.381
1982	4,679.1	3,212.5	1.457
1983	5,230.6	3,545.8	1.475
1984	5,985.4	3,851.8	1.554
1985	6,851.0	4,104.4	1.669
1986	7,678.9	4,288.1	1.791

Debt figures refer to end-year, GNP figures to fourth quarter, seasonally adjusted.

Sources: US Department of Commerce, Bureau of Economic Analysis, and *National Income and Product Accounts of the United States*, table 1.1

Figure 1 The USA's debt/income ratio starts to rise just as real interest rates move ahead of the growth rate, 1971–1985

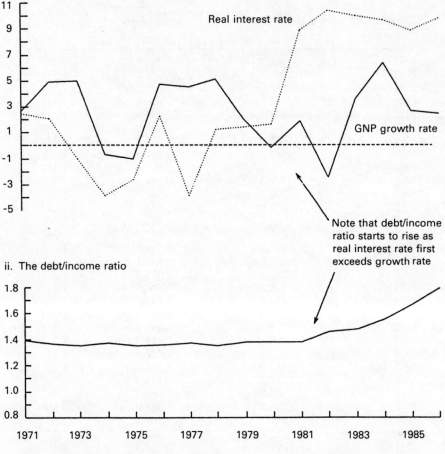

i. Real dollar interest rates compared with the growth rate

Real interest rate

GNP growth rate

Note that debt/income ratio starts to rise as real interest rate first exceeds growth rate

ii. The debt/income ratio

Sources: See tables 1 and 2

should be placed on the timing of the change in the rate of debt growth. It coincided almost exactly with the emergence of very high real interest rates in 1981 and early 1982.

The debt/income ratio has been increasing since 1981 at over 5 per cent a year, above the 1 or 2 per cent a year which we said earlier was sustainable in the long run. It follows that the present trend in debt growth is unsustainable. We have suggested that the jump in real interest rates between 1979 and 1981 was the prime cause of the deterioration in debt trends. It therefore also follows that, while real interest rates remain at current levels, the debt/income will continue to increase and the position of debtors in the American economy will worsen. To make the point more concisely, but also more provocatively, the American debt problem is insoluble while real interest rates stay as high as at present.

This is the nub of our argument – the conclusion which motivates this book. As we said at the beginning, it is self-consciously and deliberately alarmist. Its implication is that, without a major change in certain key macroeconomic variables, the American financial system is headed for continuing and potentially drastic upheaval. Perhaps 'headed for continuing and potentially drastic upheaval' is a rather weary phrase and it begs the question of how 'drastic' and 'upheaval' are to be defined. All one can say for certain is that the ratio of bad loans to good loans will increase, more banks will find that their loans losses exceed their capital and, even if the afflicted institutions do not have 'to close their doors' in the same way as their predecessors did in the 1930s, they will be increasingly under the control of regulators, lawyers and financial bureaucrats rather than their own managements and shareholders. Whether or not this constitutes the breakdown of the financial system is a matter of semantics. There will still be organizations which are recognizably 'banks', there will still be people working in them and there will still be customers who go to them to conduct financial transactions. But there will also be severe dislocation of existing business relationships. Chapter 7 gives a fuller discussion of the forms this dislocation may take and the challenge they could pose to American capitalism.

Of course, some qualifications must be made. Three deserve particular emphasis. First, the tendency for debt to grow explosively in a high-interest-rate environment can be checked if borrowers are able to achieve surpluses of income over non-interest expenditure. The evidence so far in the 1980s is that debtors have not been able and willing to curb their spending enough, hardly surprising perhaps in view of the abruptness of the change in interest rates between 1979 and 1981. Secondly, the malaise in the financial sector arises essentially because losses on old business are so large that they can wipe out the capital of vulnerable organizations. But there may still be ample profit potential in new credit business, which attracts capital back into the financial services industries. The process of securitization, which we will examine in the final chapter of this book, exemplifies the possibilities. Thirdly, a useful drop in real interest rates occurred in early 1987, with the gap between prime rate and the increase in producer prices down to about 6 per cent from the 10 per cent level which had prevailed between 1981 and 1986. However, it remains to be seem how durable the decline in

real rates proves to be, while 6 per cent is still above the trend rate of
real income growth.

In one respect the discussion so far has not been sufficiently
pessimistic. It has concentrated on the USA itself, focussing on
American inflation, an American interest rate and the American debt/
income ratio. Very little has been said about the developing countries.
But the external debt situation for many of them is much worse than the
internal debt problems within the USA. To obtain an insight at a
general level into their troubles we can carry out much the same exercise
on the interest rate and price level relevant to their debt dynamics.

The overwhelming majority of developing country debts are denominated in dollars and the critical interest rate is therefore again a dollar
interest rate. The usual practice in the syndicated credits which
dominated Third World lending in the late 1970s was to specify a margin
over the dollar inter-bank rate in London (known as LIBOR, for
London inter-bank offered rate). But, as LIBOR and prime rate move
together quite closely, it is not misleading to rely once more on prime
rate as a guide to borrowing cost.[13] The appropriate price index,
however, is different. As primary commodities account for the bulk of
developing countries' exports, we need a price index for commodities at
an early stage of processing, not for finished goods. In table 3 we have
chosen the US producer price index for crude materials.

Table 3 shows that the contrast between the 1970s and the early 1980s
was even greater for commodity-producing dollar borrowers than for
the 'typical' dollar borrower considered in table 1. The switch from rapid
inflation and moderate interest rates to negligible inflation and high
interest rates was highly concentrated in the two years from 1979, and
was extremely sharp. The real interest rate confronting commodity
producers changed from −3.7 per cent in 1979 to 10.1 per cent in 1981
and to 18.3 per cent in 1982. Over the five years to 1985 this rate
averaged 13.1 per cent, whereas in the first half of the 1970s it was
negative by 4.5 per cent and in the second half only mildly positive at 0.7
per cent.

Against this background it is hardly surprising that commodity-
exporting nations in the Third World have had difficulty servicing their
debts. It is a commonplace for Latin American economists to refer to
the 'interest rate shock' of the early 1980s just as their counterparts in
the USA and Europe talk of the 'oil shock' of 1973 and 1979. The blow
to living standards delivered to their countries by the change in interest
rates was similar in character to that in the developed countries due to
the two increases in the price of oil.

But there are also commodity producers within the USA. For them
the adverse movement in the relationship between the commodity price

Table 3 The strain of high interest rates on commodity producers in the early 1980s

	Increase in US Producer prices, crude materials (%)	Prime rate charged by banks (%)	Implied real interest rate (%)
Average of five-year periods:			
1951–5	−1.1	3.0	4.1
1956–60	0.0	4.2	4.2
1961–5	0.5	4.5	4.0
1966–70	2.6	6.7	4.0
1971–5	12.6	7.5	−4.5
1976–80	9.3	10.1	0.7
1981–5	0.2	13.3	13.1
Annual series:			
1971	2.5	5.7	2.5
1972	10.9	5.3	−5.0
1973	36.4	8.0	−20.8
1974	12.7	10.8	−1.7
1975	0.4	7.9	7.5
1976	3.0	6.8	3.7
1977	3.2	6.8	3.5
1978	12.1	9.1	−2.7
1979	17.0	12.7	−3.7
1980	11.0	15.3	3.8
1981	8.0	18.9	10.1
1982	−2.9	14.9	18.3
1983	1.3	10.8	9.4
1984	2.2	12.0	9.6
1985	−7.4	9.9	18.7
1986	−8.5	8.3	18.4

Implied real rate is obtained from the same formula as in table 1. There are again some problems with rounding.

Source: *Economic Report of the President*, 1986

increases and interest rates has been as unwelcome as for indebted developing countries. The internal American debt problem in the private sector is highly specific to certain economic activities and localized in certain regions. The worst-affected industries are farming, oil and mining, all of which ran up large debts in the lush years of the 1970s and now find that they cannot service them effectively. The specific and localized nature of the debt problem makes it all the more dangerous, because there are more likely to be bankruptcies if 10 per cent of borrowers face 25 per cent declines in incomes than if 100 per cent face 2½ per cent falls.

American commodity producers were not the only beleaguered private sector debtors of the 1980s. Rising debt/income ratios have been observed in most other industrial countries (see table 4). The contribution made by public debt to the process wil be discussed in the first part of the book, but the misbehaviour of private debt, while also important, will not be considered in any detail except in the USA. The justification for this neglect is that – so far – the growth of private sector debt outside the USA has not threatened the stability of national financial systems. It may do so in future, but there are limits to how much this book can cover.

Table 4 The behaviour of debt/income ratios outside the USA, 1975–1986

	Public sector	Corporate sector	Personal sector	Implied national total
Japan				
1975	39	94	33	166
1985	90	102	46	238
1986[a]	91	102	47	240
West Germany				
1975	25	63	42	130
1985	41	72	56	169
1986	41	71	55	167
UK				
1975	63	46	33	142
1985	60	46	51	157
1986[a]	58	48	55	161
Canada				
1975	53	65	52	170
1985	83	64	50	197
1986	84	64	54	202

Figures relate to the ratio of the three sectors' and the nation's debt to GNP.

[a] Third quarter.

Source: Bank for International Settlements *Fifty-Seventh Annual Report* (Basle: 1987), p. 75

IV

The remainder of the book is an elaboration of the themes developed in this Introduction. The reader will have the main point – that the debt crisis was caused by the sharp rise in real dollar interest rates between 1979 and 1981 and is insoluble unless real interest rates return to a level closer to the underlying growth rate of real incomes – if he proceeds no further. Nevertheless, the themes need to be illustrated and developed. Examples of the debt trap, and worse, are to be found all over the world, testimony perhaps to man's seemingly universal 'strange supinness' when it comes to matters of debt.

The approach will be to apply our analytical tool-kit, which enables us to dissect the impact of differentials between interest rates and growth rates on the dynamics of debt, in three areas. The first will be to public sector finances in the developed countries, particularly the USA. There has been a gradual change in attitudes towards fiscal policy in the USA and the other leading industrial countries over the last 50 years. In essence, governments have become more permissive about budget deficits and the growth rate of public debts has increased. At the same time, the underlying rate of growth of national income – which determines the rise in government tax revenues – has decelerated in many countries. When real interest rates soared in the early 1980s public debts ran out of control. Remedial action has subsequently been taken on a sufficient scale in the majority of European countries and Japan, but not in the USA, Canada, Italy and some small European nations. The outlook is highly conditional on fiscal policy in the USA, because a return to responsible government finances in the world's largest economy would reduce real interest rates there, which would induce a sympathetic downward movement in borrowing costs elsewhere and so help control the growth of public sector debt throughout the world.

Nowhere would the benefits be greater than in Latin America and other over-borrowed regions of the Third World. In the second part of the book the debt threat to the developing nations, which has tended to appropriate almost exclusively the title of *the* Debt Crisis, will be discussed. In fact, the causes of the developing nations' debt difficulties are – as we have already seen – the same as the causes of financial strains in the USA, particularly where these financial strains are felt by commodity producers like farmers and mining companies. There are some significant differences, however, between the debt problems of Latin America and those of private sector borrowers in the USA. In Latin America gross misgovernment, various kinds of mischief-making by businessmen and the vexed issue of sovereign debt add colour to the rather drab financial details. The resolution of debt troubles is more straightforward within the USA because the parties involved, both debtors and creditors, are members of the same legal jurisdiction and are subject to the same regulatory guidelines.

The third part of the book will deal, nevertheless, with the plight of private sector borrowers in the USA. We have argued that the debt/income ratio in the USA has started to rise sharply in recent years because the change in the relationship between interest rates and income growth has made it impossible for borrowers to service their debts. But this is only the basic plot. The story also contains many important subplots and digressions.

The conclusion for policy will, by now, be predictable. It is that the worldwide debt threat to public sector finances and private sector economic activity can be removed only by a substantial reduction in real interest rates. Some piecemeal responses, such as the substitution of commercial high-interest loans to developing countries by concessionary low-interest finance and the trend towards securitization in financial markets, can alleviate the debt problem. But two proposed large-scale 'solutions' – the increase in lending to Third World debtors envisaged by the Baker plan and coordinated fiscal reflation to boost economic activity – are misguided. They are not based on the correct diagnosis and might even aggravate debtors' difficulties if they are applied.

PART I

The Debt Threat to the Industrial Countries

1

From the Old-Time Fiscal Religion
to Voodoo Economics

Over the last 50 years, thinking about fiscal policy has had a consistent pattern of evolution. Theories and analysis have become steadily more sophisticated, while the sense of moral obligation and financial responsibility among policy-makers has weakened. The net effect is that budget deficits are now regarded as the norm, and a balanced budget or budget surpluses as aberrations. As in so many other areas, political leaders no longer feel themselves hemmed in by convention and precedent or even – it seems at times – by elementary arithmetic. Members of the Reagan administration in the USA once professed belief in the idea, which can be mildly described as counter-intuitive, that lowering tax rates would cause the American economy to generate more tax revenue. Senator Bush, later appointed Vice-President in that administration, had no hesitation while he could still express his own views in labelling this as 'voodoo economics'. There could hardly be a clearer indication that, whatever the rigour and subtlety of contemporary academic analysis, a shared understanding about the appropriate conduct of fiscal policy no longer exists at the highest policy-making levels. In this chapter we shall discuss the breakdown of traditional views on sound finance and their replacement by a welter of confusing, and often conflicting, doctrines.

But, before we examine the history of ideas about these topics, we should emphasize that government debt can be analysed with the analytical tool-kit developed in the Introduction. There are some special nuances compared with private or external debt, but the key proposition – that a borrower's debt/income ratio rises indefinitely when the rate of interest exceeds the growth rate of his income and he is not maintaining a sufficiently large surplus of income over non-interest expenditure – can be readily adapted for the purpose of discussing public sector finances. The relevant version is that public debt rises explosively when the average real interest rate on the debt exceeds the economy's real growth rate and the government's tax revenue is either less than or equal to non-interest expenditure, or exceeds non-interest expenditure by an insufficiently wide margin. If we define the difference between revenue and expenditure minus interest payments as the primary fiscal balance, this can be simplified a little. When the average interest rate on its debt exceeds the growth rate, a government must run a primary surplus to stop its debt situation running out of control. These statements are rather long-winded, but the technicalities are important, as we shall see later.

The logic behind this fiscal version of our central idea is straight-forward. The government's income is its tax revenue. On the reasonable assumption that tax schedules cause revenue to grow in line with gross national product (GNP), the government's income also grows at the same rate as GNP. So interest charges cause the debt to grow faster than tax revenue when the rate of interest exceeds the growth rate of the GNP.

There are several refinements to these basis ideas. They are of great practical significance in the analysis of fiscal policy options for over-indebted modern governments. But, for most of the last two centuries, it would have been unnecessary to labour the technical points with any thoroughness. Views about the right way to conduct fiscal policy were crude and honest. The orthodox doctrine – now termed with nostalgia the 'old-time fiscal religion' by the American economist Professor James Buchanan – was not that governments should balance their budgets but that they should plan for budget surpluses in order to minimize the risk of deficits.[1] The budget concept here was not the sophisticated 'primary balance', but more simply the difference between all revenues and all expenditure. Moreover, according to the old-time religion, the best kind of national debt was one that had been fully repaid. In the rest of this chapter we shall see how, over the last 50 years, the old-time religion has lost adherents and been replaced by less devout fiscal beliefs.

II

John Stuart Mill's *Principles of Political Economy* was the bible of economic policy in the English-speaking world for a long period after its publication in 1848. Its remarks on government debt, although brief, were a sermon on the iniquity of departures from the old-time religion. By covering expenditure by borrowing rather than taxation, the state remained 'charged with the debt besides, and with its interest in perpetuity. The system of public loans, in such circumstances, may be pronounced the very worst which, in the present state of civilization, is still included in the catalogue of financial expedients.'[2] An equally emphatic and more extended criticism of budget deficits is to be found in a manual on *Public Finance* prepared by C. F. Bastable, a professor of political economy at the University of Dublin, and first published in 1892. Its third edition, which appeared in 1903, included the following stricture:

> Outlay should not exceed income, or – and this is more often the way in which the case is presented – tax revenue ought to be kept up to the amount required to defray expenses.

But there could be logistical difficulties in the management of large sums of public money which meant that

> The safest rule for practice is that which lays down the expediency of estimating for a moderate surplus, by which the possibility of a deficit will be reduced to a minimum.[3]

In a later section, Bastable judged that

> a permanent debt ought to be avoided. If loans should be contracted under great pressure, and to prevent the exhaustion of the agency of taxation, and, if, while they exist, they act as a drag on the financial power of the State, it cannot be disputed that their speedy redemption must be eminently desirable.[4]

The quality of the economic reasoning behind Mill's and Bastable's assertions may not be notably high by modern standards. But that is not what matters for our purposes. It is much more to the point that the ideas were taught to generations of students who subsequently became politicians, civil servants, financiers, bankers and journalists. These attitudes towards public finance, with their strong emphasis on responsibility, prudence and caution, were deeply ingrained in the collective psyche of the governing elite in Victorian and early twentieth-century Britian.

They were also fully reflected in policy. In the 65 years from the publication of *Principles of Political Economy* to the First World War the budget was balanced or in surplus on 45 occasions. The exceptions were nearly all during wartime. Over the whole period the burden of the national debt was reduced appreciably. In 1850 it exceeded national income; by 1913 it represented only a quarter of national income.

The USA was governed throughout the nineteenth century with similarly strict rules of public finance, but they were applied even more rigorously than in Britain. Whereas Britain managed by balancing its budget with reasonable consistency to prevent its national debt expanding too rapidly, the USA succeeded – through long periods of budget surplus – in twice virtually repaying its national debt. The first episode was in the early nineteenth century. In 1815, after deficits incurred in the War of 1812 and its immediate aftermath, the gross national debt was $127m. Over the 21 years from 1816 there were 18 years of surplus and the gross debt had fallen to $337,000 by the end of 1836. After a period of varying fiscal fortunes in the middle of the century, the Civil War led to a drastic increase in the debt to $2.7b at the end of 1865. The return to peace was followed by 28 consecutive years of surplus and by 1893 the debt had been cut to under $1b, a modest figure in relation to national income of over $12b.[5]

The origins of the fiscal conservatism of nineteenth-century America are to be sought in the very early years of the republic. In the first decade after Independence the USA's public finances were chaotic, partly because of uncertainty about the proportion of expenditure to be covered by Federal taxation rather than states taxation. In 1777 and 1778 Congress issued an excessive quantity of Continental bills to finance its expenditure. They rapidly lost value, unleashing a severe inflation. In March 1780 Congress resolved that it would redeem them at one-fortieth of their face value, an act of outright repudiation which was humiliating for the young nation. The next few years saw sporadic attempts to put the currency on more solid fiscal foundations which culminated in Alexander Hamilton's *Report on Public Credit* in 1790. He had just been appointed the first Secretary of the Treasury when he wrote the *Report* and over the next five years he had the chance to implement its main proposals. They brought a new stability to American public finances.

On his resignation Hamilton prepared a *Valedictory Report* which outlined the cardinal principles on which the nation's finances should be run. He warned that 'The progressive accumulation of debt must ultimately endanger all Government' and recommended that a sinking fund be established to extinguish the debt over a 30–year period.[6] In response a Sinking Fund Act was passed in 1795, earmarking substantial revenues for debt retirement. A historian writing in 1887 judged that the Act had been based on 'three essential principles':

> First of all it established distinctive revenues for the payment of the interest of the public debt as well as for the reimbursement of the principal within a determinate period; secondly, it directed impera-tively their application to the debt alone; and thirdly it pledged the faith of the Government that the appointed revenues should continue to be levied and collected and appropriated to these objects until the whole debt should be redeemed.[7]

The prose is cumbersome, but the underlying sentiment is clear. In particular, the concern about the possible misbehaviour of debt interest is evident. We see here the set of beliefs which resulted in the USA's cutting a national debt of $127m in 1815 to $337,000 in 1836 and a debt of $2.7b in 1865 to under $1b in 1893. These beliefs survived as unchallenged orthodoxy until well into the twentieth century.

III

The decay of the old-time fiscal religion was a gradual process which spanned several decades. But, although the change in attitudes was protracted and occurred at different speeds in different countries, there is no doubt about the event which initiated the shift in thinking. It was the Great Depression of the early 1930s. Before this catastrophe hit the world economy there had been numerous well-defined cycles in business activity, with prosperity giving way to recession and recession to prosperity. Few observers questioned the ability of the free market economy to recover from periods of weak demand without special action by the government, as it had always done so in the past.

But the Great Depression was an economic disaster on a scale never before experienced. In the mid- and late 1930s, the revival from the trough of 1933 was regarded, particularly in the USA, as weak and unconvincing.[8] This disappointment was interpreted as a failure of the capitalist system and was therefore thought to provide justification for a more interventionist approach by government. The intellectual case for intervention – and, more specifically, for an active fiscal policy – was given by the English economist, Lord Keynes, in his 1936 book *The General Theory of Employment, Interest and Money*. It is this book, with its unusual combination of technical rigour and polemical acerbity, which is generally thought to have broken the hold of the old-time fiscal religion on the policy-making establishments of the major countries. Many economists, and probably the majority of economists in Britain and the USA, believe that the abandonment of balanced-budget notions had been completed by the late 1940s. For them the 1950s and 1960s can be described as 'the Age of Keynes'.[9]

The truth is more complex in at least two respects. First, it is uncertain exactly what Keynes himself thought about fiscal policy. This may seem an extraordinary remark in view of the countless volumes written on the worldwide 'fiscal revolution' which is supposed to have been attributable to his influence. But, in fact, his work does not anywhere set out specific principles to guide fiscal policy-makers in all circumstances. There are articles on the virtues of public works and on the multiplier effects of extra public spending in conditions of high unemployment.[10] There is also a great deal of derogatory comment on sound finance scattered throughout his writings, much of it in the form of witty allusions and literary sneers. In 1929 he mocked Treasury officials and Conservative politicians for their obstructiveness over extra public spending as 'a few old gentlemen tightly buttoned-up in their frock coats, who only need to be treated with a little friendly disrespect and bowled over like ninepins'; in 1931 he remarked, on government proposals to cut teachers' pay, that to make them the object of an economy campaign as 'an offering to the Moloch of finance' was 'sufficient proof of the state of hysteria and irresponsibility into which cabinet ministers have worked themselves'.[11] It is all great fun and very difficult to argue against, but it is not a clearly formulated guide to fiscal policy.

   The General Theory is perfunctory in its discussion of budget deficits. The only directly relevant pages refer to the benefits to economic activity from extra 'loan-expenditure', which is defined rather furtively in a footnote as public spending 'financed by borrowing from individuals' or, in effect, the budget deficit.[12] Keynes's apparent nervousness about the forthright recommendation of budget deficits may stem from doubts about their political acceptability to a governing elite still strongly attached to 'strict "business" principles'. This is confirmed by a curious episode in the last years of his life. In the early 1940s the American economist Abba Lerner did develop, with Keynes's own ideas as the basis, a theory of so-called 'functional finance' in which the budget position was to be varied to alter the level of economic activity. It as an integral and explicit part of the theory that budget deficits were to be used as an antidote to inadequate private spending. Lerner pointed out the advantages of budget deficits in this role in a seminar Keynes gave at the Federal Reserve in 1943. Keynes retorted that deficits which expanded the national debt were 'humbug' and, according to one account, paraphrased Lincoln's 'you cannot fool all of the people all of the time'.[13] Although he later retracted these remarks or at least qualified their fierceness, the conclusion must be that Keynes was not sure about the wisdom of a deliberate, aggressive policy of unbalancing the budget. These doubts, even in his later years after the publication of *The General Theory*, are not altogether out of character. In the early 1920s he had witnessed the financial chaos and social turmoil which had accompanied excessive budget deficits in several European countries. Indeed, in January 1926 he had poured scorn on the French government because of its failure to balance its books and the consequent rapid circulation of finance ministers. The impudent title of the piece – *An open letter to the French minister of finance (whoever he is or may be)* –

indicates what he felt about this particular instance of fiscal humbug.

The idea of an 'Age of Keynes' misleads, secondly, because his views about fiscal policy were not universally adopted after a short and decisive intellectual battle which saw their triumph over supposedly more primitive pre-Keynesian alternatives. The change in thinking in American and British universities certainly was abrupt. By the early 1950s Keynesianism, not the old-time fiscal religion of balanced budgets, was orthodoxy at the academic level throughout the English-speaking world. Lerner's theory of functional finance captured adherents more successfully than Keynes's own writings. It quickly infiltrated important centres of economic research and instruction, and was soon sanctified by its inclusion in elementary textbooks. Professor Paul Samuelson, later to write the most influential of these textbooks, said that many of his contemporaries reacted with Wordsworthian ecstasy when they understood the new ideas. 'Bliss was it in that dawn to be alive, but to be young was very heaven!'[14]

But Keynesianism made less progress with policy-makers, with the civil servants, politicians and advisers who deliberated about and took the vital decisions. True enough, in 1946 the US Congress passed a Full Employment Act which was intended to herald an era of conscious government action to promote high levels of employment. The reality, however, is that until the mid-1960s attitudes towards budgetary policy in Washington were rather reactionary. President Eisenhower seemed in many of his policy statements to be quite impervious to the Keynesian paradigm which dominated academic macroeconomics. In a prepared preamble to a news conference in October 1953 he said

> Balancing the budget will always remain a goal of any administration
> that believes as much as we do that the soundness of our money must
> be assured, and that an unbalanced budget has a very bad affect on it.

His hidden fears were revealed in a more spontaneous answer to a press conference in February 1958. Commenting on the advantages and disadvantages of a tax cut, he did not doubt that it would have 'a very real, great stimulus on the economy' but

> . . . on the other hand, this is something you can take hold of and,
> going too far with trying to fool with our economy, then you get
> something else started. And you just remember, all of you here, a
> year ago, how we were always talking about inflation . . .[15]

This is too bumbling and incoherent in manner, and much too virtuous in tone, to allow the interpretation that the Eisenhower Presidency marked the US government's conversion to modernity in matters of fiscal management. The period is surely better understood as transitional between the continued ascendancy of the old-time religion in the 1930s and the 1940s and the acceptance of a fully fledged Keynesianism in the mid-1960s.[16]

President Kennedy played an important role in securing this acceptance. Unlike Eisenhower, he cultivated the image of being a strong supporter of new and radical ideas. His academic advisers were predominantly chosen from those Keynesians who, as young men completing further degrees in the late 1940s, had so warmly embraced the Lernerian doctrines. In 1961 and 1962 the American economy grew, but not by as much as the administration wanted. On 7 June 1962, a tax reduction was promised to give extra vitality to demand and output, even though it would lead to an increased budget deficit. When it was passed into law by President Johnson on 26 February 1964, the balanced-budget doctrine was widely regarded as outmoded and irrelevant. The economy's response to the tax cut was enthusiastic. The sequence of percentage growth rates of real GNP over the five years from 1962 to 1966 was 5.3, 4.1, 5.3, 5.8 and 5.8; in the previous five years it had been 1.7, −0.8, 5.8, 2.2 and 2.6. The contrast seemed to represent an impressive endorsement of the New Economics of deliberate budget imbalance over the fuddy-duddy economics of the Eisenhower years.

One of the most influential advocates of the 1964 tax cut was Walter Heller, chairman of the Council of Economic Advisers. In testimony before the Joint Economic Committee of Congress in January 1963 he argued that a tax cut 'would multiply itself into an increment of GNP' which would boost revenues and so strengthen the budgetary position, at least as measured by a concept known as 'the full-employment budget'. (This is the budget balance that would obtain if full employment has been achieved and tax revenues and government expenditure are at the levels associated with it.)[17] This line of argument has an uncanny similarity to certain so-called supply-side propositions of the late 1970s and early 1980s. In fact, as we shall see later, Heller has a special position in the development of recent American economic policy since, almost uniquely, he acted as an intellectual bridge between the Kennedy and Reagan tax cuts.

Kennedy himself acknowledged Heller's contribution. In a well-received speech he gave at a dinner to the Economic Club of New York in December 1962 the President emphasized the burden of high taxes, the incentive effects of low taxes and the consequent virtues of tax cuts. He later called Heller to say, 'I gave them straight Keynes and Heller, and they loved it.'[18] It is not altogether clear what Kennedy may have meant by 'Keynes' in this remark, but Keynesianism – or, at any rate, some amalgam of Keynes, Lerner and Heller – had captured the loftiest citadels of policy formation as well as the most influential ivory towers in academe. It had taken 30 years from the publication of *The General Theory*, but the achievement appeared to be genuine and substantial for all that.

IV

In fact, Keynesianism maintained its hold on Washington for only a few years. By the mid-1970s it was in retreat before monetarism and, later, it was supplanted by more exotic economic creeds. In the USA the period of undoubted Keynesian primacy in policy-making was much briefer than implied by the familiar, but exaggerated, notion of an 'Age of Keynes'. In Britain also, despite its reputation as the heartland of Keynesianism, the new fiscal doctrines enjoyed a rather short reign over policy.

A distinction must again be drawn between the academic community on the one hand and practitioners on the other. In the universities Keynesianism and macroeconomics were virtually indistinguishable between the later 1940s and the early 1970s. In Whitehall, however, the situation was very different. Many of the most important organizational principles on public spending date back to Gladstone's day or even earlier. The doctrine of 'Treasury control', by which the Treasury concentrates into its hands the power to monitor and police the budgets of all the spending departments, is particularly strongly entrenched. Another well-established convention used to be that spending should be divided between above-the-line and below-the-line items. Roughly speaking, above-the-line items are recurrent, while those below-the-line are incurred only in a particular year and are not to be repeated. This and a number of associated rules may seem to lack functional utility in modern conditions, but they buttressed the Treasury's power against other ministries. Senior civil servants in the Treasury were therefore reluctant to abandon them.

The standard practice in the early twenieth century was to balance the budget above-the-line. Improbable though it may seem to the many middle-aged economists brought up to believe that they have always lived in 'the Keynesian era', this continued to be a key principle of fiscal management until the late 1960s. The purpose of the distinction between above-the-line and below-the-line is outlined in *The British Budgetary System* by Sir Herbert Brittain, a Treasury civil servant, which was published in 1959. 'Over a period of years the Budget should certainly be balanced above-the-line; otherwise that part of the debt not covered by new assets will increase indefinitely.'[19] The quality of economic reasoning here may not have impressed Keynesian academics, but it has an obvious affinity with the ideas expressed in the Introduction to this book. Brittain was concerned about the indefinite expansion of debt not covered by tangible assets, perhaps because he realized that the interest on such debt would have to be paid by taxation. The higher the debt, the higher also would be the required level of taxation.

As in the USA, the Keynesian element in fiscal policy formation became dominant only in the mid-1960s. The Labour Government elected in 1964 recruited a large batch of economic advisers from the universities and, in accordance with the fashionable new fiscal per-missiveness which most of them espoused, ran a substantial budget deficit in 1967. The relaxation of fiscal policy may have contributed to the devaluation of the pound in November of that year. At any rate, after this first change in the sterling parity and the scrapping of the more antique rules on public expenditure and borrowing, the old constraints on budgetary policy had been removed. In 1969 and 1970 the budget deficit, now measured by the public sector borrowing requirement (PSBR), was kept under tight control as Britain complied with an International Monetary Fund programme to improve its balance of payments. But in the early 1970s public finances lurched heavily into deficit, with the full blessing of the Keynesian economists who constituted the overwhelming majority of the British academic pro-fession. This was followed by large oscillations in the PSBR around a high average figure, a period which was termed the 'fiscal frenzy' by one contemporary observer.[20]

A few years' experience of hyperactive fiscal policy was enough to convince most policy-makers, and a large number of economists close to policy-making, that Keynesianism was overrated. Apart from the lack of evident benefits in terms of more stable output and higher employment, Britain was beginning to suffer from the problem of rapidly growing debt interest. In 1975 the Expenditure Committee of the House of Commons asked Treasury officials several awkward questions about why debt interest had risen so much faster than the Government had envisaged. The answer, in part, was that higher inflation was associated with higher interest rates, but too rapid underlying growth in the debt was also responsible.[21] The PSBR was regarded as excessive in another, increasingly noticed, respect. Policy-makers found that the higher the PSBR, the more difficulty they had persuading people to buy government debt and more they had to rely on the banking system to finance the deficit. This added to the money supply with potentially inflationary consequences. From the mid-1970s onwards, therefore, official attitudes moved towards the subordination of fiscal decisions to the overriding priority of monetary control and away from the previous commitment to demand management. In his speech to the Lord Mayor's dinner on 19 October 1978 Mr Healey, the Chancellor of the Exchequer, stated that the Government was determined 'to make its fiscal policy consistent with its monetary stance'. The connection between budget deficits and monetary growth was formalized in the medium-term financial strategy introduced by the Thatcher government in 1980. It is clear from the passage of events and from the sequence of official statements that Keynesianism had little influence on British policy in the late 1970s and early 1980s. This is interesting, as there is no doubt that Keynesian ideas held undiminished sway in the universities. The gap between the academics and the practitioners became very public in a letter to *The Times*, signed by 364 university economists, in March 1981. It condemned the large tax increases announced in the Budget of that year as too deflationary and predicted that the Government would have to reverse its monetarist policies. Whatever the rights and wrongs of the case, these policies have not yet been reversed and academic economists continue to protest against so-called 'PSBR monetarism'.[22]

Keynesianism had only a brief period in which it commanded a monopoly of policy advice in the USA and Britain. In other important industrial countries it never really determined governments' financial behaviour. In Japan, West Germany and France political habits, bureaucratic traditions and, above all, folk memories have been more important influences on fiscal policy than the theories of Keynes and Lerner.

This is most obvious in the German case. The starting point for any understanding of Germany's post-war economic policy has to be the currency reform of June 1948, which both liberalized markets and established a sound currency. Its architect was Ludwig Erhard, later Chancellor of the Republic, who wrote that, 'An undigested Keynesianism is no less discredited that the *laissez-faire* idea that the state should play no part in economic life'.[23] In the 1950s and 1960s German public finances at both the Federal and the local levels were frequently in surplus. It was as late as 1967 before Karl Schiller, finance minister in a Social Democrat government, introduced a law on economic stabilization and growth which made reference to Keynesian principles. There were budget deficits in the 1970s, sometimes of considerable proportions. The most deliberate resort to fiscal policy was after the Bonn Economic Summit of June 1978, where Chancellor Schmidt's delegation pledged stimulation equivalent to 1 per cent of GNP in response to international demands that Germany assume a 'locomotive' role in the world economy. Two years afterwards the balance of payments was in massive deficit and inflation increased sharply. As an understandable reaction to these setbacks, the early 1980s saw a return to the fiscal conservatism that had characterized the first 20 post-war years. Under the direction of Stoltenburg, finance minister in the Christian Democrat government of Helmut Kohl, the budget was restored to a condition of virtual balance.

In Japan also fiscal policy was almost completely passive throughout the 1950s and 1960s, with the government's finances in balance, small deficit or small surplus year after year. It was only in the 1970s that continous and sizeable deficits were recorded. As in the German case, 1978 saw the most conspicuous fiscal expansion in the post-war period after international pressure at the Bonn Summit. The results were soon felt. By 1980 Japan had a depreciating currency, a widening payments deficit and accelerating inflation. The early 1980s were marked by fiscal retrenchment, not only to end these classic symptoms of mistaken policies, but also because the unduly rapid growth of the national debt had started to generate anxieties about the future burden of debt service.

Behind the German resistance to Keynesian policies, which are regarded as liable to provoke price increases through the over-stimulation of demand, lies a deeply ingrained suspicion of inflation. This suspicion can be attributed to memories of the Weimar hyper-inflation of the early 1920s. France has never suffered such a complete breakdown of the monetary mechanism, but it has had several periods of moderate or severe financial disorder in the twentieth century, usually associated with weak governments. The last significant phase of this kind, in the early and mid-1950s, was brought to an end by the creation of the Fifth Republic under de Gaulle in 1958. De Gaulle appointed Jacques Rueff, known for his conservative views on financial management, to the chairmanship of the Economic Commission. The restoration of a balanced budget was part of the comprehensive stabilization plan that the commission introduced in late 1958. Like Eisenhower, de Gaulle intruded his own values into an apparently technocratic area of policy and said that he approved the plan because its object was 'to establish the nation on a basis of truth and severity'.[24] A more or less exact balance between central government revenue and expenditure remained an integral feature of the system of government under the Fifth Republic until the late 1970s. Apart from a short interruption under the Socialist administration of President Mitterand in 1981 and 1982, careful control of public finances has continued until the present.

Italy is an exception to the strict post-war control of public finances which characterized most of the major nations. After financial chaos in the immediate aftermath of the war, expenditure and revenue came into better contact from 1950 onwards. Although tax receipts grew somewhat faster than expenditure in the 1950s and early 1960s, there was always a budget deficit, even if it was sometimes very slight. Between 1947 and 1961 the public debt rose from 488b lire to 2,352.2b and the floating debt from 986b to 3,548.4b.[25] Public finances have always been rather ramshackle in Italy and we see here the beginnings of a much graver problem in the 1970s and 1980s.

We can summarize our survey of the development of attitudes towards fiscal policy so far. Most of the Western industrialized world never experienced a Keynesian era, but only a Keynesian episode. The exact timing and duration of this episode varied from country to country. It could reasonably be argued that fiscal policies in Japan, West Germany and France, throughout the post-war period, have reflected domestic financial and political forces rather than intellectual input from the Anglo-Saxon nations. In the USA the first indisputably Keynesian policy measure was the tax cut of 1964. It is a matter of taste when one dates the subsequent decline and fall of demand-side fiscal activism, but no one would have considered it still dominant in the mid-1970s. Even in Britain a strong case can be argued that the Keynesians' window of opportunity opened wide only in the mid-1960s and that it was shut rudely in their faces after the financial muddles of the mid-1970s.

The Keynesian episodes may have been short, but that does not mean they had little significance. As will become clear in the next chapter, the growth of national debts was profoundly conditioned by fluctuations in intellectual fashion. Five- or ten-year periods of deficit financing may seem incidental in the long histories of sound public finance in countries such as the USA and Britain, but they were enough to affect savers' attitudes towards their governments and so to change expectations about appropriate interest rate levels. Most obviously, they tended to increase real interest rates. We shall pick up this point, and its importance for the sustainability of fiscal policy, later in the chapter.

V

Until the late 1970s thinking about fiscal policy evolved in broadly the same direction in the major nations. Afterwards there was a bifurcation between the USA and the rest of the large industrialized countries. In the early 1980s Britain, West Germany, Japan and France all – for their separate reasons – adopted structures of economic policy-making which left little scope for large and deliberate budget deficits. By contrast, the

USA embarked on the most ambitious programme of deficit financing in its peacetime history.

The intellectual origins of this remarkable policy shift are still not properly understood, but the subject invites comparison with such recognized watersheds in the development of economic theory as the Keynesian revolution. The most familiar portrait of Lord Keynes has him seated, not altogether comfortably, in an armchair. It is not obvious what he is thinking about, but the viewer has to presume that his ruminations relate to the liquidity preference theory of the rate of interest, the marginal propensity to consume, the future of capitalism and similar topics. Keynesian ideas, with all the benefits they have reputedly conferred on mankind, may therefore be said to have started in an armchair. The supply-side revolution, by contrast, began at the dinner tables of Washington or, to be more precise, on paper napkins.

This may seem trivial and unfair, but the anecdotal evidence has now been codified and is well on the way to acquiring the status of historical truth. Even Henry Kaufman, the eminent Wall Street economist, reports in his book *Interest Rates, the Markets, and the New Financial World* that, 'Rumor has it that a university professor sketched a diagram on a dinner napkin showing that lower tax rates would generate so much economic growth that the result would be an *increase* in tax receipts. On that basis, with no additional theoretical or empirical evidence, Congress bought the 1981 tax package – and has been regretting it ever since'.[26] Although Kaufman's comment may not be the whole story, or even most of it, it is certainly an important part. But what, more exactly, happened between the first diagram-strewn paper napkin and the 1981 Economic Recovery Tax Act? Why and how were supply-side ideas absorbed so readily by policy-makers in Washington?

The starting point does indeed seem to have been a lunch or dinner in 1976 between Representative Jack Kemp and Professor Arthur Laffer at which Laffer explained that at tax rates of both 0 per cent and 100 per cent no revenue is collected. At 0 per cent, there is no tax; at 100 per cent, there is no income left to the taxpayer, hence there is no point in working and again no tax. Between these points various combinations of tax rate and revenue collected are possible. There must, as a matter of logic, be a range in which lower tax rates lead to extra tax receipts for the government. The whole 'theory', if it can be so dignified, is readily portrayed in a diagram showing the relationship between tax rates and the proportion of income paid in tax. This diagram, which is certainly ideal for drawing on paper napkins, is known as the Laffer curve. Of course, it is one thing to claim that there are some circumstances in which lower tax rates boost tax receipts and quite another to assert that those are the circumstances of the American economy at any particular period of time.

A little-remarked occasion on 7 February 1977 may therefore have had some importance in moulding opinion. Walter Heller, who has been so effective in spreading Keynesian ideas under Kennedy, was again giving evidence to the Joint Economic Committee of Congress. He told the Committee that the 1964 tax cut was 'the major factor' that led to a $3b surplus on government finances in 1965, because the extra economic activity caused by the fiscal boost had increased revenues and reduced expenditure. Paul Craig Roberts, a particularly diligent campaigner for supply-side ideas, has recognized the value of Heller's statement. It seemed to provide solid, impressive and relatively recent empirical support for his case. If that had been the economy's response to the Kennedy tax cut, it no longer appeared totally implausible to say that the American economy in the late 1970s was on the lucky part of the Laffer curve where tax cuts could *reduce* the budget deficit.[27] Arguably, there is a thread of continuity in economics between the Keynesianism of the mid-1960s and the supply-side economics of the late 1970s, as there is in politics between Kennedy's vision of a New Frontier and Reagan's rhetoric about a New Dawn of American prosperity.

According to Roberts, the next important step was on 23 February 1977 when Representative Rousselot suggested, as an amendment to the third budget resolution for fiscal year 1977, 'a simple across-the-board tax reduction for every American'. It was the first of a sequence of such amendments over the next 18 months. They were all rejected, but their impact on political attitudes was considerable and cumulative. Kemp and Senator William Roth were the leaders of the movement in Congress, with a proposal for a 30 per cent reduction across the board in tax rates which they urged on several occasions. Finally, in October 1978 a new amendment from Senator Nunn of Georgia combined tax reductions with provisions limiting the growth of federal spending and envisaging a balanced budget in 1982. As with so many other proposals of the same genre, the tax cuts were immediate and definite, while the balanced budget was remote and conjectural. Despite these problems, the Nunn amendment was passed by both houses of Congress and rejected only because of a veto by President Carter. The insider's verdict was that 'by the autumn of 1978 a majority of Congress had clearly demonstrated that supply-side economics was irresistible'.[28]

Influential newspapers, notably *The Wall Street Journal* where a supply-side leader-writer, Jude Wanniski, was active, supported the new Congressional consensus. The bandwagon for tax cuts was now such that they had to form part of the Republican platform in the Presidential Election of 1980. Although the terms 'supply-side economics' and 'Reaganomics' have sometimes been used interchangeably, President Reagan's own contribution seems to have been that of a disciple rather than an originator. Nevertheless, he did have the political nous to realize that tax cuts, rather than the balanced budget aim traditionally favoured by the Republican establishment, would gain votes and enable him to defeat President Carter. His main rival for the Republican nomination, Senator Bush, did not have that insight and was soon overshadowed. His most quotable remark, about Reaganomics being voodoo economics, has been repeated many times since he first said it, but not by him.

Supply-side economics was translated into legislation on 31 July 1981 when Congress passed the Economic Recovery and Tax Act, knowing that it would receive President Reagan's signature. It endorsed a $749b tax cut over a five-year period, the largest in American peacetime history.

VI

The supply-side revolution can be interpreted as the result of Washington political manoeuvring, particularly infighting between Congressional factions. But these factions were not operating in a vacuum. Instead they reflected underlying trends in American public opinion. There is no doubt that in the late 1970s a majority of the American people resented the intrusiveness and the cost of Big Government. In Reagan's words, 'Runaway government threatens our economic survival, our most cherished institutions, and the very preservation of freedom itself.'[29] Supply-side ideas gave this resentment an analytical focus and their expositors had remarkable skills in managing the media, influencing key figures in public debate and changing the agenda of political action. The 1981 tax cuts were very popular. Reagan's opponent in the 1984 Presidential Election, Senator Mondale, is widely believed to have spoiled his chances by saying, with an admirable but disastrous frankness, that a tax increase would be necessary to restore a sustainable budgetary position.

At a more fundamental level, the easy acceptance of free-lunch ideas in economic policy is symptomatic of both the breakdown of old notions of fiscal responsibility and the overburdening of the political process in the late twentieth century. We have seen that in the nineteenth century, and for most of the early twentieth century, governments in the USA, Britain and other industrial countries maintained balanced budgets as a matter of principle. The thinking behind their self-restraint had some subtlety, but not much. It rested mostly on the moral conviction that decisions in fiscal policy were a choice between good and evil and that balanced budgets were virtuous and deficits were wicked. It owed little to any profound technical appreciation of the likely results of deliberate deficit financing.

Keynesian ideas were the pivot of the tilt away from the old-time fiscal religion towards less strict attitudes of fiscal management. Without their corrosive influence on the principles of sound finance, the voodoo economics of Laffer, Wanniski and Paul Craig Roberts could never have achieved credibility in top policy-making circles or made headway in public debate. Most obviously, they supplied the analytical apparatus which – through the indirect route of the Lernerian theory of functional finance and its practical application in the Kennedy tax cuts of 1964 – gave the supply-siders the real-world example, or in their words 'the empirical evidence', needed to substantiate their policy recommendations.

Keynes as an individual was also interesting in a perhaps more fundamental sense, as both a symbol and a symptom of deep trends in the intellectual life of the twentieth century. As a member of the Bloomsbury Group as well as a world-renowed economist, he was placed in the cultural midstream of the 1920s and 1930s. He did not devote himself exclusively to following recent developments in economic theory but also kept a close interest in new movements in the arts, philosophy and politics. He recognized in a paper in 1938 on 'My Early Beliefs', that the mood of the opening decades of the twentieth century – which he fully shared and enjoyed – was 'immoralist'. He and his circle of friends 'entirely repudiated a personal liability on us to obey general rules. We claimed the right to judge every individual case on its merits, and the wisdom, experience and self-control to do so successfully. . . . We recognized no moral obligation on us, no inner sanction, to conform or to obey.' In view of these attitudes, it is hardly surprising that Keynes and other economists of his generation, and even more so of a younger generation, should have no qualms about deriding 'the Moloch of sound finance' and the hocus-pocus of balanced budgets. What is surprising, and today little remembered, is that by late middle age Keynes had mixed feelings about his 'Early Beliefs'. One of the final paragraphs of the 1938 paper includes the sentence, 'We were not aware that civilisation was a thin and precarious crust erected by the personality and the will of a very few, and only maintained by rules and conventions skilfully put across and guilefully preserved.'[30] Would Keynes – perhaps somewhat ruefully after the publication of *The General Theory* have included the balanced budget principle among these rules and conventions? Does this help in explaining his denunciation of Lernerian functional finance as 'humbug'?

At any rate, by the time of his death in 1946 the damage had been done. Keynes had made it intellectually fashionable, indeed almost essential as a mark of professional competence, for economists to scorn the old-time religion of balanced budgets. When Eisenhower and de Gaulle gave their approval to pre-Keynesian ideas about fiscal policy in the late 1950s, and reduced or eliminated budget deficits, their accompanying rhetoric appealed strongly to pre-Keynesian ideas of public morality. Their own systems of belief were more humdrum and traditional than Keynes's, and they remained attached – in economic policy as in other areas – to exactly those rules and conventions which had been 'skilfully put across and guilefully preserved' in the nineteenth century.

By the 1960s skill and guile were instead being used to complete the destruction of old fiscal traditions. Most American academic economists regarded Eisenhower's public utterances on financial policy as quaint and charming, but in the era of Keynesian enlightenment also rather ridiculous. In Britain clever young men in newspaper offices pointed out the former President's intellectual shortcomings. Nigel Lawson, later to become Chancellor of the Exchequer in the Thatcher government, wrote in a *Sunday Telegraph* article of 11 March 1962 against 'the Eisenhower school of economic commentators, who see mystical significance in an overall budget balance, since this is a muddled amalgam of Gladstone and Keynes without the logical consistency of either'.[31] Scorn for balanced-budget ideas has continued in the British press since then. Samuel Brittan, perhaps Fleet Street's most influential economic writer in the post-war period, has been particularly dismissive. In *The Financial Times* of 5 February 1976 he claimed that 'Events in the last few months have shown that monetary control is the important element of "sound finance" and that the balanced budget doctrine is, for a thousand and one reasons, as absurd as Keynes once thought it to be'. Almost ten years later, his weekly column had the title 'No magic rule for setting budget deficits'. It included such judgements as that it was 'not sensible' to take a zero PSBR as a benchmark for government decisions and that 'fiscal policy can play a part in demand management in the short-to-medium term'.[32]

Lawson's and Brittan's remarks are, of course, distinctly Keynesian, not just because they mention his name and regard the budget deficit as a policy instrument, but also because of their subjective and provisional approach to economic truth. In the 1985 article Brittan said that he would refrain from defining a neutral fiscal position and instead watch how the economy responded to any particular fiscal stance. 'If you like, it is a policy of "suck it and see".' The later Brittan, like the early Keynes, rejects general rules and is very much prepared to look at individual cases on their merits.

It is not an exaggeration to see the abandonment of the old-time fiscal religion as an aspect of a larger deterioration in public morality. But, rather than preach about the wickedness of our times, we need to emphasize the effect of the change in attitudes towards budget deficits on our central concern, the sustainability of current trends in the growth of debt. Actual or potential investors in public debt are aware that nowadays governments in countries such as the USA and Britain have no particular commitment to balancing the books. Although these governments do set out medium-term financial projections which contain targets for budget deficits and by implication some restriction on the expansion of debt, their attitude towards the targets is pragmatic and flexible. The pragmatism and flexibility have a serious cost. The financial community comes to believe that politicians will compromise their duty to control inflation because of competing responsibilities to maintain high employment and economic growth. This belief cannot be blamed on the innate nervousness of investment advisers, but is amply justified by the terms and substance of contemporary public debate. Political willingness to tolerate or even sometimes to encourage inflation undermines savers' confidence in the state. Governments are no longer perceived as having an overriding loyalty to people who buy their debt, but instead as adjusting the size of the budget deficit according to the vicissitudes of the business cycle and intellectual fashion. To compensate for this new and highly political form of risk, savers demand a higher rate of interest on new issues of government debt. This adds to debt servicing costs and increases the burden of the debt.

It also – and here we come to the connection with our main theme – makes the danger of an explosive rise in public debt more likely. At the beginning of the chapter we said that the key determinant of the long-run growth of public debt is the relationship between interest rates and the growth rate of nominal GNP. Clearly, the looser is the government's commitment to sound money, the greater is the weakening of savers' confidence, and the weaker is savers' confidence, the higher are interest rates. It then follows that, for any given growth rate of nominal GNP, the more unfavourable is the relationship between interest rates and the increase in tax revenue for the long-run control of public debt.

The argument is given added piquancy if it is expressed in real rather than nominal terms. To persuade savers to overcome their aversion to self-confessedly inflationary governments, they must receive higher real interest rates on new debt issues. If the real growth rate of the economy is constant, there is an increased risk of an indefinite and uncontrollable rise in the ratio of public debt to national income. The dangers are heightened if the upward movement in real interest rates coincides with a deterioration in underlying growth performance. In such circumstances, both the interest rate and the growth rate have changed adversely from the standpoint of long-run fiscal management. This is a very important and disturbing conclusion, because there has been a pronounced slow-down in the pace of economic advance in most countries since the early 1970s.

In the first 25 years after the Second World War growth rates were high throughout the industrialized world. In Europe the typical annual increase in GNP was between 5 and 10 per cent, while in Japan it lay in the 10–15 per cent range. These historically unprecedented rates of economic expansion made it easy for governments to keep public debt a low or negligible fraction of national income, for two reasons. Not only did the rapid growth in national income boost tax revenues and so enable governments to increase expenditure without incurring budget deficits, but also it arithmetically increased the denominator in the debt/income ratio. Even in the USA and Britain the same line of reasoning applied. Growth rates were much lower than in Europe and Japan, but they were impressively fast by the standards of the inter-war period or the nineteenth century.

But around 1973 the vigour of the growth impulses which had driven the Western economy in the immediate post-war decades began to wane. Since then the annual GNP increase in Europe has usually been under 5 per cent, with a tendency towards further deceleration to 2 or 3 per cent in the 1980s. In Japan the figure is now down to under 5 per cent. In the USA and Britain, exceptionally, growth rates in recent years have remained similar to the post-war average. Overall the economy of the Western industrial nations is growing in the mid-1980s at less than half the rate recorded in the 1960s. The environment for policies of deficit financing is therefore much less congenial. To prevent increases in the ratio of public debt to national income governments must run smaller budget deficits than would have been permissible in the early post-war years.[33]

Our argument contains a simple message for government leaders. The relationship between the real interest rate and the growth rate could be regarded as the political terms of trade, which it is their duty to keep as favourable as possible. They may have many delusions of grandeur and they may waffle endlessly about New Frontiers and New Dawns, but in truth there is not much they can do to increase the underlying growth rate of productivity in a two- or three-year period. But they must try to sustain the demand for government debt and maintain low or moderate borrowing costs.[34] However cynical their private motives and however inflationary their programmes, they must always insist in public that their intentions are angelic and that their first economic objective is the restoration of price stability. For them to talk in any other terms is to alienate financial markets, raise the yield on government bonds and so worsen the fiscal terms of trade against themselves. It is altogether defensible, as well as very predictable, that as Chancellor of the Exchequer Mr Lawson should have declared himself in 1983 as a supporter of 'eventual' price stability. He would no doubt not have liked to be reminded that, as a financial journalist 20 years earlier, he had written 'The great social justification, to my mind, for a mildly inflationary economy is that a society in which borrowers do better than lenders of money is fundamentally more attractive than one in which the reverse is true.'[35]

If politicians must be expected, indeed have an obligation, to mislead the investing public, that does not give them any excuse to mislead themselves. There are strong temptations to base projections of future increases in tax revenue on rosy, but quite untenable, forecasts of economic growth. A particularly crass, and also particularly important, example has been the tendency of the Reagan administration in the USA to publish numbers on GNP and inflation two or three years ahead which no well-informed observer considers credible. In his book *The Triumph of Politics* David Stockman, Director of the US Office of Management and Budget between 1980 and 1985, has written of his despair in early 1981 at colleagues who wanted to worsen the budget (through tax cuts and extra defence spending) by $900b, cut non-defence spending by only $450b and yet still pretend that a balanced budget was within reach. The only way the numbers could be reconciled was by an extraordinarily bullish GNP forecast, which, according to Stockman, was 'the work of a small band of ideologues' including Laffer, Wanniski, Kemp and Paul Craig Roberts. 'The newcomers to the supply-side revolution – the President, the Secretary of the Treasury and the White House senior staff – were almost entirely innocent and uninformed.'[36] In practice, the GNP forecasts were far too high and quite wrong, and very large budget deficits of $200b a year soon emerged.

Stockman had the sense to realize that budget deficits on this scale would cause real interest rates to rise. Although other contributory influences need to be mentioned as well, it certainly was true – as we showed in the Introduction – that the early 1980s saw a substantial increase in real interest rates. This change has complicated the task of restoring equilibrium between the growth of the USA's government debt and the growth of its national income. The issue has now, like the excesses of Big Government in the late 1970s, became one of the most contentious in American domestic politics.

But the international repercussions also need to be highlighted. Because the USA has the world's largest economy, the interest rate on its government debt has a powerful influence on interest rates in other government bond markets. International investors have the choice to commit money to a variety of bond markets and, if everything else is equal, they will buy where the interest rate is highest. The more funds are allocated to US Treasury bonds, the less is available for the Japanese, German or British markets. These countries must then retaliate by increasing their interest rates. The problem of long-run fiscal management caused by the American budget deficit and the associated rise in real interest rates is therefore generalized to all the major industrial countries.

Perhaps even worse are the implications for indebted developing countries. As their own currencies have no prestige in international financial markets, they have had to borrow in dollars and, to a much smaller extent, in deutschmark, yen, sterling and other freely convertible currencies. In consequence, when real dollar interest rates rise, indebted developing countries suffer an increase in borrowing costs. The long-run difficulties in the management of their external debt are worsened by a development over which they have no control. In this way the work of 'a small band of ideologues' can have a profound effect on living standards in São Paulo, Buenos Aires and Lima.

We can now summarize the main points of this chapter. The sustainability of a policy of deficit financing largely depends on the relationship between interest rates and the rate of economic growth. In the last 50 years there has been a deterioration in standards of public morality, and more particularly in the sense of responsibility politicians and their advisers feel towards the public finances. Savers are well aware of this deterioration. As they no longer have the same confidence in the financial integrity of their governments, they require a higher real interest rate on new issues of public debt. The consequent worsening in the fiscal terms of trade has been aggravated in the last 15 years by a slow-down in the underlying rate of economic growth in the Western world. The relationship between interest rates and the growth rate is more hostile to deficit financing, and more dangerous for long-run fiscal control, than at any time in the post-war period. Indeed, arguably it is more worrying today than ever before. The contrast with the past is most vivid in the American case because the old-time fiscal religion, which was observed through most of the nineteenth century and twice enabled the public debt to be substantially repaid, has been replaced by the voodoo economics of a small group of supply-side fanatics. This group has done great damage not only to the public finances of the USA itself, but also to fiscal management in other countries and to the control of external debt in the Third World.

In the following chapter we shall amplify these themes in the context of the major industrial countries. Whereas the present chapter has traced the evolution of thinking about fiscal policy in general, the next will examine the likely consequences of particular fiscal stances and assess the seriousness of recent trends in the ratio of public debt to national income.

2

The Mismanagement of the Public Household

I

In the course of the twentieth century the state sector has expanded as a share of the economy throughout the industrialized world. As this trend has paralleled the decline of the old-time fiscal religion, there seems to be some justification for associating the eclipse of the balanced budget doctrine with the emergence of Big Government. With the state no longer confined, as it was during the nineteenth century, to law, defence and the relief of poverty, a new question of social organization has arisen. A Marxist writer has remarked that, 'The volume and composition of government expenditure and the distribution of the tax burden are not determined by the laws of the market but rather reflect and are structurally determined by social and economic conflicts between classes and groups.'[1] The reference to social conflict may be rather strained, but the contrast between allocation by market mechanisms and distribution according to political pressures is well drawn. The consequent problem for economic policy has been termed 'the management of the public household', a phrase which is more evocative than 'the control of the public finances'.[2]

The notion of a public household accords well with the now widely shared attitude that governments exist to minister to the material needs of their citizens. It is this attitude which lies at the root of the fiscal problems of the modern state. Not only are there constant demands for extra expenditure to meet a variety of social objectives, but there is also a general acceptance that these demands are valid even if the beneficiaries have no intention of paying for them. The legitimacy, indeed the warm and frank approval by leaders of opinion, of these social demands subverts the common-sense principles on which public finance used to rest. It should not require statement that governments cannot pluck resources out of thin air and that their expenditure must be matched, sooner or later, by taxation. But much of political debate, and even more of media comment on social issues, appears to proceed on the assumption that public spending is financed by a nebulous but supposedly omnipotent entity known as 'the state' and not by taxpayers. As Brittan has remarked, contemporary political discussion is penetrated by the myth of Good King Wenceslas that 'there exist tiny handfuls of people known as "governments" who could so act to increase the supply of satisfactions enjoyed by the population if only they chose to do so, but through malevolence or inefficiency do not'.[3] Against this background the history of the last 20 years is best described as the mismanagement, not the management, of the public household.

The degree of mismanagement has varied between countries, but there are common themes throughout the industrial world. In this chapter the main symptom of deterioration is taken to be an increase in the burden of public debt. This is perhaps tendentious, since there may be good reasons for the creation of debt by governments. The most convincing is that, when faced by a sudden and temporary increase in expenditure due to war or a large programme of public works, it causes less harm to the economy to spread the cost over a period of years than to pay for it straightaway. Deferred payment involves the incurral of debt, immediate payment requires taxation. But, considered by itself and aside from any benefits it makes possible through the more flexible timing of expenditure, public debt is an unqualified misfortune for any society. To service it the government must levy taxes, imposing two kinds of cost. Not only are there the disincentives to working and saving associated with any taxation, but also people have to be employed to assess and collect the taxes. These costs have virtually no offsetting net benefit to society because the revenues are raised merely to make transfer payments. The money passes, through the maws of the revenue authorities and the central bank, from taxpayer to bondholder. Since taxpayers and bondholders are members of the same political community it is a case of taking from Peter to give to Paul. Even worse, because in today's circumstances many taxpayers are also – either through direct ownership or indirectly through their insurance policies or pension funds – owners of government debt, it may be a case of taxing Peter to pay Peter. This is pure waste. Moreover, bond dealers and financial commentators find that the demand for their services is strongly correlated with the level of government debt. Turnover in the US Treasury bond market now frequently exceeds $100b a day, with all that entails in terms of contract notes, computer time and skilled man-hours. The paper-churning adds nothing to the quantity of goods and services available to society, however much it may increase the quantity of goods and services available to the paper-churners.[4] Their skills could perhaps be more productively used elsewhere in the economy.

We explained in chapter 1 that the behaviour of the ratio of public debt to national income (from here on, the 'public debt ratio') depends on the relationship between the real interest rate and the growth rate as well as on the size of the budget deficit. In the remainder of chapter 2 we shall see how, partly because of the relentless rise in public expenditure, budget deficits have tended to increase in industrial countries since the 1960s. Heavy emphasis has to be placed on the late 1960s and early 1970s as the starting date for the process. Deficits did not become commonplace in public finance 'since Keynes' or 'since the War', as many sloppy writers on recent economic history suggest. They began, on a recurrent basis, only when Keynesianism had captured a strong hold on policy-making establishments and we have seen that this was much later than 1936 or 1945. The practice of fiscal policy was consistent, therefore, with the evolution of ideas described in chapter 1. It confirms that we should think in terms of a number of separate and brief Keynesian episodes in the major countries and not in terms of a global Keynesian era. Unhappily, it was much easier to start deficit financing than to stop it. When the world economy entered a cyclical recession in 1974, most governments suffered a cyclical loss of revenue and were forced to incur unusually large budget deficits. They have subsequently had great difficulty restoring their fiscal positions to the same healthy condition as in the 1950s and early 1960s. Indeed, the malaise has been aggravated by the budget deficits themselves because their existence and perpetuation worsen the relationship between interest rates and the growth rate. This tendency, for the mismanagement of the public household to become self-reinforcing once it has begun, is one of the main themes of the present chapter. But, before we develop it, we need to survey fiscal practice in the industrialized nations in the 1950s and 1960s.

II

American public finances were managed with great care in the 15 years after the Second World War. In 1945 the Federal deficit, at $47.6b, was equivalent to almost a quarter of GNP, a state of affairs which obviously could not be allowed to continue for long.[5] Sharp reductions in military expenditure led to a surplus of $14.4b in 1947. Over the 14 years from 1947 to 1960, which we have argued are better regarded as the Era of Eisenhower Economics than the Age of Keynes, there were seven surpluses and seven deficits. The cumulative sum of these surpluses and deficits was a minus figure of $0.8b, an impeccable record of balancing the budget over a sequence of minor business cycles.

The numbers are more impressive still if we adjust them to fit in with our conceptual tool-kit. We have seen that, in understanding the behaviour of the debt/income ratio, we need to look at the primary budget balance (i.e. subtracting debt interest from expenditures). On this basis, there were only three years of deficit between 1947 and 1960 and over the whole period the cumulative surplus was substantial. The strong position of the primary balance was combined with a favourable differential between the growth rate of nominal GNP and the interest rate on public debt. As table 5 shows, the early 1950s saw nominal GNP expanding on average by 7.1 per cent a year, while the yield on ten-year Treasury securities was little more than 2½ per cent. In the late 1950s the growth rate of nominal GNP dropped to 4.9 per cent, but it was still above the yield of 3.7 per cent on Treasury securities.

With both the primary fiscal balance and the relationship between the GNP growth rate and the interest rate on government debt helpful, the ratio of Federal debt to GNP fell heavily from over 100 per cent in 1946 to under 50 per cent in 1960.[6] Eisenhower left Kennedy an extremely favourable fiscal legacy. The achievement is the more remarkable because the reduction in the public debt ratio owed little to the effect of inflation in reducing the real value of the debt. Over the 15-year period bondholders enjoyed a worthwhile, although far from munificent, real return in most years. Nevertheless, there does seem to have been some weakening of financial respect for government. Bond yields crept upwards in the late 1950s, despite both the reassuring words from President Eisenhower and the responsible budgetary actions taken by his administration. It is clear, in retrospect, that this upward creep in bond yields was fully justified by emerging trends in American public finance. Good King Ike could not reign for ever.

The deterioration was gradual. The Kennedy Presidency may have seen the first conscious application of Keynesian ideas, but it was certainly not marked by wild fiscal adventurism. Although there were Federal deficits of $4.3b and $3.8b in 1961 and 1962 respectively, these figures were both under 1 per cent of GNP. The 1964 tax cut was followed by enough economic buoyancy and sufficiently strong revenues for the budget to be in surplus of $0.5b in 1965 and only modest deficit of $1.3b in 1966. The reasonably satisfactory condition of public finances was accompanied by moderate inflation. In no year in the early 1960s did the consumer price index rise by more than 2 per cent. However, this was not good enough to halt the slow attrition of financial confidence. The yield on ten-year Treasury securities increased from 4.12 per cent in 1960 to 4.98 per cent in 1966.

The halcyon years of financial stability came to an end in 1966, when the USA increased its military involvement in Southeast Asia. In the late 1960s inflation was always above 2 per cent and in 1970 exceeded 5 per cent. The largest post-1945 Federal deficit until then, amounting to $14.2b, was registered in 1967. It is possible to blame the Vietnam War for this slippage, but also important was advice from many Keynesian economists, now dominant in policy-making circles, that the deficits were not grounds for particular concern. The yield on ten-year Treasury securities rose once more, reaching 7.35 per cent by 1970. Despite this, the ratio of Federal debt to GNP was still falling for most of the 1960s. There may have been a greater intellectual preparedness to incur budget deficits, but in every year except one (1967) they were less than interest payments and the primary budget balance remained in surplus.[7] The yield on public debt may have been rising, but it continued to be less than the rate of increase in nominal GNP. By 1970 Federal debt was equivalent to only 30 per cent of GNP.

In West Germany and Japan government finances were controlled even more tightly than in the USA. The avoidance of deficits reflected a good starting point and favourable economic conditions as well as the political commitment to responsible public finance described in the last chapter. In West Germany the Nazi debts were repudiated in 1945, while rapid inflation in the immediate post-war years wiped out the real value of any financial obligations incurred by public authorities before the 1948 currency reform. In the 1950s there were more years of surplus than of deficit. In Japan the situation was similar.

But how can we talk about public debt when governments are in financial surplus over a period of several years? To resolve this apparent conundrum we need to differentiate between gross and net public debt. Gross debt is the sum of all liabilities owed by a government; net debt is the gross debt minus the value of the financial assets it holds. In West Germany and Japan government debt was issued, mostly as national savings instruments or in short-term form to facilitate open market operations. But debt issuance was exceeded by the acquisition of financial assets. These assets were held in part as deposits at the central bank and in part in the form of vast surpluses in national insurance funds. They were invested either in foreign exchange reserves, which rose spectacularly in West Germany and Japan in the 1950s and 1960s, or in bonds issued by the domestic private sector.

Economists at the Organization for Economic Cooperation and Development (OECD) have estimated that in 1972, five years after the passage of Schiller's law on economic stabilization and growth, West Germany's net public debt was negative (i.e. there was an excess of assets over liabilities) by 5.8 per cent of GNP. There was a positive gross debt, but it was modest at only 18.8 per cent of GNP. The numbers for Japan were remarkably close. Net public debt was −6.5 per cent and

Table 5   American public finances, and the relationship between the growth of nominal GNP and the rate of interest on Treasury securities 1951–1970

	Federal surplus (+)/ deficit (−)	*Increase in money GNP*	*Yield on 10–year Treasury securities*	*The 'fiscal terms of trade'*
	($b)	*(%)*	*(%)*	*(%)*
1951	6.1	15.7	2.56[a]	13.1
1952	−1.5	5.5	2.66[a]	2.8
1953	−6.5	5.7	2.85	2.8
1954	−1.2	0.2	2.40	−2.2
1955	−3.0	9.0	2.82	6.2
1956	3.9	5.5	3.18	2.2
1957	3.4	5.3	3.65	2.6
1958	−2.8	1.3	3.32	−2.0
1959	−12.8	8.5	4.33	4.2
1960	0.3	3.9	4.12	−0.2
1961	−3.3	3.6	3.88	−0.3
1962	−7.1	7.6	3.95	3.6
1963	−4.8	5.6	4.00	1.6
1964	−5.9	7.1	4.19	2.9
1965	−1.4	8.5	4.28	4.2
1966	−3.7	9.5	4.92	4.6
1967	−8.6	5.8	5.07	0.7
1968	−25.2	9.3	5.65	3.6
1969	3.2	8.0	6.67	1.3
1970	−2.8	5.4	7.35	−2.0

[a] Series not available for 1951 and 1952. Figures are Moody's corporate bond yield (Aaa) (%) minus 30 basis points.

The 'fiscal terms of trade' is the excess of the percentage rate of growth of nominal GNP over the percentage yield on 10–year Treasury securities.

Source: *Economic Report of the President* (Washington: US Government Printing Office, 1986), table B–1, B–68, B–73

gross public debt was +17.5 per cent of GNP.[8]

Britain, France and Italy were not blessed by the same degree of fiscal prudence as West Germany and Japan. The British Government, still hemmed in by the archaic above-the-line and below-the-line conventions, was more responsible than the French or Italian governments. There were budget deficits (as measured by a comprehensive measure such as the public sector financial deficit) throughout the 1950s and 1960s, but they were typically between 2 and 3 per cent of GNP. As nominal GNP grew much faster than the average interest rate on the debt, the ratio of public debt to GNP fell from over 200 per cent in 1945 to 75 per cent in 1972. The very high value in 1945 reflected the large deficits, and consequent accumulation of debt, during the Second World War.

France, which had carried such a heavy debt burden during the 1930s, did not repudiate its state obligations after the War, but they were much reduced in value by rapid inflation. Consumer prices were more than 15 times higher in 1950 than 1939. The ratio of public debt to GNP was under 50 per cent throughout the 1950s, although the condition of the government's finances left much to be desired. The reforms of fiscal administration in 1959, following the Rueff package, resulted in a further decline in the ratio during the 1960s. By 1972 gross public debt was equivalent to 26.4 per cent of GNP, while net debt was a meagre 9.1 per cent.

Italy's performance was far less satisfactory. The deficit financing of the 1950s continued, with only brief intervals of fiscal restraint to check the build-up of debt, during the 1960s. By the early 1970s its ratios of gross and net public debt to GNP were approaching Britain's, although Italy did not have the excuse that it had inherited a substantial load of debt from the War. The blemished record of Italian public finance cannot be attributed to Keynesian ideas, but seems almost to be an abiding feature of its national life. Of the smaller European countries, the same comment seems to apply to Belgium which in 1972 had a gross public debt amounting to 71.4 per cent of GNP. Other nations which fell into the debt trap in the 1980s, such as The Netherlands and Sweden, had well-managed budgetary positions in the 1950s and 1960s.

This survey of public finances in the industrial world in the first 25 post-war years has been rapid and perhaps cursory. It does suffice, nevertheless, to establish that the almost universal pattern was to maintain low or negligible budget deficits. This pattern, in conjunction with the favourable gap between growth rates and interest rates, ensured that public debt ratios either declined or remained at very low levels in nearly all the major industrial countries. The only important exception was Italy.

Despite the universality of small budgetary imbalances and the trend towards low public debt ratios, a distinction may be drawn between the English-speaking nations (the USA and Britain) on the one hand and West Germany and Japan on the other. (France does not fit neatly into either category.) At the beginning of the period the English-speaking nations had large public debts which had originated in the War. Their task, and their achievement, in the 1950s and 1960s was to prevent the expansion of these debts from imposing further strains on taxpayers.

Although the academic community in both countries was heavily contaminated by Keynesian theories, policy-makers had a strong and perhaps fortunate resistance to intellectual innovation. They continued to draw up the public accounts and watch the balance between revenue and expenditure in much the same way as their predecessors in the 1930s and 1940s. However, as their conservatism was not enough to persuade savers that price stability would be maintained, government bond yields drifted upwards. In West Germany and Japan, by contrast, there was virtually no public debt in the early post-war years and governments organized their finances with such rigour that they even became net creditors.

In one sense, virtue was rewarded. The yield on West German government debt *declined* for most of the 1950s and 1960s, touching a low point in 1968. It may be symbolic that this low point coincided almost exactly with Schiller's welcome for Keynesian fiscal principles. Afterwards German bond yields began increasing, just as they had been in the USA and Britain since the early 1950s. Nevertheless, West Germany's and Japan's submission to Keynesianism came late enough not seriously to tarnish their reputations for good financial management. Investors, particularly those with large resources and an international outlook, have long memories. They have been prepared – throughout the late 1970s and 1980s – to accept lower returns on holdings of German and Japanese government debt than on US Treasury bonds and British gilt-edged securities. This is a significant comment on the need for governments to retain savers' loyalty and an illustration of our argument in chapter 1 that, the stronger is investor confidence, the lower are a government's debt servicing costs.

But, whatever the Keynesian peccadilloes of the English-speaking nations, budget deficits were nowhere too large to make the control of public debt a major problem. In the early 1970s public debt ratios in the industrial world as a whole were at their lowest levels in the post-war period. The data in table 6 show that in 1970s and 1975 the mean value of the ratio of central government debt to GNP was about 25 per cent in 18 OECD countries. The public debt ratio itself, somewhat higher because of the addition of local authority and nationalized industry obligations, was 37.1 per cent in 1975. Debt at these levels gave policy-makers few headaches. Since public debt ratios had been declining for so many years, they may have become complacent about the medium- and long-run dangers of deficit financing. In the mid-1970s they relaxed their guard and allowed abnormally large budget deficits to emerge. The seeds were being sown for the harvest of fiscal problems in the 1980s.

The severity of the fiscal deterioration is shown in table 6. In 1973 the industrial countries as a group had approximate balance on their general

Table 6 The growth of public debt and budget deficits in the industrial world, 1960–1986

Note that public debt ratios were generally falling until the mid 1970s, but rose sharply in the 1980s. Budget deficits were always under ½ per cent of OECD GDP until 1974 and always (except 1979) above 2 per cent of OECD GDP thereafter.

i. Ratio of public debt to GNP

The period 1960–80:

Country	Central government debt as percentage of GNP					Total public debt as percentage of GNP	
	1960	*1965*	*1970*	*1975*	*1980*	*1975*	*1980*
USA	46.6	37.6	29.3	28.1	28.0	49.1	47.4
Japan	6.0	4.3	6.8	10.4	24.6	17.8	41.9
West Germany	7.4	7.2	7.0	10.5	15.6	24.8	31.4
France	28.4	17.4	12.6	8.9	10.1	15.0	14.0
UK	n.a.	n.a.	52.9	42.9	40.1	68.3	57.2
Italy	37.0	32.3	35.9	53.7	60.8	58.4	49.5
Canada	44.6	36.7	29.2	22.6	28.4	n.a.	n.a.
Mean of 18 OECD countries	34.2	28.1	24.7	24.5	26.8	37.1	45.1

n.a., not available.

Sources: L. Hakim and C. Wallich 'OECD deficits, debt and savings, structure and trends, 1965–81: a survey of the evidence' in D. Lal and M. Wolf (eds) *Stagflation, Savings, and the State* (New York: Oxford University Press for the World Bank, 1986), p. 329

The period from 1980:

	Gross debt of general government as percentage of nominal GDP/GNP								
	1980	*1981*	*1982*	*1983*	*1984*	*1985*	*1986*	*1987[a]*	*1988[a]*
USA	37.7	37.1	41.1	44.0	45.1	48.5	50.5	51.6	52.2
Japan	52.0	57.0	61.1	66.9	68.4	69.4	69.1	69.5	68.8
West Germany	32.5	36.3	39.5	40.9	41.7	42.3	42.4	43.2	44.4
France	25.0	25.9	28.3	29.8	32.6	34.6	36.4	38.3	39.9
UK	54.9	54.9	53.6	54.0	55.3	53.7	53.8	53.0	52.4
Italy	67.4	70.5	76.8	84.4	91.1	99.6	102.4	107.1	112.7
Canada	44.7	45.1	50.5	54.5	58.2	63.7	67.4	70.2	72.5

[a] Forecasts.
1986 partly estimated.

Source: OECD *Economic Outlook*, June 1987, p. 20

Table 6 (*Continued*)

ii. Ratio of budget deficits to GNP

	General government surplus (+) or deficit (−) as percentage of nominal GNP/GDP as market prices									
	1971	*1972*	*1973*	*1974*	*1975*	*1976*	*1977*	*1978*	*1979*	*1980*
USA	−1.7	−0.3	0.5	−0.2	−4.2	−2.1	−0.9	0.0	0.6	−1.3
Japan	1.4	0.4	0.5	0.4	−2.6	−3.8	−3.8	−5.5	−4.8	−4.5
West Germany	−0.1	−0.5	1.2	−1.4	−5.7	−3.4	−2.4	−2.5	−2.7	−3.2
France	0.7	0.8	0.9	0.6	−2.2	−0.5	−0.8	−1.9	−0.7	0.3
UK	1.5	−1.2	−2.7	−3.8	−4.6	−4.9	−3.2	−4.2	−3.2	−3.3
Italy	−7.1	−9.2	−8.5	−8.1	−11.7	−9.0	−8.0	−9.7	−9.5	−8.0
Canada	0.1	0.1	1.1	1.9	−2.4	−3.8	−4.6	−4.9	−3.2	−4.2
GDP-weighted average of 15 OECD countries	−0.5	−0.4	0.1	−0.5	−3.8	−2.7	−2.1	−2.3	−1.9	−2.5

	1981	*1982*	*1983*	*1984*	*1985*	*1986*	*1987[a]*	*1988[a]*
USA	−1.0	−3.5	−3.8	−2.7	−3.4	−3.3	−2.7	−2.6
Japan	−3.8	−3.6	−3.7	−2.1	−0.8	−0.9	−0.9	−0.2
West Germany	−3.7	−3.3	−2.4	−1.9	−1.1	−1.2	−1.5	−2.0
France	−1.8	−2.7	−3.1	−2.9	−2.6	−2.9	−2.7	−2.5
UK	−2.8	−2.3	−3.6	−3.9	−2.7	−2.9	−2.7	−2.7
Italy	−11.9	−12.6	−11.7	−13.0	−14.0	−12.6	−12.6	−12.2
Canada	−1.5	−5.7	−6.6	−6.6	−5.4	−4.9	−4.6	
GDP-weighted average of 17 OECD countries	−2.7	−4.0	−4.2	−3.4	−3.4	−3.3	−3.0	−2.8

[a] Forecasts.

Sources: To 1980, Hakim and Wallich, p 325; from 1981, OECD *Economic Outlook*, June 1987, p. 18

government finances, a satisfactory position by any standards. (General government includes both central and local government.) In 1975 they had a deficit equivalent to 3.8 per cent of their combined national products, the worst figure in the post-war period until then. This change could be attributed to the intensity of the worldwide recession. Output in the OECD area fell by 0.4 per cent in 1975, also the worst figure in the post-war period, and the weakness in economic activity had the usual adverse effects – through the consequent loss of tax revenues and increase in unemployment benefit – on the budgetary position. The harshness of the cyclical downturn was interpreted as the main reason for the widening budget deficits. This view carried the comforting message that the 1975 figures were a temporary lapse and that, with the return of more normal levels of demand, budget deficits would decline without further government action. Moreover, the recession could be blamed on the oil price shock, which was quite beyond the control of policy-makers in the industrial nations. It followed that there was no strong case for reversing the trends in revenue and expenditure which had characterized the 1960s.

This assessment was too sanguine in two respects. First, it rested on the assumptions that the level of economic activity, and the associated rates of unemployment and capacity utilization, were normal in 1973 and unusually depressed in 1975. This was not an unreasonable belief at the time, but subsequent experience suggests that it was over-optimistic. Secondly, it failed to recognize that certain elements in public expenditure, especially various kinds of social welfare payment, had been growing in the late 1960s and early 1970s at rates much in excess of the potential long-run growth in GNP. This imbalance was disguised by the remarkably rapid advances in industrial productivity, and so in national output, achieved in the Golden Age of the first 25 post-war years. Politicians were misled into thinking that these advances were guaranteed into the indefinite future, whereas in fact they were – from a very long-run historical perspective – a fortunate aberration. The slower growth of output after 1973 also implied slower growth in the tax base and so denied the state the resources needed to finance more generous welfare arrangements. As Daniel Bell has put it, the public household was threatened by 'the pressure of rising entitlements.'[9]

The scale of these rising entitlements should have caused governments to pause for thought. In the seven major industrial countries the share of government expenditure on public goods (defence, administration, economic services) fell from 16.4 per cent to 10.9 per cent of GNP between 1954 and 1980. By contrast, the share on social goods and income maintenance rose from 10.5 per cent to 23.4 per cent over the same period. 'In essence, the entire purpose of government was changing.'[10] Because of the increasingly widely held presuppositions of the public household, and because more voters saw the nation as having as its prime end the improvement of their living standards, it was difficult for political leaders to curb the growth in welfare expenditure.

The political inconvenience of correcting unsustainable trends in expenditure and revenue could, in any case, be avoided if the growth rates, unemployment levels and tax buoyancy of the Golden Age were to return. In most nations it was only in the 1980s that this hope had to be abandoned. By then, as table 6 demonstrates, there had been several years of significant deficit financing. Governments finally came to recognize that expenditure plans had to be trimmed back into line with increases in GNP. But the damage had been done. National debts had acquired their own growth momentum.

III

To understand the self-feeding character of the public debt problem it may be helpful to reiterate and develop the fiscal version of our key proposition about debt growth. This was stated in the last chapter as 'when the average interest rate on its debt exceeds the growth rate of nominal GNP, a government must run a primary surplus to stop its debt situation running out of control'. A primary surplus is an excess of tax revenues over public expenditure minus interest payments.

There is a complication which should be mentioned at this stage. It can be argued that the *post-tax* average interest rate is more appropriate than the *pre-tax* interest rate in statements about the long-run behaviour of public debt. The reason is that the post-tax interest rate represents the true cost of borrowing to the government. Debt does not grow each year by the addition of interest charges, but by the addition of interest charges *less the tax on them*. This is important. Even when the pre-tax interest rate is above the growth rate, the post-tax rate can still be beneath it if tax rates are high enough. Perhaps not surprisingly in view of its significance for policy, there has been a debate about the relative validity of pre-tax and post-tax interest rates. The conclusions are difficult and will not be reviewed here, but in broad terms the post-tax interest rate is the correct one to use.[11] The amended version of the key proposition then becomes 'the public debt ratio rises explosively when the average post-tax interest rate on government debt exceeds the growth rate of nominal GNP and the government is not running a sufficiently large primary surplus'.

This more complete statement of the determinants of debt growth is valuable in identifying the options available to a financially embarrassed government. Let us suppose that the conditions on sustainability have been breached and that, unless something is done, the ratio of public debt to national income ratio will rise explosively. Our statement shows that the government has four variables it can influence to escape from the debt trap. The first and most obvious is the primary fiscal deficit. If this can be reduced enough, by cuts in non-interest expenditure or increases in taxation, sustainability may be restored. But this is politically unpalatable, particularly in nations where certain kinds of non-interest expenditure – such as welfare entitlements – are regarded as sacrosanct. The three other variables are the average interest rate on debt, the growth rate of nominal GNP and the tax rate on debt interest receipts. If the interest rate can be reduced and the growth rate and tax rate increased, the government may be able to return to a viable fiscal position. In practice the only permanent and genuine answer normally is a cut in the primary deficit. Attempts to alter the other determinants of debt growth may work as palliatives in the short or medium run, but they are counter-productive in the long run. This is another of those many cases where democratic governments facing an electoral deadline have a strong temptation to misbehave. An economist's lag is often a politician's nightmare, but here it can be his deliverance. Indeed, it is in the contrast between these short-run and long-run effects that an important part of the self-feeding character of deficit financing and debt growth is to be explained.

In the next three sections we shall consider each of the potentially mischievous variables in turn.

IV

When there is a free market in public debt, there is nothing wrong with a government trying to sell its debt at the lowest possible nominal interest rate. Indeed, as taxpayers obviously benefit if debt interest costs can be limited, it has a duty to market its debt in the most cost-effective way. However, when a government has trouble finding enough purchasers of its debt, there is a temptation to meddle with financial markets and force savings institutions to buy new issues of stock at artificially high prices. Unhappily, in most countries governments do succumb to this temptation. The typical encroachment on the savings pool is a requirement that financial institutions hold a minimum proportion of their assets in the form of public debt.

If these institutions would otherwise have held – at the prevailing price of public debt – a lower proportion, their commercial freedom has been infringed. There are two damaging effects. First, as the saving institutions would have willingly bought public debt in the prescribed amount only at a lower price, the gap between this price and the actual price paid represents a levy on their operations – in effect, a kind of tax. The levy appears to fall on the institutions, which are large and impersonal and are tagged in the media as 'unpopular'. In fact, financial institutions are merely intermediaries between one set of people and another and the tax is paid by their shareholders, their customers, their depositors (in the case of banks) or their policy-holders (insurance companies). Even if the formalities are conducted with more courtesy, the underlying realities are little different from the forced loans (the so-called 'benevolences') of Stuart England.[12] Secondly, because mandatory ratios of public debt to assets apply to institutions but not to persons, there is a disincentive to save through institutional channels. Instead individuals prefer to keep financial assets in their own names. This fragments the financial system, impairs its ability to exploit economies of scale, reduces its efficiency and undermines the marketability of government debt. Perversely, the long-run effect of heavy-handed government intrusion into the financial system may therefore be to reduce the community's willingness to hold public debt.

Exchange controls can be interpreted in similar terms. They commonly oblige people to hold money or other financial assets in domestic currency rather than a preferred mix of domestic and foreign currency. Since in modern conditions virtually all money is a liability of the central bank or the commercial banking system, and since both the central bank and commercial banks lend to government, the obligation to hold money in domestic currency is tantamount to an obligation to invest in government debt. Again, although its interference with currency choice may appear to be far removed from a government's financing problem, the truth is that exchange controls are a form of taxation.[13] Arguably, their long-run effect is also to exacerbate the problem of financing a budget deficit. As they complicate the purchase and sale of a currency, they restrict its convertibility, stain its reputation and reduce people's preparedness to hold it. In consequence, the sale of government debt denominated in a currency subject to exchange controls is more difficult than in a freely convertible currency. This may seem paradoxical, but a casual inspection of the relative liquidity of the major government bond markets justifies the conjecture. Of course, the more liquid a financial market, the greater in general is its capacity to absorb new issues of debt.

In short, attempts to bend the terms of public debt sales – either by direction of investment or by exchange controls – recoil on the governments which make them. The efficiency of financial markets, and so their willingness and ability to purchase government debt, is inevitably undermined. Indeed, the damage is worse than that. When governments intrude aggressively into the financial system and try to grab an excessive share of a nation's savings, the private setor has more difficulty raising money for its own investment needs. The eventual result is to reduce the economy's dynamism, causing an unfavourable change in the relationship between interest rates and the growth rate. We shall return to this point in chapter 3.

V

The second way for a government to escape from the debt trap without curbing its primary fiscal deficit is to increase the growth rate of nominal GNP sufficiently. In fact, the phrase 'increasing the growth rate of nominal GNP' is misleading. The rise in nominal GNP has two components, the increase in real output and inflation. Since it is fantasy to imagine that governments can improve the trend rate of real output growth over a mere two- or three-year time-frame, policies which boost the growth rate of nominal GNP tend in practice to be policies which boost inflation.

There is no doubt that through one important and obvious mechanism inflation eases any government's debt management problem. It reduces the real value of debts incurred in the past. This lowers the tax burden necessary to service the debt and so facilitates the task of keeping the budget deficit down. To take a simple example, suppose that the public debt ratio is unity (i.e. public debt is equal to national income) and the average interest rate on the debt is 10 per cent. Assume also that the budget deficit is entirely accounted for by interest payments, which must then of course also be 10 per cent of GNP. If nominal GNP is rising at any rate less than 10 per cent a year, the government is in the debt trap. But let it now embark on a programme of deliberate inflation which doubles the price level in a matter of a few weeks. As national income has doubled as well and the nominal value of the debt is unchanged, the public debt ratio is reduced to 0.5. Debt interest payments are also fixed in money terms, and both they and the budget deficit are lowered to 5 per cent of GNP. It is clear that the burden of the debt has been cut drastically. Moreover, despite being in the debt trap initially, the once-for-all jump in prices has led to a fall in the debt/income ratio.[14]

Few governments have ever behaved with this degree of cynicism. To enact a doubling of the price level, virtually by fiat, is hardly distinguishable from outright theft. Holders of the debt have lost half of their assets. The consequent reduction in the real value of the taxes needed to service the debt is a straightforward transfer of spending power from them to taxpayers, which the taxpayers have done nothing to deserve. It requires some cheek to pretend that arbitrary shifts in wealth distribution on this scale are socially beneficial.

But many governments in all ages have behaved with a somewhat lower level of cynicism which can fairly be called legalized fraud. Inflation may not be allowed to double prices and halve the real value of debts in a few weeks, but it has not been prevented from having these effects over a five-, ten- or fifteen-year period. If at the outset the public debt ratio was high – say, greater than 1 – the resulting erosion of the real value of the government's liabilities amounts to a substantial tax on bondholders. Of course, when this process of debasement is associated with a sufficiently high inflation rate, the rate of increase in nominal GNP exceeds the average interest rate on its debts and the government cannot be caught in the debt trap.

Indeed, in the 1970s all the governments of the main industrial countries – with the exception of West Germany – ran inflation rates so high that holders of their debt earned a negative real return. In other words, the inflation rate exceeded the interest rate paid out to savers. It would be less circumlocutory and more honest to say 'savers lost money'. Aware that the process of debt debasement had simplified, at least temporarily, the task of fiscal control, none of the governments concerned was loud with apologies for what they had done. The OECD has prepared estimates, for six large economies, of both the real return on government debt and the extent to which inflation eroded its value. They are given in table 7.

The numbers are particularly instructive because they isolate the

Table 7 Central government debt in six major OECD countries, 1973–1982

	Average annual change in central government debt as % share of GDP	*Change in share (% of GDP) attributable to:*			*Average real return (%)*
		Inflation	*Interest payments*	*New issues*	
USA, 1973/4–1981/2	−0.3	−1.5	+1.6	+0.7	−0.1
Japan, 1973/4–1981/2	+3.5	−1.5	+1.2	+4.3	−2.8
West Germany, 1973–1982	+1.3	−0.6	+0.7	+1.3	+1.4
France, 1973–81	+0.3	−0.8	+0.7	+0.6	−1.8
UK, 1973/4–1981/2	−0.5	−5.4	+2.5	+3.2	−6.7
Canada 1973/4–1980/1	−0.4	−3.1	+2.4	+1.4	−1.7

Component changes do not add to total since effect of relative price changes and real GDP growth is excluded. New debt issues are equal to change in debt outstanding, excluding interest payments.

Source: Table 7 in 'Public sector deficits' in *OECD Occasional Studies*, June 1983

relative size of the three main influences – inflation, interest payments and budget deficits – on the growth of debt. The budget deficit under consideration is the 'primary' concept, net of interest payments, which we have seen is most useful in this kind of analysis. In every country inflation reduced the ratio of central government debt to GNP. There were wide contrasts in the extent of deficit financing, with the largest primary deficits in the UK and Japan and the smallest in France. There were also wide contrasts in the behaviour of the debt/GNP ratio, with large rises in Japan and (from a very low base) in West Germany, but declines in the UK and Canada. But one feature was common to the six countries. Irrespective of whether the debt/GNP ratio was rising or falling, interest payments increased as a share of GNP. The obvious interpretation is that savers were retaliating against the losses they had incurred because of inflation. Moreover, they required an upward adjustment to nominal yields not only to match the higher levels of inflation that governments now regarded as acceptable but also to pre-empt the risk of yet faster inflation in future. As two World Bank economists commented on these trends, 'higher *real* interest rates have been required to compensate bondholders for the potentially higher risk of taking a capital loss on their bonds'.[15]

The most unattractive case among the six countries considered by the OECD was the UK. It may be difficult today to recall how much admiration and respect the financial conduct of the British government once commanded. From the Exchequer Stop of 1672 to the Second World War it had an enviable, indeed a possibly unique, record.[16] It had always honoured its obligations in nominal terms and it had never in peacetime relied on inflation to reduce the real value of its liabilities. True enough, there had been several phases of rising prices, notably during the Napoleonic Wars and again in the 1850s and 1860s, and there had also been the sharp inflation of the First World War. But after the wartime inflations Britain's rulers had made serious attempts not just to restore price stability but to return prices to the level which had prevailed before the wars.

It was this resolution and commitment, reflecting a deeply held sense of financial obligation by the British governing elite, that motivated the return to the gold standard in both 1819 and 1925. The safety of gilt-edged securities, their complete immunity to political risk and budgetary mismanagement, was an assumption of thought for many generations. Ford Madox Ford's tetralogy *Parade's End*, which chronicled the early decline of what he called the 'public official class' in the 1910s and 1920s, begins with a paragraph describing a train journey in southeast England just before the First World War. The central character in the novel is Christopher Tietjens, a senior civil servant.

The compartment smelt faintly, hygienically of admirable varnish; the train ran as smoothly – Tietjens remembered thinking – as British gilt-edged securities.

If the train had 'swayed or jolted over the rail joints', his colleague 'would have written to the company. Perhaps he would even have written to *The Times*.'[17]

Nowadays no one could write in such terms of either gilt-edged securities or the British railway system, nor could they hold such expectations about the automatic efficacy of a letter to *The Times*. In the 1970s the British government debased its debt more rapidly than any other large industrial country. Inflation reduced the real value of central government debt by 5.3 per cent a year on average between 1972–3 and 1979–80, while the real rate of return to bondholders was −7.2 per cent. The government's reputation for financial probity, which had been built up and protected over three centuries, was frittered away in less than a decade. This is a serious loss, comparable to the wilful destruction of part of the national heritage, because future British governments will not enjoy the same degree of trust among savers as their predecessors and will therefore not be able to operate with such high ratios of debt to national income. They will not have the same flexibility when faced by genuine financial emergencies (such as those arising from war or extensive trade embargoes).

The British public official class of today seems little concerned. On the contrary, a well-respected school of thought among economists has argued that budget deficits are not being measured correctly because the real value of the national debt is being eroded every year by inflation. In its view, the most valid measure of the budget deficit is one where this erosion of the real value of the debt is deducted from the accounting deficit. As the loss of real value exceeded the accounting deficit during the 1970s, it is claimed that the British government actually ran a surplus during the period. In some versions, this so-called 'surplus' is criticized for having withdrawn demand from the economy and so contributed to the weakness of economic activity. The implied policy recommendation is rather anarchic. The higher the inflation rate, the larger the nominal budget deficit the Government should run, in order that debt still be injected into the economy in real terms. 'If one is concerned with the inflation-adjusted deficit, then clearly a higher rate of inflation requires a larger conventional accounting deficit to maintain the same fiscal stance.'[18]

This line of reasoning suffers from serious conceptual inadequacies even in its own terms. Economists may find it convenient to regard the national debt as an asset in the hands of the private sector. They can then argue both that the inflation-induced reduction in the real value of the debt makes the private sector worse off and that people cut their spending in response. But, in truth, the size of the national debt does not in itself add anything to or subtract anything from the wealth of a nation. It is simultaneously an asset of bondholders and a liability of taxpayers. In consequence, to the extent that inflation reduces bondholders' wealth, it also reduces taxpayers' liabilities. There should be no net effect on expenditure. In any case, the private sector holds many financial assets and liabilities, with their total value far greater than the national debt. The justification for basing a view on people's spending behaviour solely on changes in the real value of their holdings of government debt is very unclear. Why should behaviour not be much more profoundly influenced by the impact of inflation on the real value of shares, debentures, building society deposits and bank accounts?[19]

The absurdity of regarding public debt as part of the nation's 'wealth' is exposed rather obviously if we were to accept, for a few moments, that the idea was correct. The debt consists merely of bits of paper, called gilt-edged securities, Treasury bills, local authority bonds and the like to give them an identity, but just bits of paper all the same. If these bits of paper are 'wealth', the government should immediately stop all taxes, conscript the entire working population and instruct it to build factories for printing gilt-edged securities, preferably of very high denomination. If the national debt is indeed wealth, we would soon be hundreds of billions of pounds 'better off'. Laymen may marvel at what passes for economics in contemporary Britain![20]

In short, the argument for fiscal reflation to compensate for the inflationary depreciation of past debt is conceptually insecure. But let us suppose that it was soundly based in theoretical terms. What would be its practical effects? The answer is that it would complete the work of financial vandalism begun in the 1950s and 1960s and pursued so shamelessly in the 1970s. Investors in government debt were cheated at a rate of 7.2 per cent a year in the mid- and late 1970s, but they are now to be expected to acquire substantially more debt in order that the government can resume inflationary policies. They are not likely to be reassured that advocates of fiscal reflation on these grounds, notably Professor Marcus Miller and Henry Neuberger, have prepared some of the most precise, scientific and sophisticated estimates of the fraud perpetrated on them in past years; nor that Professor Miller was once an influential adviser to the Social Democratic Party and that Mr Neuberger advises the Labour Party; nor that academic research on this subject has been financed by the Bank of England and listened to with close and respectful attention at seminars with senior Treasury officials present. It is almost as if, in the Britain of today, some degree of official swindling is regarded as necessary as confirmation of the government's intellectual modernity. The simple and traditional conception of the market in British government securities – that, in an environment of broadly stable prices, yields might fluctuate between 2 and 5 per cent in nominal terms – is now considered not to be a norm but a historical curiosity of little more than antiquarian interest.

Actual and potential investors in government debt are well aware of the intellectual climate. They also have strong memories of how much money was lost during the 1950s, 1960s and 1970s. Although the position has been much better for them in the 1980s, they have no guarantee that the recent improvement can continue, particularly as debt debasement seems in some influential policy-advising circles to be treated almost as an instrument of government policy. They must therefore have a high real return on public debt whose terms are fixed in money terms to protect them against the risks of future inflation. It is obvious that this limits the government's scope to incur budget deficits and makes a slide into the debt trap more likely. We can draw two conclusions. The first is paradoxical, that the noiser are the proponents of fiscal reflation, the less effective will fiscal reflation be in practice. This follows from the damage that the prospect of increased deficit financing has on inflation expectations and hence on real interest rates. Secondly, attempts to escape the debt trap by increasing inflation are counter-productive in the long run because they drive up real interest rates and so worsen the fiscal terms of trade.

The discussion in this section has concentrated on Britain, mainly because the contrast between its long record of monetary responsibility until the Second World War and its recent financial experience is so pathetic. Similar remarks could be made about other countries. We have already seen that holders of government debt had negative real returns in the large industrial countries, except West Germany, in the 1970s. On the whole, however, intellectual trends in other countries have been healthier than in Britain. In the USA most academic economists, and certainly the overwhelming majority of Federal Reserve officials, consider price stability to be a prime official policy objective. This is not true of most academic economists and Bank of England officials in Britain. However, there have been some worrying signs even in the USA. For example, Professor Robert Eisner has argued – on the same lines as Miller and Neuberger – that estimates of fiscal thrust should be adjusted to take account of inflation and that 'official measures of the federal debt and budget deficits are misleading by any reasonable standards'.[21] If it is unreasonable for citizens to expect their government to maintain the real value of investments in its debt, this comment is justified. Otherwise it is not.

VI

The third means by which a government in the debt trap can restore sustainability without cutting the primary deficit is by raising the tax rate on debt interest. Here the myopia of the policy response is particularly transparent. An investor in government debt will be able to see very quickly that the return to him has been reduced. It would be logical for him to withhold his savings until the government has raised the pre-tax interest rate on its debt enough to re-establish the same post-tax return. The cost of debt service to the government would move back, after a relatively short interval in which the necessary portfolio adjustments were made, to the previous level and the debt trap would continue to operate. Even worse, the fact that the government had raised taxes once would give a warning to investors that it might do so again. They would have to receive not the same post-tax rate of return as before, but a higher one to anticipate future tax increases. If this were their response, the government would be in a more unfavourable position than if it had not put up taxes on debt interest in the first place. Once again, an attempt to escape the debt trap by tampering with the terms available to investors is only viable in the short run. It eventually worsens the fiscal position.

Perhaps this says enough about the folly of raising taxes to ease the debt burden. However, there is one country – Italy – where the government (or, rather, a sequence of governments) has adopted (or, perhaps one should say, stumbled upon) a remarkable combination of inflationary, tax and regulatory expedients to ease its fiscal difficulties. As Italy is more seriously caught in the debt trap than any other large industrial country, the various devices merit some discussion.

Tax evasion is and has long been part of the Italian way of life. Its eradication has been hampered by an unusual feature of its fiscal arrangements, namely a strict law on banking secrecy which prevents the tax authorities from investigating an individual's accounts. As a result, money from the 'hidden economy' finds its way into the banking system, where it is effectively immune from taxation in the ordinary sense. This is very frustrating for the government because the reduced size of the tax base hits its revenues and tends to enlarge the budget deficit. However, the money can be attacked in other ways. For many years the Italian banking system has been forced to invest a high proportion of its deposits in public debt, thus ensuring that funds saved from the hidden economy become available for the government's use. By then running a sufficiently high inflation rate, the government can reduce the real value of deposits and appropriate this loss for itself. One observer has suggested that 'the state acquired a vested interest in inflation, since through inflation the size of past debts would shrink . . . . Inflation thus became a substitute for unpaid taxes. In a country of prevailing wage indexation, the inflation tax was levied mainly on savings.' Indeed, the rough justice enforced by inflation could be said to have stopped the economy 'falling apart' and 'though ritually blamed for all kinds of evil became in fact a key ingredient of the economic mix'.[22]

In other words, every element in the Italian savings and tax nexus is silly considered in its own right, but the sum of the various sillinesses is a coherent fiscal machine. The truth is less flattering. It would be fine for the government, by deliberate inflation, to recapture the tax base lost through clandestine business activity if it had no effects on the legitimate economy. But, of course, both the legitimate and the hidden economies are affected by inflation. Honest savers, who pay their taxes in full, are made worse off by rising prices and have to be compensated by a better return on government debt. In Italy today interest on government debt has therefore had to be exempted from tax, while interest rates are kept attractive in relation to inflation. This may be admirable in many respects, but it aggravates the long-run fiscal dilemma. We explained earlier that part of the condition for unsustainability is that the post-tax interest rate on public debt be above the growth rate. By virtually abolishing tax on public debt, the Italian government has increased the post-tax interest rate it has to pay. Even worse, because many commentators recognize that the present growth in government debt is intolerable, there are numerous proposals in the newspapers for taxing interest or imposing an arbitrary cut in interest payments. Of course, this further increases suspicion among savers and obliges them to ask for a yet higher interest rate. So far the process has not run out of control. 'Uncoerced, Italians have shown no fear of, or antipathy towards, government securities. . . . According to the central bank, the number of members of the family sector with savings in state bonds runs into millions, with 60 per cent of holdings being worth less than 20m. lire (under £1,000).'[23] We shall consider later whether the Italian citizen's confidence in his government is altogether warranted.

It is time to restate our theme. Governments are ill-advised to attempt to escape from the debt trap by distorting the market for savings in their favour, by eroding the value of public debts by inflation or by taxing bondholders' income at an excessive rate. All three courses of action are counter-productive in the long run because they raise real interest rates. If the economy's underlying productivity performance is unchanged, the differential between growth and interest rates will have changed unfavourably and the stability of fiscal policy is further jeopardized. As we shall argue later that large budget deficits can cause serious injury to financial markets, weaken the efficiency of private investment and therefore reduce the growth rate, another strand of analysis has still to be added to reinforce the pessimism of our conclusions.

VII

An important outcome of the argument so far is that, once a government has fallen into the debt trap, it should try to restore a sustainable fiscal position by acting on the primary budget balance. It should, at the very least, reduce the primary budget deficit. Indeed, if the average interest rate on its debt is above the growth rate, it has to achieve a primary surplus to prevent an unstable increase in debt. The larger the debt has grown, and the higher the burden of debt interest, the greater must this surplus be to restore sustainability.[24] What has been the record of the advanced nations since the mid-1970s in controlling expenditure on debt interest and maintaining satisfactory primary budget positions?

We have already seen in table 7 that debt interest payments rose, as a share of national income, in six of the large industrial countries during the 1970s. Those figures related to central government debt interest. The OECD economists to whom we referred in an earlier context have also prepared figures for net interest on all public sector debt. They show a more drastic, and arguably more frightening, increase in the 1980s. In the seven major OECD economies as a whole net interest on public sector debt went up from 4.1 per cent of total government expenditure in 1972 to 6.0 per cent in 1979; in the following seven years, to 1986, it is estimated to have risen to 9.5 per cent. In the OECD area (which includes another 11 small countries) net interest was 4.3 per cent of government expenditure in 1972 and 5.9 per cent in 1979 and is estimated to have been 9.8 per cent in 1986.[25] These statistics may seem bad enough, but since total public expenditure rose appreciably faster than national income debt interest must have increased even more as a proportion of GNP.

There have been large differences between countries, some of them perhaps unexpected. The growth of debt interest has been faster in Japan and West Germany than in the English-speaking nations. This is partly explained by the lower intitial level of debt in Japan and West Germany, but also relevant in the Japanese case have been the extremely high budget deficits incurred in the late 1970s and early 1980s. In 1986 gross interest on public debt is estimated to have been twice as high, as a share of government expenditure, in Japan as in the USA.[26] In the UK debt interest is no longer rising quickly, although it is higher as a share of national income than five or ten years ago. In 1984 the British government published a Green Paper on *The Next Ten Years: Public Expenditure and Taxation into the 1990s*, containing explicit and quite detailed projections of debt interest in Annex 4. The hope was that, on plausible assumptions about the budget deficit, growth and real interest rates, the ratio of debt interest to GNP would decline in the late 1980s.[27] Some of the numbers amounted to little more than wishful guesswork, but they were nevertheless very significant as signalling concern about this aspect of budgetary policy. Whatever its record in the 1970s, the British government at present stands moderately well in international comparisons of fiscal control. But the West German government stands even better. The share of debt interest in government expenditure went up rapidly from 3.7 per cent in 1979 to 6.3 per cent in 1983, but then stopped rising. In the next few years it is likely to fall.

The most alarming cases, in terms of both the level of the debt interest burden and its rate of growth, are Italy, Canada and a number of small European countries. In Italy interest on public debt was 5.5 per cent of government expenditure in 1972, 12.8 per cent in 1979 and 16.1 per cent in 1986. As a share of GNP the explosion in debt interest is even more disquieting. In the early 1970s the figure was about 2 per cent; it is now in excess of 10 per cent. It does not require much common sense to see that, if this trend continues, the Italian people will be paying an extremely high proportion of their taxes merely to meet the claims of the bondholders. If – as most projections envisage – debt interest is a quarter of government expenditure by the mid-1990s, they will resent the amount of money being spent on debt interest and tax evasion will increase further. No doubt, in such circumstances a few muddle-headed commentators will be even more vocal about the merits of inflation as a means of extracting resources from the hidden economy and so preventing the nation from 'falling apart'. There is a risk that the process of financial disintegration will accelerate, with increasingly mad policy proposals being taken seriously by politicians unwilling to accept the necessary austerity measures. Every increase in debt, debt interest and the budget deficit would bring forward the date of the plunge into ungovernability by raising real interest rates and worsening the terms on which further debt issues were sold.

Even if the pace has quickened in recent years, the deterioration in Italian public finances has been continuous in the post-war period. It can at least be sanctioned, although hardly in a flattering sense, by tradition. Canada has no such excuse. As another English-speaking country, Canada is both an inheritor of war debts and a natural consignee of Keynesian ideas, but this does not really explain why debt interest should be 8 per cent of national income and 18 per cent of government expenditure. One possible rationalization is that Canada regards itself as part of a North American financial zone. Because it can tap the savings pool of the USA its government does not feel as constrained, in its budgetary behaviour, as if it were limited to borrowing in domestic financial markets.[28]

The same argument can be extended to small countries generally, providing a reason for their undoubted tendency in recent years to let debt and debt interest rise at unsustainable rates. For example, the idea may apply to Ireland which remained a member of the sterling area, with access to British savings, for several decades after its formation as an independent republic. Debt interest, already very high at about 12½ per cent of government expenditure in the late 1970s, almost reached 20 per cent in 1985. By ending the link between its currency and sterling in 1979, the Irish government may actually have worsened its fiscal problem. Other European countries suffering from an explosion in interest costs in the early 1980s were Belgium, The Netherlands, Sweden and Denmark. The ready marketability of their debt in offshore financial markets, supplied partly with savings from the large and low-deficit West German economy, may account for their procrastination in reversing adverse fiscal trends. They did not feel under the same degree of pressure as if they had had to rely exclusively on local financial resources.

It is clear from this account that many industrial countries have been in the debt trap in the early 1980s. As we warned in the Introduction, because interest is being charged not only on the principal but also on the accumulating interest which is constantly being added to it, the problem is exacerbated. The difficulties are the more unwelcome because debt interest, unlike many other items of public expenditure, is a contractual obligation and cannot be escaped. 'The major reason for concern about an increasing debt interest burden is the implied reduction in the flexibility of fiscal policy. With one component of expenditures committed to increase as a share of GNP, fiscal restraint is required (either tax increases or expenditure cuts elsewhere) just to maintain . . . the deficit at a stable share of GNP.'[29]

This is not to say that all political leaders have allowed the situation to slither from bad to worse. On the contrary, several governments have taken strong corrective measures. Unable to halt the growth in debt interest payments, they have had to curb the primary fiscal deficit. The rigour and extent of this kind of fiscal action has varied between countries. Some of the most prodigal governments of the late 1970s and early 1980s have taken the necessary steps. The British is one example, all the more surprising and creditable in view of the attitudes of most British academic economists. More important, because of the size of its economy, is the Japanese. Its primary fiscal deficit, which peaked at 4.9 per cent of GNP in 1978, had been transformed to approximate balance in 1984, 1985 and 1986. Even some of the smaller European countries have made major efforts to restore long-run fiscal stability. Belgium cut its primary budget deficit from 7.5 per cent of GNP in 1981 to 0.6 per cent in 1985, Ireland from 6.8 per cent in 1982 to 2.4 per cent in 1985 and Sweden from 5.8 per cent in 1982 to 0.6 per cent in 1985. Nevertheless, all these European nations are still in the debt trap because they have not achieved sufficiently large primary budget surpluses to outweigh the malign effect of interest rates that exceed growth rates.

But, once more, it is the numbers for Italy which are the most disturbing. Its primary budget deficit peaked at 5.1 per cent of GNP in 1981, fluctuated between 2½ per cent and 5 per cent in the years to 1984 and was then 4.7 per cent in 1985.[30] In other words, little progress has been made in dealing with the root cause of its public finance problem even in a period when debt growth has been uncomfortably high and is giving clear signals of unsustainability. Strong emphasis should again be placed on the self-feeding character of this kind of fiscal imbalance. If corrective action is postponed and public debts are allowed to grow faster than national income, the public debt ratio rises. For any given adverse differential between the interest rate and growth rate, a larger primary surplus must then be recorded to stabilize the public debt ratio in future.[31] If the adverse differential also worsens because of a probable deterioration in financial confidence, the improvement needed in the primary surplus is even greater.

This may sound convoluted and abstract. It is given more pungency if we fill in some details. In the debt trap the constant addition of interest to outstanding debts itself enlarges the overall budget deficit (i.e. the primary balance plus interest costs) as a share of GNP. Moreover, this enlargement of the budget deficit continues year after year. To try to stop the slide into fiscal anarchy after five years therefore involves a *larger* cut in the primary deficit than if the attempt had been made after one year. In essence, because the bondholders' incomes are growing as a share of both national income and public expenditure, there has to be an adjustment somewhere else in the government's accounts. The longer the bondholder's incomes grow too fast, the larger this adjustment has to be. So a country can end up in a socially divisive situation where spending on schools, hospitals and roads has to be lowered to ensure that the costs of servicing the national debt can be met. If austerity is deferred, the necessary expenditure cuts are more severe when they are finally made. What seems in the short run to be a display of economic self-indulgence proves in the end to be an example of financial sado-masochism.

Italy has been learning this lesson in the 1980s, but it does not yet appear to have learnt it fully. It may seem to be ironic, even perverse, that the quality of public services is declining because the government is spending too much money and running an excessive budget deficit. But that is the unhappy logic of inadequate fiscal control. France, when beset by similar troubles in 1984 and 1985, sensibly cut the primary deficit to manageable levels. According to a report in *The Financial Times* on 18 June 1985, 'France faces some of the sharpest cuts in public spending since the war next year as a result of an increasing rise in interest payments on the debt . . . . On the expenditure side, the Government has asked all ministries for a 3 per cent nominal cut in their running expenses, exclduing salaries. It has also required them to put 15 per cent of their expected capital appropriations into a reserve fund.'[32]

Behind the Italian problem lie the assumptions and thought patterns of the public household. Most Italians believe that the state must honour not only its legal obligations to owners of government debt but also its social obligations to pensioners, the unemployed and other recipients of social welfare. Of course, if social expenditure is untouchable, any cut in the primary budget deficit must come from larger reductions in other parts of public spending than would otherwise have been required. The attitudes are understandable – although not necessarily wise – in an old European country with strong corporatist traditions.

But such attitudes are not widely or strongly held in the USA, which is the last but most important country we need to consider. It would surely be plausible to expect, if the USA fell into the debt trap, that corrective measures on the primary deficit would include cuts in welfare expenditure. Indeed, as the rhetoric on the virtues of individualism and self-reliance has been unusually forthright under the Reagan adminis-tration, this prospect of welfare reductions might have been thought certain. In fact, President Reagan seems by his actions, if not by his words, to have been as susceptible as any of his predecessors to the assumptions of the public household. Very early in the life of his administration he had the chance, by curbing welfare entitlements, to stop excessive deficit financing.

The occasion arose on 10 February 1981 when budget director Stockman told a full cabinet meeting that $58b of expenditure cuts were needed to achieve a balanced budget and listed five benefit programmes which, until then, had been left untouched. He wanted them to be considered for abolition or pruning. The other cabinet officers completely misunderstood the purpose of his remarks and thought he was suggesting that the programmes be exempted from the economy drive. President Reagan, sensing the mood of his colleagues, immediately decided that seven areas of social expenditure should be spared any cuts. As Stockman later commented,

> The fact was that these seven programs accounted for $240 billion of baseline spending – more than 40 per cent of the domestic budget. And we had just neatly built a fence around them.[33]

Thereafter the task of budgetary management became increasingly difficult. Reagan was 'too kind, gentle and sentimental' to give Stockman the support he wanted, too much – one might say – of a Good King Wenceslas to achieve a revolutionary reduction in the role of government. 'Despite his right-wing image, his ideology and philosophy always take a back seat when he learns that some individual human being might be hurt.'[34]

The immunity of welfare spending, combined with the supply-siders' 1981 Economic Recovery Tax Act and the massive increase in defence spending needed to support a more active American foreign policy, were responsible for the emergence of very large budget deficits in 1982 and 1983 and their persistence in the mid-1980s. In fiscal 1981 the Federal deficit was $78.9b. It then rose to $127.9b in 1982, $207.8b in 1983, $185.3b in 1984, $212.3b in 1985 and a record $220.7b in 1986, to bring the cumulative increase in debt in the Reagan years to over $1,000b.[35] Because the public debt ratio was low at the beginning of the 1980s, this torrent of red ink has been mopped up without too much trouble by the government bond market. Forecasts that the extra debt would be monetized, and hence cause an acceleration of inflation, have so far been mistaken. Indeed, a strong dollar and heavy capital inflows enabled the American economy to achieve an unusually impressive recovery from a recession in 1982.

As the gap between government expenditure and tax revenue cannot be attributed entirely to debt interest, the American government is now running a significant primary deficit. OECD economists have estimated that the general government sector in the USA instead needs to run a primary surplus of 0.6 per cent of GNP if it is stabilize the debt/GNP ratio.[36] The American situation is less bad than in many other countries. Because the sizeable Federal deficit is offset by healthy surpluses in the finances of local authorities and the states, a cut in the budget deficit equivalent to 1½ to 2 per cent of GNP would be sufficient to restore a sustainable fiscal position. Nevertheless, the American deficit has an importance beyond the simple arithmetic of correcting it. As we showed in chapter 1 and earlier in this chapter, the public finances of the USA were kept under tight control from the mid-1970s to the mid-1960s, apart from wartime periods. The contrast between this long record of financial responsibility and the rather cavalier attitude towards the budget under the present administration has a special symbolic significance. Not only does the USA have the world's largest economy, but also its patterns of public policy have often been copied elsewhere. Moreover, the early successes of Reaganomics – or, more accurately, the common perception that the USA ran deficits for quite a long period with impunity – could give future administrations the pretext to be equally careless about fiscal control. The breakdown of old standards of fiscal rectitude is undoubtedly one reason for the high level of dollar interest rates in real terms.[37] As real interest rates are now far above the American economy's trend rate of economic growth, the long-run problem of restoring fiscal control has been both exaggerated and made more complex.

The mismanagement of the American public household has also aggravated the fiscal difficulties of other countries by pulling in capital from the international financial markets and increasing real interest around the world. But perhaps it is invidious to target criticism solely on the Americans and the Reagan administration. We have seen that in the 1980s the financial problems facing governments of developed countries have been similar mainly because they have shared both intellectual trends and policy mistakes. Of course, they have not shared these trends and mistakes to the same degree. But there does seem to have been a common origin for their troubles, a sharp increase in budget deficits in the mid-1970s initially attributed to cyclical causes but fully endorsed by the Keynesianism which had held sway over policy-making since the mid-1960s. It eventually became clear that the budget deficits had more permanent roots in unsustainable trends in public expenditure growth, while the new dilemmas of budgetary management discredited naive Keynesianism. The breakdown in fiscal control could be interpreted as symptomatic of a basic inconsistency in the idea of a public household. To imagine that governments can perform their eleemosynary deeds at the whim of politicians and at no expense to the community is to sever totally the connection between input and output, between effort and reward, and between revenue and expenditure, on which all sustainable economic activity depends. Even worse, the violation of the traditional principles of budget control damaged financial confidence, raised real interest rates and so made the deterioration in public finances self-feeding. Although many governments have struggled in the 1980s to achieve a more viable budgetary position, their achievements remain limited and precarious while interest rates on their debts exceed the growth rates of their economies. In chapter 3 we shall consider whether an improvement in the relationship between these variables is to be expected. We shall also have to consider what the consequences might be if an improvement does not occur.

3

Finding Out about Budget Deficits

I

American economic policy was more successful in its stabilization aspects under President Eisenhower than before or since. Nevertheless, the conduct of fiscal policy was censured by Keynesian economists in leading universities for being too strict. In his memoirs, written in 1965, Eisenhower tried to answer their objections.

> Critics overlooked the inflationary psychology which prevailed during the mid-fifties and which I thought it necessary to defeat. In 1957, for example, consumer prices were rising at an unacceptably high annual rate of 3.2 per cent. Ten years of this could devalue the current dollar by more than 30 per cent while, if the rate accelerated, we would have had an entirely intolerable situation on our hands . . . . The anti-inflation battle is never-ending, though I fear that in 1959 the public was apathetic, at least uninformed, regarding this issue. This attitude caused me to recall a laconic comment of Winston Churchill when someone asked him during World War II what the allies were fighting for: "If we stop," he replied, "you will find out."[1]

In the 1970s and 1980s the industrial countries have indeed found out about the dangers of excessives budget deficits. They have done it the hard way, by experience.

Governments have learned, for example, the unsurprising truth that budget deficits must be restricted if public debt is not to expand at an unsustainable rate. We have also seen that a favourable relationship between the average interest rate on government debt and the economy's growth rate is needed. In the present chapter shall consider some aspects of this relationship, which we have called the fiscal terms of trade, in the developed nations. The purpose of the discussion is to seek further insights on the chances of a return to the sustainable fiscal situation which most of them enjoyed in the 1950s and 1960s.

Our first task is to consider whether the condition of public finances itself has any effect on the underlying rate of economic growth. The conclusion that heavy and persistent budget deficits may reduce growth rates, is disappointing for long-run fiscal viability. It is a further illustration of the theme that, once a nation's budget position has deteriorated, the deterioration becomes cumulative and self-feeding. We then describe in more detail the events which led to the sharp rise in real interest rates in the late 1970s and early 1980s. This account is a prelude to an initial discussion of whether real interest rates can be reduced, in the foreseeable future, to historically more normal levels. There are a few hopeful signs. Finally, we shall examine the eventual consequences – notably, for inflation and the balance of payments – of unchecked deficit financing.

But, before we set out, it may be helpful to present the facts on the deterioration in the relationship between the interest rate on debt and growth rates since the mid-1960s. The relevant statistics are given in table 8. The actual numbers used have some drawbacks. Their most important weakness is that the measure of real interest rates is not the average interest rate on all public sector debt, but instead the rate on a representative long-term bond issued by central government. This may be somewhat misleading because part of government debt (such as the note and coin issue) bears no interest, while there is always room for debate about what constitutes a 'representative' bond. But simplifications of this kind are inevitable to some extent. The basic trends are adequately described by the statistics in the table.

The main point to emerge is that, whereas between 1965 and 1979 the interest rate on government debt was generally beneath the growth rate of the seven economies under consideration, in the early 1980s the interest rate was above the growth rate. If we look at the average for all the countries, the most favourable period for limiting the expansion of debt was in the early 1970s when the growth rate exceeded the interest rate by 3.7 per cent. In contrast, in the early 1980s the interest rate exceeded the growth rate by 2.1 per cent.

The comparisons between countries do not agree altogether satisfactorily with some of our arguments. We have seen that the worst sinner against the old-time fiscal religion had consistently been Italy. If the logic of our case is right, then the Italian government should have suffered the harshest revenge from its savers and should now be paying the highest real interest rate on its debt and facing the most adverse differential between interest rates and growth rates. Instead the real interest rate on Italian government debt averaged only 1.1 per cent between 1980 and 1984, while the West German government had to pay 4.2 per cent. However, there are serious objections to naive comparisons

Table 8 The deterioration in the relationship between interest rates and growth rates, 1965–1984

	GNP/GDP growth rate (%)	Real long-term interest rate on government bonds (%)	Growth/ interest differential (%)
USA			
1965–9	4.4	1.8	+2.6
1970–4	2.5	0.7	+1.8
1975–9	3.3	0.3	+3.0
1980–4	2.0	4.9	−2.9
Japan			
1965–9	10.1	2.1	+8.0
1970–4	5.7	−3.4	+9.1
1975–9	4.6	0.5	+4.1
1980–4	3.9	4.1	−0.2
West Germany			
1965–9	4.3	4.7	−0.4
1970–4	3.4	3.2	+0.2
1975–9	2.8	3.0	−0.2
1980–4	1.0	4.2	−3.2
France			
1965–9	5.2	3.2	+2.0
1970–4	5.1	1.3	+3.8
1975–9	3.1	0.5	+2.6
1980–4	1.7	3.6	−1.9
UK			
1965–9	2.5	3.1	−0.6
1970–4	2.8	1.0	+1.8
1975–9	2.0	−2.2	+4.2
1980–4	0.6	2.9	−2.3
Italy			
1965–9	5.8	4.3	+1.5
1970–4	4.2	−0.7	+4.9
1975–9	2.4	−3.2	+5.6
1980–4	1.2	1.1	+0.1

Table 8 (*Continued*)

	GNP/GDP growth rate (%)	Real long-term interest rate on government bonds (%)	Growth/ interest differential (%)
Belgium			
1965–9	4.3	3.2	+1.1
1970–4	5.1	1.0	+4.1
1975–9	1.9	1.3	+0.6
1980–4	1.1	5.2	−4.1
Average of seven countries			
1965–9	5.2	3.2	+2.0
1970–4	4.1	0.4	+3.7
1975–9	2.9	0.0	+2.9
1980–4	1.6	3.7	−2.1

Real long-term interest rate is yield on representative long-term bond minus change over 12 months in consumer prices. Figures are averages for the period.

Sources: Growth rates taken from OECD *Economic Outlook*, May 1986, table R.1, p. 174. Real interest rates taken from Bank for International Settlements *Fifty-Fifth Annual Report*, 1985, p. 81

of this sort. As explained in chapter 2, it is the post-tax, not the pre-tax, interest rate which is strictly valid in these exercises. Because the Italian government exempts interest on its debt from tax, it would emerge less favourably from a comparison of post-tax interest rates. Moreover, the damage done by the Italian budget deficit cannot be fully understood by looking at interest rates on public debt. Not only are these rates held down artificially by mandatory reserve ratios on the banks and by other restrictions, but also the diversion of savings to finance the budget deficit starves the private sector of investment funds. We shall discuss this problem in the next section, but before we move on one further warning has to be given about the numbers. There have been significant and disturbing changes since the early 1980s. The estimates were made at the Bank for International Settlements in spring 1985. In the first quarter of that year, the real interest rate on government debt had risen to 4.1 per cent in Italy, 5.4 per cent in the UK, 6.2 per cent in Belgium and 8.2 per cent in the USA. There has not been much subsequent improvement in any of these countries.

II

In the simplest and crudest Keynesian fables an increase in the budget deficit is good for growth because it injects new spending power into the economy and the extra demand stimulates extra production. Unfortunately, this sort of story applies only to the short run and is altogether inadequate for analysing the effects of large budget deficits maintained over several years. In the medium and long runs we need to consider the extent to which budget deficits displace, rather than supplement, private spending. There is a particular danger when they absorb a disproportionate share of a nation's savings. We shall see that, over the more extended time-frame, deficit spending is more likely to be bad for growth than good.

To appreciate the damage that can be done, consider how an increase in the deficit is to be financed. Let us suppose that the pool of savings is fixed in size. It follows that, because more money has to be diverted from this pool to the government, less is available to companies for investment. In economists' jargon, the private sector is 'crowded out'. The price signal involved is an increase in interest rates as the government competes for a finite quantity of funds. If investment declines as a share of national income, the capital stock expands more slowly and the growth rate of the economy as a whole declines.

This account highlights the principal mechanisms by which an increase in the budget deficit reduces the growth rate and serves as an initial warning against allowing the government's borrowing requirement to dominate financial markets. But, like vulgar Keynesianism, it is a fable. There are many details and complications to add.

The first and most important qualification is that it may be wrong to assume that the pool of private saving is fixed. Instead it is possible that an increase in the budget deficit is accompanied by a similar or identical increase in private saving. If so, there may be little change in the availability of funds for private investment and no serious impact on the growth rate. This issue is closely related to one of those most debated in contemporary economics: whether government debt is net wealth to the private sector. One strand of thought, associated with the American economist Robert Barro, is that it is *not* net wealth because the incurral of a deficit entails an increase in future taxes needed to service the extra debt. If a number of assumptions hold, the extra debt should be regarded as equivalent to the present value of these future taxes. In such circumstances, an increase in the budget deficit should be associated with an increase in private savings and there is little or no crowding out.[2] The question then becomes 'how realistic are the assumptions behind

Barro's model?'. There has been a flood of learned articles in reply, with no clear-cut conclusions but with the weight of evidence being that people regard government debt, as least in part, as net wealth. As a result some degree, perhaps only limited, of crowding out of private sector investment should be expected to follow deficit financing by the public sector. Moreover, even those economists who believe that higher budget deficits are offset by more private savings recognize that the extra taxes needed to service the increased debt have disincentive effects on work and investment.[3] On balance, it seems reasonable to conclude that budget deficits cannot be favourable to capital accumulation or economic growth over the long run and are very likely to be unfavourable.

One fascinating recent exercise by Professor James Tobin of Yale University, a winner of the Nobel Prize for economics, analyses the dynamics of a 'hypothetical' economy with a deficit-prone government. The word 'hypothetical' is put into quotation marks because the model is readily applied, by inserting appropriate values for the parameters, to the USA of the mid-1980s. The exercise pivots on the assumption that government debt is net wealth and therefore that crowding out can be total. If an increase in interest rates does not improve the supply of savings but does squeeze capital investment, simulations of the model 'end in catastrophes, which can be precisely described and dated'.[4] With the primary deficit at 3 per cent of GNP, the real pre-tax interest rate on government debt 7.3 per cent, the public debt ratio 40 per cent, the growth rate 3 per cent and various other economic variables set at levels similar to those in the contemporary USA, crowding out occurs for 11.6 years after the starting point of the main simulation. Private sector investment still exceeds depreciation of the capital stock and the economy continues to expand, but both investment and growth are lower than they would have been without the budget deficit. Tobin remarks that the 'shortfalls' in the first 11.6 years are 'trivial' and that 'the visible penalties of gradual crowding-out are undramatic'. (In fact, the growth rate is reduced only from 3 per cent to 2.61 per cent, while consumption is unaffected.) Thereafter, the financial system dissolves and the economy deteriorates radically. Government debt overwhelms the stock market and depresses share prices to the point at which no new investment takes place. The capital stock actually declines. 23 years after the beginning of the process government debt absorbs all private wealth and 'the surviving capital stock is valueless'. The economy continues to expand, but the growth rate is cut by about a third from its original level.

Tobin is careful not to exaggerate the gloom. As he points out, the simulations are not 'predictions' and 'are designed only to illustrate why remedial policies should and will be adopted'. Nevertheless, they do 'make concrete the vague forebodings about runaway government debt' and contain an explicit message for policy-makers. Given a choice of parameters and initial conditions which is reasonably close to those prevailing in the USA today, Tobin finds that the debt/GNP ratio can be stabilized if the primary budget is balanced.[5] Of course, primary budget balance is not the same thing as a balanced budget as understood by the old-time fiscal religion, but the reappearance of the notion of 'balance' in some form deserves comment. Indeed, it may not be entirely frivolous to compare Tobin's reference to the primary or non-interest budget position to one aim of the 1795 Sinking Fund Act which 'established distinctive revenues for the payment of interest of the public debt as well as for the reimbursement of principal'.[6]

What is particularly interesting and remarkable here is that Tobin is perhaps the most distinguished Keynesian economist in the world. His anxiety about the long-run implications of large budget deficits is symptomatic of the shift of academic attention away from their short-run demand effects. Ironically, Professor Milton Friedman, the leader of the monetarist school of thought and a strong opponent of inflationary policies, takes a much more relaxed view of the deficit problem in the USA. On 4 September 1984 he wrote a letter to *The Wall Street Journal* saying that he did 'not regard the deficit as a major issue or cause for concern', and that he strongly opposed a tax increase and favoured 'further reductions in marginal tax rates'.[7] It is paradoxical that the world's foremost Keynesian thinks that excessive budget deficits can end in catastrophe, while its most well-known monetarist seems not to care about them at all. Conflicts of advice like this may help to account for President Reagan's delay in taking firm action to eliminate the Federal deficit. If Tobin is right, the eventual result of his procrastination will be to reduce the growth rate of the US economy.

Indeed, the logical structure of the argument – that budget deficits, by diverting savings away from the private sector and so restricting investment, do reduce the rate of economic growth – seems difficult o assail. However, there is the possibility that funds raised by government debt sales may themselves be directed towards investment. Not only is there is an obvious outlet in public sector capital projects, but also the government may channel the proceeds of debt issues back to private sector companies. The range of options is very wide. The Italian government, which has been particularly imaginative in this area, has channelled money to companies through production subsidies, invest-ment grants and a variety of loans and participations. One estimate is that between 1970 and 1978 all public sector transfers to the corporate sector grew at an average annual rate of 23.8 per cent, appreciably in excess of inflation. In effect, the government became a 'hidden banker' to companies, to some extent substituting for 'open bankers' in the private sector. The private financial system's ability to extend credit was increasingly limited because it was forced to invest in government debt, but the government used the proceeds of its debt issues to assist companies. This large and growing flow of transfer payments helped to explain 'why the corporate sector had not been financially suffocated at a time of ever-increasing public sector appropriation of credit'.[8]

If Italian industry has not been financially suffocated by the increase in the budget deficit, the interposition of the state between banks and companies has certainly made it more difficult for the private sector to breathe easily. As companies have to pay taxes as well as apply for the miscellany of government hand-outs, this is another case of taxing Peter to pay Peter. An unnecessary layer of bureaucracy and another set of distortions are imposed on the directly productive sector of the economy. Many of the subsidies and credits are awarded not on the basis of relative profitability but according to political priorities and even personal favouritism. The consequent misdirection of investment disturbs the efficient allocation of resources and reduces the productivity of capital. It seems likely that the assumption of a 'hidden banker' role by the Italian government is one reason why the rate of GNP growth fell from almost 6 per cent in the late 1960s to a mere 1 per cent in the early 1980s.

The Italian situation illustrates the problem of excessive government inroads on private saving most graphically. In the six years 1981–1986, the budget deficit was equivalent to over half of gross private savings in Italy and over 85 per cent of net private savings. Even in the USA, the budget deficit amounted to almost 60 per cent of net private savings over the same period. In the previous six years, before supply-side economics and the Reagan tax cuts, it had absorbed only 17.7 per cent of American net private savings.[9] The tendency for the budget deficit to engross the savings pool can also be observed in other industrial countries. Although it has generally been more muted than in Italy and the USA, it may have contributed to a decline in investment as a share of output in the Organization for Economic Cooperation and Development (OECD) area. In the six years to 1974 gross fixed capital formation was 22.3 per cent of the OECD's GDP; in the six years to 1980, 21.7 per cent; and in the four years to 1984, 20.3 per cent.[10] This may not seem a marked change, but the difference is more striking if we make an adjustment for depreciation of the capital stock. According to some estimates, savings net of depreciation fell from almost 15 per cent of the OECD's GDP in the early 1970s to under 10 per cent a decade later.[11] It would require remarkable changes in other characteristics of the economy for a drop of this size not to lower the trend rate of economic growth.

There seem to be strong reasons, both on theoretical grounds and because of experience over the last decade, for believing that increased budget deficits reduce the medium-term growth rate of industrial economies. Crowding out and excessive government intrusion into the capital markets reduce both the quantity and quality of investment. It follows that, while budget deficits continue on their present scale, they will act as a brake on economic growth. By restricting the increase in tax revenues, this check to output will compound the fiscal dilemmas facing modern governments. The balance between growth rates and interest rates will remain unfavourable for the long-run control of public debt. Reductions in budget deficits, or the restoration of balanced budgets, would be beneficial because they would not only curb the increase in debt directly but also indirectly promote a faster pace of economic expansion.

III

What, then, of interest rates, the other side of the fiscal terms of trade? If the budgetary position in some of the major industrial countries promises no early easing of the threat to fiscal control posed by low growth rates, is there more hope of a fall in interest rates? And what would declines in nominal interest rates, if they can be taken further than they have been so far, imply for real interest rates? To answer these questions we need to recapitulate some points already made and to discuss certain critical developments in American monetary and fiscal policy in the late 1970s and early 1980s. The focus has to be on the USA, because dollar interest rates have a contagious effect on interest rates in all currencies.

In the Introduction we saw that real dollar interest rates increased suddenly and sharply between 1979 and 1981. The real rate, as measured by the difference between prime rate and the increase in the US producer price index, reached 10 per cent and remained at that level throughout the early 1980s. In chapters 1 and 2 we argued that the rise in American interest rates, and indeed in interest rates throughout the industrial world, could be interpreted as an attempt by holders of financial assets to seek compensation for the losses they had suffered since the mid-1960s. At one level they were retaliating against inflation. At a deeper level they were protesting against the decay of the old-time fiscal religion, the political endorsement of the 'something-for-nothing' fallacy implicit in the idea of the public household, and the widespread acceptance of persistent budget deficits as a norm. However, both the inflation and the trends responsible for it had been under way for many years before the abrupt change in real interest rates. We have yet to explain the precise timing of this change.

If we are to understand why monetary conditions changed when they did, we have to discuss the personalities involved. The most important figure in the monetary history of the early 1980s is undoubtedly Paul Volcker who, after a long and distinguished career in central banking, was appointed Chairman of the US Federal Reserve in 1979. His motives are to some extent a matter of conjecture at present (August 1987). Although he is no longer Chairman of the Federal Reserve he has not yet given any revealing interviews on his work or published any memoirs. But there seems to be no doubt that he decided, sometime in the late 1970s, that it should be his personal mission to eliminate inflation and to restore trust in the American currency. The need for action had become compelling. After reaching 12.2 per cent in 1974, the US inflation rate (as measured by the December-on-December change in the consumer price index) declined in the mid-1970s, but then accelerated once more. In 1976 it was 4.8 per cent, in 1977 6.8 per cent and in 1978 9.0 per cent. In 1979 it was to hit 13.3 per cent. Apart from that in the 1780s, and certain years in the aftermath of the First and Second World Wars, this was the worst inflation performance in American peacetime history.

The rise in inflation was partly due to the deterioration in fiscal discipline described in chapters 2 and 3. But also relevant – and, in the immediate circumstances of the late 1970s, perhaps more important – was the rapid growth in credit to the private sector and consequent excessive monetary expansion. (Under President Carter the Federal deficit was usually quite modest, being $40.2b or only 1.6 per cent of GNP in 1979.) The low or negative real interest rates which prevailed in the 1970s were extremely advantageous for borrowers. Indeed, a comparison of nominal interest rates with the increase in prices of goods and services understates just how favourable credit terms were to many sectors of the American economy.

For the most part people do not borrow in order to buy the goods which enter the consumer or producer price indices. Instead they borrow in order to acquire capital assets, including factories, farms and mines, but very commonly real estate and houses. In the 1970s the prices of most of these capital assets were increasing more quickly than the prices of goods and services. For example, it has been estimated that the value of farmland increased at an average annual rate of 14.4 per cent between 1972 and 1981, compared with an average annual rise of 9.9 per cent in the producer price index.[12] In these circumstances people who were prepared to go heavily into debt could make large speculative fortunes. They borrowed from their banks at interest rates of under 10 per cent in order to purchase assets appreciating at 15 per cent a year. The past record of continuous asset price appreciation encouraged expectations of further appreciation in future, which in turn stimulated more demand for credit. The consequent acceleration in the growth of bank credit led to faster increases in the rate of monetary expansion, because every bank loan creates a new deposit. Faster monetary expansion added to the pressure for higher prices and consolidated inflationary expectations. As we shall discuss in more detail in chapter 6, by the late 1970s most Americans took it for granted that borrowing to buy a house would be profitable, in the sense that the increase in its price would exceed mortgage costs, and many believed that borrowing to buy any kind of tangible asset was a wise financial decision.

Moreover, certain features of the American tax system stimulated the appetite for credit. Interest costs used to be fully deductible in the USA not only from business profits but also from personal incomes. (As we shall see, this is changing, but it was true throughout the 1970s and early 1980s.) For someone facing a marginal tax rate above 50 per cent, the post-tax rate of interest on a 10 per cent loan was therefore under 5 per cent. An individual in this situation would have been ill-advised not to borrow and acquire assets rising in value at 15 per cent a year. In the USA of the late 1970s, with inflation rampant and incomes rising fast in money terms, more people were beginning to pay high tax rates because of their upward migration through the progressive personal income tax system. Because this phenomenon of 'bracket creep' increased the number of taxpayers who could benefit from the tax-deductibility of interest, it also strengthened the demand for credit. A tax avoidance industry, employing thousands of lawyers and accountants, developed to advise people on the best ways to borrow and minimize their tax bills. It successfully preached the beneficence of credit to an American middle class which had believed for three centuries in the Puritan virtues of hard work and thrift. The idea became fashionable that the easiest way to amass a fortune was to fall heavily into debt. At the level of society as a whole this is, of course, a self-contradiction and an absurdity, but to particular individuals it appeared to make sense.

When Volcker took charge of the Federal Reserve his first task was to break the inflationary psychology which had captured the mind of the American public in the 1970s. Most economists were sceptical that Federal Reserve officials could judge what level of interest rates would be adequate to moderate the demand for credit and dampen inflation. The preferred technique of inflation control was to specify a target for the maximum growth of the money supply, in the conviction that over the medium term the increase in national income could not proceed at a markedly different rate. Although money supply targets had been set since 1975, the Federal Reserve's record in attaining them was not particularly good in their early years. Several monetarist economists argued that the method of control should be changed, with a move away from the traditional arrangements to a system known as monetary base control. The details are technical, but in essence the central bank would have to refuse to supply reserves as freely as in the past and instead restrict the amount available. If the banks wanted more reserves, they would have to pay for them by bidding up interest rates.

Volcker was attracted to the idea, perhaps largely on the pragmatic grounds that it gave an opportunity for making a decisive break with the past. On 6 October 1979 the Federal Reserve announced that it would in future try to control the growth of the money supply by reserve targetting. The precise implications were complex and caused considerable confusion at the time. But the broad intention was plain enough. The Federal Reserve would no longer keep interest rates down at levels inadequate to thwart the spirial of inflation expectations, but would instead let them rise sufficiently to check credit expansion and meet preordained, anti-inflationary monetary targets. The eventual objective would be to restore at least the same degree of price stability that the USA had enjoyed in the 1950s and early 1960s. 6 October 1979 is, indeed, the most significant date in recent monetary history. It divides the low-real-interest-rate, rising-inflation 1970s from the high-real-interest-rate, falling-inflation 1980s. Although the successful final outcome was not to be known for some years, from this point onwards Volcker and the Federal Reserve were winning the battle against inflation.

The significance for interest rates of the new monetary control procedures soon became apparent. When the procedures were announced prime rate was 13½ per cent. This was already sharply higher than in 1977 and 1978, when prime rate averaged 6.83 per cent and 9.06 per cent respectively, but much loftier rates were still to come. By the end of October prime rate had risen to 15 per cent. It remained at about this level until March 1980 when it moved upwards to 19½ per cent. A substantial drop in interest rates occurred in the summer, possibly because the Federal Reserve was required to accommodate political demands for lower interest rates and more buoyant economic conditions ahead of the November presidential election. But, after touching a low point of 11 per cent in August, prime rate headed back towards and above its previous levels. In the autumn it leapt upwards from one month to the next. At the end of September it was 13 per cent, at the end of October 14½ per cent, at the end of November 17¾ per cent and at the end of December 21½ per cent. Like the inflation rate which have preceded it, this was the highest interest rate in American peacetime history. There was a little abatement in 1981, but not much, and over the year as a whole prime rate averaged 18.87 per cent.[13]

From a political standpoint, the move towards these stratospheric interest rates was shrewdly timed. Volcker had no illusions that a reduction in inflation could be achieved painlessly. He knew that it would involve an unpleasant recession, with substantial losses of output and employment, and that the consequent political unpopularity would fall on the incumbent President who would in turn blame the Federal Reserve. The Federal Reserve is nominally independent, but in reality it bends with the political wind and has to do so if it is to retain any autonomy at all.[14] It was therefore essential to engineer depressed business conditions while the next presidential election deadline, which was November 1984, was distant. Volcker had to manipulate the time-path of the economy to reconcile his ambition to conquer inflation with Reagan's ambition to secure re-election. The ideal pattern would be to have the trough of the cycle, when the anti-inflationary pressures would be at their fiercest, in mid-1982 and a strong upturn throughout 1984. Because of the lags in the system, this dictated that interest rates should be at their highest and most deflationary in 1981.

However, in almost every other respect, the timing of Volcker's campaign could not have been more unfortunate. Other changes in economic policy were conspiring to increase inflation, just as the Federal Reserve was making an unusually determined effort to defeat it. The first and most critical problem was that economic policy-making in the White House was in the hands of the supply-siders. The consequent emergence of very large budget deficits had some short-term stimulatory impact on the economy, which tended to sustain rising prices, and also, more importantly, provoked fears that a strict monetary policy would not be viable in the long run. The collision between inflationary fiscal policy and anti-inflationary monetary policy seriously complicated Volcker's task.

But it was not just the extent of the Reagan administration's fiscal largesse which was to cause trouble. The character of the tax reforms incorporated in the 1981 Economic Recovery Tax Act intensified the Federal Reserve's discomfort. We have seen that in the 1970s the American tax system had encouraged borrowing and so had fuelled inflationary pressures. The 1981 Act, instead of removing the credit-stimulating features of the tax system, actually strengthened them. New investment incentives were given to business, with the most important being a generous arrangement for depreciating capital assets (known as the accelerated recovery cost system) and an investment tax credit for some types of equipment. Their intention was to increase the after-tax return available on new projects. They therefore reduced the required pre-tax return, which widened the range of potentially profitable investments and increased companies' demand for external finance. As it remained worthwhile to meet this demand largely by borrowing rather than by the issue of new equity, the effect was to motivate even faster growth in debt.

Some parts of the 1981 Act led to frank and conspicuous waste. A 25 per cent tax credit was given on research and development spending, ostensibly to help the USA recapture its pre-eminence in high technology. But, as one economist has remarked, it 'has primarily turned into just one more tax shelter. Admittedly, the R & D tax shelter has been around for years and has been used for (among other things) motion pictures, books, records, computer programs for options trading, a new version of the Learjet, and the ill-fated DeLorean sports car. But more innovative and extensive uses sprang up after the passage of the 1981 tax bill, with the resulting revenue loss to the Treasury expected to reach $5b. per year'.[15] Even more damaging was the indulgent tax treatment of real estate investment, which was partly responsible for excessive building and a surplus of new office space, and eventually – as we shall see in chapter 7 – contributed to the crisis in American banking.

The tax reforms of 1981 would have bedevilled the Federal Reserve's efforts to restrain private credit growth if the financial system's ability to supply credit had remained unchanged. Unfortunately, the ability to supply credit was about to be expanded considerably, further complicating the anti-inflationary task. Since the 1930s, American financial institutions, particularly the banks, had been subject to elaborate regulations. These were designed to prevent a recurrence of certains abuses which were commonly believed to have been responsible for the 9,000 bank failures, and other calamities, which the USA suffered in the Depression. The regulations may have hindered the abuses but by the late 1970s they were also causing serious distortions and reducing the efficiency of financial intermediation. As part of the more general deregulatory movement which reflected the trend away from Big Government, the Depository Institutions and Monetary Control Act was passed in 1980 and inaugurated a sequence of measures to liberalize the financial system. The aim of promoting a more efficient financial system may have been admirable but the result was to release credit demands which had been pent up artificially in previous years. Like the 1981 tax changes, this tended to increase the growth of credit to the private sector.

In short, Volcker's assignment in the early 1980s – to eradicate the inflationary psychology which had driven the excessive credit and money growth of the 1970s – could hardly have been carried out in more unfavourable circumstances. The Federal Reserve was handicapped by unhelpful and virtually simultaneous changes in the financial structure and tax regime, and by the most daring and extravagant programme of fiscal stimulus the USA had ever seen. It was the conflict between Volcker's objectives and these contemporaneous developments in other policy areas that drove real interest rates to such exceptionally high levels. Because the level of real interest rates is the most fundamental single reason for the debt problems of the mid-1980s, the untoward American policy developments of the early 1980s are central to understanding the current plight of borrowers in both the USA and other countries.

IV

It was not immediately obvious how high real interest rates would become. The leap in prime rates in 1980 coincided with the rush of price increases which caused the American inflation rate to reach its peacetime peak. So real interest rates did not appear excessive at first. As usual, monetary restriction caused a slow-down in the economy and a slow-down in the economy was followed by a decline in the inflation rate. Although the responses were a little delayed, they did come through. In 1979, when consumer prices rose by 13.3 per cent, GNP expanded by 2.5 per cent; in 1981 GNP increased by 1.9 per cent and consumer prices by 8.9 per cent; but in 1982 GNP contracted by 2.6 per cent and consumer price inflation dropped to 3.9 per cent. In a standard business cycle a fall in inflation on this scale would have been accompanied by a similar decline in nominal interest rates, to leave real rates broadly unchanged.

On this occasion, however, nominal rates did not fall in the normal way. Prime rate had been cut in late 1981, but it stayed as high as 16½ per cent throughout the spring and early summer of 1982. Meanwhile inflation – particularly as measured by commodity prices or the producer price index – fell quickly and real interest rates therefore increased very sharply. In July there was some relief, with another cut in prime rate. It was only in the second half of the year, following Mexico's announcement of its inability to service its external debts on schedule, that a series of interest rate reductions brought prime rate down to 11½ per cent by December. However, the producer price index had more or less stopped rising. In the new environment of approximate price stability nominal rates above 10 per cent implied real rates above 10 per cent. In the event prime rates were not to fall beneath 10 per cent until June 1985 and, as we saw in the Introduction, very high real interest rates persisted throughout the early and mid-1980s.

As present levels of real interest rates are doing great harm to all dollar borrowers as well as contributing to the US public debt problem, it should be a top policy priority to reduce them. The primitive approach is to reduce nominal interest rates, irrespective of concurrent economic and political circumstances, on the assumption that inflation will remain under control. Since it was the Federal Reserve which forced up nominal rates in 1979 and 1980, the implication is that the Federal Reserve should be mandated to cut rates in 1988 and 1989. Demands of this kind are often accompanied by calls to reduce the central bank's independence. For example, in 1984 Senator Melcher from Montana brought a lawsuit challenging the constitutionality of the Federal Reserve Open Market Committee (FOMC), which makes the critical decisions on monetary policy. His aim was to increase the number of FOMC members subject to Senate approval and therefore answerable to Congress. The cost of the lawsuit was covered by the Committee for Monetary Reform, whose founder is reported to have said, 'The goal is to remove the influence of banks from our monetary system'.[16] This is rather like asking a meteorologist to remove the influence of clouds from rainfall.

It also expresses, perhaps rather whimsically, an old anti-banker, hard-money tradition in the USA, which dates back to the early nineteenth century and was reinforced by the Depression. Although the ideas have no serious analytical content, their origins are easily understood and very excusable. They are to be sought in the losses inflicted on many less well-off savers by the bank failures and stock market collapses which have punctuated American financial history. When poor families have been ruined – or, at least, regard themselves as having been ruined – by bankers and Wall Street brokers, and when the memories are passed down from generation to generation, it is not surprising that hostility to the banking system should become deeply rooted. There is no need to say anything more here about the strong vein of anti-bank sentiment in American society, but we should remember it when we discuss possible solutions to the debt crisis.

Large and deliberate reductions in nominal interest rates, if undertaken in isolation, would be ill advised. They would merely incite renewed credit demand from the private sector, and so stimulate faster money supply growth and higher inflation. Instead nominal rates can be reduced safely only when the structural causes of dear money – the excessive Federal deficit and a tax system that is too friendly to borrowers – have been removed.

On the first of these, there is growing recognition – indeed, now an almost unquestioned consensus – that the budget deficit must be cut. In 1985 the Balanced Budget and Emergency Deficit Control Act, also known as the Gramm–Rudman–Hollings Act after its Congressional sponsors, became law. It prescribed a gradual reduction in the Federal deficit for every year until a balanced budget was reached in 1991. If Congress and the President could not agree in a particular year on the expenditure reductions needed to achieve the targets, the Congressional Budget Office would have the power to decide on across-the-board cuts which would then be enforced by Presidential order. Unfortunately, this procedure was determined to be unconstitutional by the Supreme Court in July 1986. The spirit of Gramm–Rudman–Hollings survives, with Congressmen still talking of spending cuts to achieve the targets laid down by the legislation. However, in the 1986 fiscal year the Federal deficit hit a record $220.7b. As the outcome was almost $30b above the original estimate it necessarily casts doubt on the attainability of the targetted reductions in future years. The deficit in the 1987 fiscal year is expected (August 1987) to be slightly more than $170b, better than in the preceding fiscal year, but nowhere near the $108b target envisaged by Gramm–Rudman–Hollings. Many observers believe that – without policy changes – the deficit will be rising again in fiscal years 1989 and 1990.[17]

Sooner or later, something will be done and the USA will return to fiscal prudence. But it makes a great deal of difference whether action is taken willingly soon or reluctantly later. The longer the necessary measures are postponed, the more painful they will have to be. As we have emphasized, the accumulation of debt and the growth of debt interest are self-reinforcing. The stumbling block before the Gramm–Rudman–Hollings legislation was the fear, shared by both Congressmen and the President, that they would appear responsible for particular expenditure reductions and so alienate identifiable electorally powerful interest groups. In other words, they were hemmed in by the political constraints imposed by the attitudes associated with the public household, that government does have gifts to hand out and that it is sheer meanness and perversity for elected representatives to withhold them. It is regrettable that the Supreme Court could not accept the politically attractive idea of passing responsibility for specific cuts to the bureaucracy. The lack of political courage in Congress does not bode well for an early return to low budget deficits.

Much more encouraging are prospective changes to the American tax system. In the 1960s and 1970s the steady accretion of exemptions, loopholes and special allowances superimposed complexity on complexity and made the preparation of tax returns increasingly time-consuming. The ground swell of support for tax cuts, which was exploited by the supply-siders, was accompanied by a growing feeling that the system was too complicated, a feeling shared by the overwhelming majority of economists including those who favoured responsible fiscal policies. Officials at the US Treasury and elsewhere put together proposals for reform which combined the withdrawal of exemptions and allowances with the reduction of tax rates. The most comprehensive of these reform plans was published in December 1984 and was widely welcomed. President Reagan praised it as 'the best and most complete' he had seen, although he withheld support for the details.[18] The next two years saw a sequence of reform ideas being discussed in Congress. Apart from the drive for simplification, their theme was that any revenue shortfall from the reduction in tax rates on individuals should be offset by an increase in the burden on business. The negotiations were protracted and difficult, which was perhaps not surprising in view of the subject matter, but a breakthrough came suddenly in the summer of 1986.

On 24 June the Senate agreed by a vote of 97 to 3 on a tax simplification plan proposed by Senator Packwood, the Finance Committee chairman. Its political appeal rested on the promise of a top tax rate of 27 per cent, which could be reconciled with keeping revenue constant if a variety of tax deductions were scrapped. The House of Representatives disagreed with many of the provisions of the Packwood proposals, but most of its members sympathized with their general tenor. After two months of bargaining the House and the Senate reached a compromise which respected the essentials of the original plan. This has subsequently passed into legislation. Instead of the previous 14 tax brackets with a maximum 50 per cent rate, there are to be two brackets of 15 and 28 per cent. Interest on personal loans, formerly deductible in full from taxable income, may now be deducted only for mortgages on the first two homes; a miscellany of deductible expenses have been repealed; and losses incurred in certain investments (i.e. tax shelters) may no longer be charged against income. The standard rate of corporate tax is also to be lowered, but the overall tax bill for business will increase because of the repeal of investment tax credits and a return to economic depreciation.

The simultaneous elimination of tax breaks and cut in rates have dealt a double blow to the conventional fallacy of the late 1970s, that debt is the passport to prosperity. The elimination of tax breaks means that individuals and companies can no longer lower their taxable income by borrowing; the cut in rates means that the tax efficiency of borrowing is much reduced for those deductions that survive. The result is certain to be a significant weakening in credit demand from the private sector and a consequent fall in real interest rates. In this respect tax reform is perhaps the most promising development in American economic policy in the 1980s. The simpler and more rational tax code will both make redundant much of the socially wasteful tax avoidance industry and lead to a more efficient allocation of resources.

Some reduction in the budget deficit and tax reform should together result in a fall in real interest rates. Because of the associated improvement in the fiscal terms of trade, this would be unambiguously helpful in restoring the long-run viability of American fiscal policy. However, there is another condition for a sustained decline in real interest rates. It is the full restoration and maintenance of financial confidence, particularly of confidence that inflation will remain at its present negligible levels. As we shall see in the next section, the durability of low inflation cannot be guaranteed.

V

It is time to complete our inquiry into the growth of public debt in the developed countries. We need to relate the subject to our more wide-ranging discussion in the Introduction and, more specifically, to the idea of a nation's debt/income ratio. This ratio is the sum of the public debt ratio and the ratio of private debt to GNP. We argued in the Introduction that the debt/income ratio, which is perhaps the most general measure of the debt problem, would explode in an environment of very high real interest rates. The connection between this argument and the themes of the last three chapters is evident. We have finally to explore the consequences of further rises in the public debt ratio in the developed countries.

We shall continue to focus on the USA because of the clarity with which it illustrates the issues at stake as well as its importance to the world economy. We saw in the Introduction that the debt/income ratio first started to rise sharply, in contrast with its previous stability over a 40-year period, in 1982. Between the end of 1981 and the end of 1985 the total debt of non-financial sectors rose at a compound annual rate of 12.4 per cent, not much faster than in the previous four years when the rate of increase was 11.1 per cent. The change in the behaviour of the debt/income ratio between the two periods is largely to be attributed – in terms of arithmetic – to the slow-down in the growth of money national income, a consequence of the successful pursuit of anti-inflationary policies by the Federal Reserve under Chairman Volcker. The other big difference between the two four-year periods is that, whereas in the first public debt grew more slowly than debt as a whole, in the second it grew faster. Public debt held by private investors increased by 10.7 per cent a year between 1977 and 1981, but by 18.6 per cent between 1981 and 1985.[19] In this purely numerical sense, budgetary policy under President Reagan can be blamed for the break in the trend of the debt/income ratio in the early 1980s. Indeed, the indictment is more extensive. The deterioration in fiscal responsibility lay behind the increase in real interest rates which then contributed to persisting fast growth in private debt and so added another twist to the spiral in the debt/income ratio.

In view of the over $1,000b of new debt incurred by the Reagan administration, it is hardly surprising that the public debt ratio increased in the 1980s, reversing the decline which had characterized the first three post-war decades. Gross public debt was 37.1 per cent of GNP in 1981, but rose to almost 48.5 per cent in 1985 and is projected to exceed 50 per cent in the next two or three years. This larger debt has to be serviced at more onerous interest rates than those prevailing in the late 1970s (see table 9). Interest payments on public debt are estimated to have been 5.0 per cent of GNP in 1986, compared with 2.7 per cent in 1979.[20] Strong emphasis has to be placed on the eventual need to charge higher taxes on the American people to cover the cost of these interest payments. This paradoxical and unfortunate outcome is, of course, implied by the logic of the debt trap. It is the most forceful criticism, indeed the virtual self-refutation, of supply-side economics.

There have been other unhappy results. The outpouring of new government debt has been on such a scale that domestic savings have not been able to absorb it in full. Foreign investors have had to fill the gap by substantially increasing their holdings of American government debt. These investments are the financial counterpart to a trade deficit which has grown continuously since 1982. The excess of imports over exports, which was $114.1b in 1984, $124.3b in 1985 and $147.7b in 1986, is by far the largest the world has ever seen. The current account of the balance of payments has also been in the red. So far the deficit has not been on quite the same scale as that on the trade account because the USA has traditionally recorded a surplus on invisibles, particularly receipts of capital income on its foreign assets. Nevertheless, its foreign liabilities are now larger than its assets and, within the next two or three years, the USA's payments of interest, dividends and profits to foreigners will become larger than foreigners' payments to it. Eventually, the USA will have to run a trade surplus to service its external debt properly. To move from massive deficit to surplus will need a switch in resources to produce more exports and cause a major structural upheaval in the economy. In broad terms, the trade deficit is now 4 per cent of GNP, whereas a surplus of perhaps 1 per cent will be needed to

Table 9   American public finances, and the relationship between the growth of nominal GNP and the yield on 10–year Treasury securities, 1971–1985

	Federal surplus (+)/ deficit (−) ($b)	Increase in money GNP (%)	Yield in 10–year Treasury securities (%)	The 'fiscal terms of trade' (%)
1971	−23.0	8.6	6.16	2.4
1972	−23.4	10.0	6.21	3.8
1973	−14.9	12.1	6.84	5.3
1974	−6.1	8.3	7.56	0.7
1975	−53.2	8.5	7.99	.05
1976	−73.7	11.5	7.61	3.9
Transition quarter	−14.7			
1977	−53.6	11.7	7.42	4.3
1978	−59.2	13.0	8.41	4.6
1979	−40.2	11.5	9.44	2.1
1980	−73.8	8.9	11.46	−2.6
1981	−78.9	11.7	13.91	−2.2
1982	−127.9	3.7	13.00	−9.3
1983	−207.8	7.4	11.10	−3.7
1984	−185.3	11.0	12.44	−1.4
1985	−212.3	5.8	10.62	−4.8

1. 'Transition quarter' arose because of change in timing of US fiscal year from January-to-January to October-to-October.
2. The 'fiscal terms-of-trade' is the excess of the percentage growth of nominal GNP over the percentage yield on 10–year percentage Treasury securities.

Source: *Economic Report of the President* (Washington: US Government Printing Office, 1986), tables B–1, B–68 and B–73

satisfy foreign investors and to stop the debt growing further. The required resource shift therefore amounts to 5 per cent of GNP, equivalent to two years' growth.

It is difficult to see how the USA can accomplish such a large adjustment without a fairly long period of dollar undervaluation in which its products are cheaper (in terms of a common currency) than those of other countries. This raises the disquieting question of the continued viability of the dollar standard. The dollar, like previous key currencies such as the Venetian ducat or the pound sterling, maintained its prestige because people believed that it would retain its value compared both with goods and services and with other currencies. But, by definition, in a period of undervaluation it is not maintaining its value against other currencies. There could be an even more drastic transfer of investor allegiances from the dollar to the yen and the deutschmark than that already seen in 1985, 1986 and early 1987. The root cause of the trouble is that savers cannot respect the currency of a country whose government is increasing its indebtedness at more than 10 per cent a year. As the growth rate in debt is evidently outstripping that of national product in real terms, there is little confidence that the debt can be serviced and repaid in dollars of stable value. In the words of Morgan Guaranty's *World Financial Markets*, America 'may not be viewed forever as the "shining city on the hill" '.[21] If the loss of international financial confidence becomes severe, there is a danger of a collapse in the value of the dollar which will ignite renewed inflationary pressures within the USA. This could then damage domestic investor sentiment and force up real interest rates, undoing the beneficial effects on long-run fiscal control of tax reform and the limited reductions in the budget deficit so far implemented.

In general, the fiscal outlook in Japan and the large European nations is more satisfactory than in the USA. We have seen that the governments of Japan and West Germany have been particularly conscientious in restoring sound public finances. However, even for these countries some reservations about the sustainability of present trends have to be mentioned. In an important analysis in its May 1986 *Economic Outlook* the OECD suggested that, when making medium-term projections, it is misleading to determine the future path of the public debt ratio by assuming a constant ratio of the primary budget deficit to GNP and a particular relationship between interest rates and the growth rate. The reason is that, over a period of two or three decades, the primary budget positions of several countries are certain to come under pressure from demographic developments. Most obviously, the cost of pensions will increase because of ageing populations. If prospective changes in pension payments are not covered at all by extra taxation, but instead add to the primary deficit and the accumulation of debt, the OECD work shows that public debt ratios will rise explosively in Japan, West Germany, France and the UK.[22] This disturbing conclusion is hedged about with qualifications. In some countries, including West Germany and France, explicit mechanisms exist to match social security contributions to the cost of the pension system on a pay-as-you-go basis. In others, notably Japan, recent moves towards fiscal consolidation have been motivated in part by the need to anticipate future changes in the pension burden, which suggests that policy-makers will not let the situation run out of control. Nevertheless, the OECD analysis is a warning against complacency even for those nations where public finances are in reasonably good shape.

What, then, about the large developed countries where public finances are not in reasonably good shape? What, in particular, about Italy and Canada? The OECD study shows that, even without the pension problem, these two spendthrifts face an explosion in public debt. If the primary budget deficit remains unchanged as a share of GNP and the real interest rate is assumed to exceed the growth rate by 2 per cent, by the year 2010 the ratio of net public debt to GNP will reach 200 per cent in Italy and 110 per cent in Canada. The additional deterioration due to rising pension costs is 'relatively large' and, as the OECD economists note in rather diplomatic and guarded language, 'this reinforces the need for budgetary restraint that was already apparent without any consideration of social security'.[23] In fact, the Italian situation will become hopeless. When allowance is made for the financial strain of increased pensions, the ratio of net public debt to GNP is projected to hit nearly 250 per cent by 2010. If the average interest rate on debt were 10 per cent, debt interest would amount to a quarter of national income. The cost of servicing the national debt would absorb such a high proportion of tax revenue that taxpayers would rebel, further aggravating the deficit problem. The government would be forced to renege on its debt, with ruinous effects on the community's respect for the state and its preparedness to purchase public debt issues in future.

A pervasive distrust of the financial conduct of government is a curse on any society. If people are not willing to buy public debt in significant quantities, it is impossible to run a large budget deficit without provoking inflation. That part of the deficit which cannot be covered by sales of long-term debt to long-term savers must instead be taken up by the banking system, which increases the money supply and generates upward pressure on the price level. It is therefore a boon for a deficit-prone government to enjoy savers' confidence because a high proportion of its deficit can be financed by issues of long-term debt and serious inflationary consequences avoided. When a government has once failed to honour the terms on its debt, it cannot escape having a much harder task selling its debt in future. This lesson has been learned, and then forgotten and ignored, by Latin American governments on a number of occasions. Because of these experiences, the citizens of Brazil and Argentina are not prepared to hold public debt amounting to more than 20 per cent of national income. The worst outcome in Italy would be a financial breakdown in which the loss of confidence is so total that its citizens also refuse to hold a high ratio of public debt to income. If the value of the debt is fixed in nominal terms, the public debt ratio could fall from 200 per cent to 20 per cent only by ten-fold rise in the price level.

The problem of public debt in Italy is very serious, but it should be kept in perspective. Apart from occasional intervals of fiscal discipline, Italy has mismanaged its government finances for centuries. In *The Wealth of Nations* Adam Smith remarked that 'the practice of funding' (by which he meant government borrowing) seemed to have begun in the Italian republics and to have 'gradually enfeebled every state which has adopted it'.[24] There is no one final Day of Judgement when the public debt ratio exceeds a particular critical value and a government passes from the purgatory of fiscal unsustainability to the inferno of debt repudiation and hyperinflation. Even after a financial breakdown, with government bankruptcy and 1,000 per cent inflation, a nation still has its houses, factories and farms, and its people still have their skills and technical know-how. If a responsible and convincing new financial regime can be established amidst the wreckage of the old, the habits of producing and selling, getting and spending, and even borrowing and lending, can be resumed without too much fuss.[25] Nevertheless, the record of fiscal mismanagement and the consequent disturbance to the mechanisms of saving and investment may be important reasons for Italy's economic inferiority compared with West Germany and France. Despite the dynamism and versatility of its industry, it continues to have one of the most unsatisfactory financial systems in Europe.[26]

In fact, many nations, seemingly unable to learn from history, are condemned to repeat it. The countries of Latin America are in much worse plight than Italy. They have long been handicapped by the political instability and economic uncertainties which have their origins in almost perpetual fiscal irresponsibility. Perhaps this is the right moment to move on to a consideration of their difficulties and those of other developing countries.

PART II

The Debt Threat to the Third World

4

The Boom in Sovereign Lending

The phrase 'debt crisis', despite being repeated endlessly in the media in recent years, has not become stale. It may owe its power to command attention to the combination of two short and evocative words. As there is something unsettling about the notion of debt and alarming about a crisis, to put the two ideas together is to demand interest from any audience. The interest is well justified. Developing countries' debt has soared from under $100b in 1970 to almost $1,000b today while the ability to service and repay has not risen commensurately. However, before we consider the causes and results of this debt explosion, we need to do some preparatory homework. More specifically, we need to link the process of debt growth in developing countries to the analytical framework set out in the Introduction and already used to consider the public debt problem in developed countries.

Although there are important differences between lending to governments across frontiers and purchasing the debt of one's own government, the same underlying principles determine the dynamics of debt. Instead of the debt being public debt owed internally, it is sovereign debt owed externally, and instead of the growth being equal to the budget deficit, it is closely related in size to the current account deficit on the balance of payments. We can separate a nation's payments deficits into two parts – the deficit on interest costs and the deficit on non-interest items. We can call the deficit on non-interest items the primary payments deficit, by analogy with the concept of a primary budget deficit used in the discussion of fiscal policy. It can be regarded as broadly equivalent, for the majority of developing countries, to the trade deficit. It can also be thought of as measuring the net flow of resources from the rest of the world to the developing country under consideration. For this reason it has been termed the 'resource transfer'.[1]

Only a few rich industrial countries are able to repay their external debts in their own currencies. Because of exchange controls, the currencies of developing countries are not fully convertible and, because of the past record of inflation and depreciation, they are not widely respected. Developing countries must therefore honour their external debts in terms of other nation's currencies. In practice, by far the most common currency is the dollar. Indeed, the share of the dollar in the currency denomination of developing countries' public long-term debt rose between 1974 and 1983 from 65.1 per cent to 76.3 per cent.[2] An implication would seem to be that their ability to repay depends on their receipts of dollars and other hard currencies, which in turn depend on exports. A favourite yardstick of developing country creditworthiness is therefore the ratio of debt to exports. If the debt/export ratio is stable over time, the country concerned is deemed to be in a sustainable situation and its creditors can feel relaxed. In fact, there is considerable room for debate about the suitability of the debt/export ratio in credit assessment. Although exports may measure the current level of dollar receipts, a higher proportion of a nation's output could be mobilized and sold abroad if the political will was there. This suggests that the debt/GNP ratio is the appropriate variable to watch. Alternatively, some economists believe that the ratio of debt service (i.e. amortization plus interest) to exports is the key measure because it indicates the pressure on a country to direct hard currency receipts to meeting debt obligations. The drawback to the debt service ratio is that it is more an indication of the urgency of financial difficulties than of a nation's ability to switch resources to the benefit of foreign creditors in the long term. In the circumstances of the 1980s, when banks have been more or less forced to renew maturing loans, its usefulness has been less obvious than in earlier decades. In this section we shall focus the discussion on the debt/export ratio which, whatever its weaknesses, has the virtue of being easy to relate to general economic trends.

The analysis of sustainability has the same structure as with public debt. If the rate of interest exceeds the growth rate of exports, a developing country must achieve a primary payments surplus if it wishes to keep the debt/export ratio constant. The situation is less demanding if the rate of interest is equal to or less than the growth rate of exports. When the two variables are equal, primary payments balance maintains stability in the debt/export ratio. Even better, when the interest rate is less than the growth rate of exports, it can run a primary payments deficit and still be impressing its creditors with a stable debt/export ratio. In other words, it can be borrowing money and so receiving resources from the rest of the world, while simultaneously persuading the rest of the world that it can eventually send back enough goods and services to meet its debts.

This is, from the viewpoint of an indebted developing country, the best of all possible worlds. It presents a wonderful opportunity to be indulgent and virtuous at the same time. For most of the 1970s it was the happy situation facing the Third World. The prices of commodities, which represented the majority of developing country exports, rose quickly in dollar terms, while interest rates – before the sea change in American monetary policy in 1979 – remained moderate. Table 3 gave figures on the increase in crude material prices, up by 12.6 per cent a year on average between 1971 and 1975 and by 9.3 per cent between 1976 and 1980, and on US prime rates, 7.5 per cent on average in the first period and 10.1 per cent in the second. This comparison was very favourable by itself for indebted commodity exporters, but it was further improved by the expansion in the volume of exports achieved by a number of countries. At the time it did not seem absurdly Panglossian for the banks to be expanding their lending to developing countries by 35 per cent a year.

Several aspects of the debt build-up have to be discussed. In the first section we shall consider why the lending occurred and examine its main characteristics. This is important because the form of their debts left the borrowing countries particularly vulnerable to interest rate fluctuations. In the next section we shall see that the debt growth of the 1970s had some favourable effects, which may have contributed to the complacent view many bankers took of the whole process. The bad effects undoubtedly outweighed the good only after 1979, which saw both the second oil shock and the change in American monetary control procedures. As we shall discover in the final section, this should have been obvious to participants in what has been termed the 'international debt game' by 1981, which was actually the peak year for lending.[3] The discussion will pay more attention to Latin America than other continents because it received the bulk of the loans and is, commonly and rightly, regarded as typifying the problem of over-indebtedness. However, it should be noted that, relative to their more limited resources, African nations have suffered more severely than Latin American nations. The absolute size of low-income Africa's debt is small – $27b in 1984 – but in relation to income and exports it is the highest in the less-developed world.[4] Several Asian countries, notably Turkey and South Korea, have incurred heavy external debts, but we shall refer to them only if they illustrate a point particularly well.

II

Sovereign lending has a long and discouraging history. In 1327 the English king Edward III renounced his debts to Italian financiers, causing the failure of the Bardi and Peruzzi banks. Even the USA has had its delinquents. The states of Mississippi and Louisiana defaulted on their debts, mostly to Britain, in 1839 and their subsequent refusal to reach a settlement with their creditors led to the formation of the Council of Foreign Bondholders in 1868. But the most notorious record is held by Latin American countries. They have had an almost regular 50-year cycle of borrowing, default and rehabilitation, and then renewed borrowing and default, since they secured their independence from Spain and Portugal in the early nineteenth century.

The first wave was between 1822 and 1825 when several newly independent republics issued bonds in London. The firms arranging the issues retained two years of interest and amortization from the proceeds, which suggests they had little confidence in the supposed recipients. Once these funds were exhausted, most of the bond issues went into default and became worthless.[5] A second phase occurred in the 1870s when a number of Latin American countries again defaulted. It coincided with loans to Turkey and Egypt which also ran into difficulties and prompted Bagehot to write an article on 'The danger of lending to semi-civilised countries', which warned that 'We lend to countries whose condition we do not know, and whose want of civilisation we do not consider, and therefore we lose our money.'[6]

There was a period of relative calm in the 20 years before 1914 when, under the watchful eyes of the European imperial powers, most 'semi-civilized countries' serviced their debts properly. After the First World War international investors embarked on another bond-buying spree, with Latin American paper once more in demand. 'Peru was a consistently popular issuer, notwithstanding the fact that its bond issues were regularly six months in arrears.'[7] The slump in world economic activity after the Great Crash of 1929 led to sharp falls in commodity prices. With their export receipts much diminished, 17 Latin American nations defaulted in the 1930s. Only Argentina honoured its debts in full and on time during that decade and the 1940s. But it had the humiliating experience of having to seek debt renegotiation in 1956, which led to the establishment of the Paris Club, the first institutionalized forum of creditor nations. (Nevertheless, meetings of the Club, which are convoked by the French Treasury, have an informal character.)

Against this background, the willingness of the international banks to lend heavily to developing countries in the 1970s may seem remarkable. However, it should be recognized that the first 25 years after the Second World War were historically unique, marked not only by the fastest growth of output and trade the world has ever seen, but also by an almost complete absence of official debt defaults. Between the Argentine episode in 1956 and 1970 there were 17 reschedulings involving seven countries. For the most part, creditors did not incur capital losses but instead merely received money somewhat later than they expected.[8] The circumspection with which less-developed countries (LDCs) handled their foreign debts was partly attributable to the influence of two organizations set up at the Bretton Woods conference in 1944, the International Monetary Fund (IMF) and the World Bank. Their function was to superintend an international financial order by the enforcement of non-discriminatory rules. More specifically, the IMF would not permit a nation to pay its debts to one group of nations, repudiate its debts to another group and continue to trade unhindered. Such discrimination against one set of creditors would be countered by the withdrawal of access to IMF standby facilities, the suspension of World Bank loans and a variety of other sanctions.

The IMF and the World Bank are therefore strictly multilateral in approach. Their activities represent a sharp contrast to the bilateralism and discrimination of the 1930s. The behaviour of Nazi Germany, which repudiated its external debts in 1932 and then blocked the payment of foreign currency to other countries until they had made purchases in Germany, would not be tolerated today.[9] In this very important sense, the post-war system is a new departure in the history of international finance. Arguably, the banks were not unreasonable to expect sovereign borrowers to honour debts more scrupulously in this environment than ever before. It could be objected that the multilateralism of the system is a sham since it rests, in the final analysis, on the economic and military might of the USA. The objection has some force, but, of course, it would not deter banks from making loans if they were themselves American or (as with all Western banks) under the American protective umbrella.

But, if the *Pax Americana* of the 1950s and 1960s ushered in the lending boom of the 1970s, it still does not explain why the banks should have wanted to lend to Latin American countries rather than to their traditional customers in the USA and other industrial countries. Although many conjectures have been made about ulterior political motives, profit maximization was the most important inducement. For some time after the disasters of the Depression years American banks kept very high ratios of capital to assets to protect them against future loan losses. In the more tranquil conditions of the 1950s and 1960s they came to believe that loan losses would never again be on the scale of the 1930s. As perceptions changed, they decided to reduce their capital/asset ratios. But, within the USA, business was extremely competitive with numerous small and medium-sized banks trying to increase market share. The large banks therefore sought to expand their lending abroad. They were further encouraged to move in this direction by restrictions on inter-state banking which reduced their ability to diversify loan portfolios. In part they could achieve their objectives by setting up operations in other industrial countries, but again they were confronted by regulatory obstacles and stiff local competition. A warmer welcome came from the governments of developing countries. These governments were typically in constant need of finance, but had access only to backward and small-scale domestic capital markets.

In the mid-1970s the developing countries' demand for external finance became insistent because of the damage to their balance of payments from the first oil shock. The decision of the Organization of Petroleum Exporting Countries to triple the oil price caused the collective payments surplus of the Middle Eastern oil exporters to increase from $6.5b in 1973 to $55.9b in 1974, with corresponding damage to the payments positions of the industrial and developing countries. In 1974 the industrial countries as a group incurred a deficit of $14.6b, but some of them – notably Japan and West Germany – were not prepared to let this situation continue and took corrective action. In 1975 the industrial countries moved back into surplus. In consequence, the only possible deficit area remaining was in the oil-importing Third World. Over the four years to 1978 the average annual surplus of the Middle Eastern oil exporters was $33.8b and the average annual deficit of the developing countries $39.5b. The international banks came in useful as intermediaries between these two groups. They received much of the oil exporters' surplus in the form of deposits and were able to on-lend, or 'recycle', them to the developing countries. The smooth circulation of funds from the newly rich Arab nations to the potentially rich nations of Latin American seemed, at the time, a signal achievement.

With the banks playing a key role in recycling, their new loans to LDCs rose from negligible figures in the 1960s to $9.7b in 1973 and to $12.0b in 1975.[10] Whereas in 1971 bank loans had represented only 12.2 per cent of total LDC external debt of $90b, in 1976 they amounted to 29.1 per cent of debt of $220b and in 1978 to 30.4 per cent of debt of $345b.[11] They were encouraged in their activities by governments and central banks in the main industrial countries who, in general, regarded recycling to the Third World as the best answer to the global payments imbalance caused by the oil shock.

The banks had no previous experience of lending on this scale across frontiers. They were not sure how to assess risks nor what rules they should be following on the size of exposure. This lack of experience was reflected in three very important characteristics of the lending boom. First, bond finance was minimal. In 1973 bond issues raised a meagre $0.6b for LDCs and in 1975 only $0.4b. Even in 1979, when bank lending had soared to $24.9b, bond finance amounted to $0.7b.[12] The limited extent of bond issuance was partly due to the work of the Council of Foreign Bondholders. It deterred new issues by countries which had defaulted in earlier decades and not reached an agreement with their creditors. But most of the defaulting countries of the 1930s had reached such agreements. In truth, the main obstacle to bond finance was that investors were far more sceptical about LDCs' ability to pay than bankers. This contrast between the ready availability of bank loans and the virtually complete absence of bond finance is intriguing. It is also critical to understanding why, at a later stage, the governments of developed countries became so anxious about the debts. Losses by bondholders are unfortunate, but they are restricted to the individuals concerned. As such, they are not a policy problem for governments or other official bodies. But losses by banks and possible bank failures have wider ramifications and do raise major questions of public policy.

Secondly, the bank lending was nearly all at variable rates of interest. The typical arrangement was to set a rate which was equal to the London inter-bank offered rate (LIBOR) plus a margin. The rate therefore varied with LIBOR, which in turn fluctuated with dollar interest rates generally. As LIBOR measured the banks' cost of funds, they made a profit as long as the margin (or 'spread) exceeded their administrative costs and other overheads. In the 1970s spread banking of this kind was the standard practice in the Euro-markets based in London, although not for domestic loans in the USA or some other industrial countries.[13] Its effect is to place the macroeconomic risks associated with interest rate changes with the borrower, while the specific risk due the borrower's own problems falls on the bank. Spread banking has subsequently become much more common within the USA itself. The acceptance of interest rate risk by developing country borrowers in the 1970s should be emphasized, as it explains their vulnerability to the violent interest rate swings of the early 1980s. In earlier phases of LDC lending bond issues had been dominant and had carried fixed rates of interest.

Thirdly, the loans were predominantly to governments or to public sector bodies with government or central bank guarantees. This is, of course, the meaning of the term 'sovereign lending'. Banks did not have to assess in detail the viability of the investments being financed with their money or even have to check that the money was being invested. Instead they had only to appraise the creditworthiness of countries, according to criteria – such as the debt/export and debt servicing ratios already mentioned – which were standard and easy to estimate. As long as the various ratios appeared satisfactory, the banks thought that they did not need to worry themselves over the uses or misuses to which their loans were being applied. This characteristic had an important advantage that the administrative costs of making sovereign loans were very low. It was necessary to have only a small number of people in a head office, usually in London, working out the ratios, preparing reports and making occasional trips. As a result modest margins over LIBOR of ½ or ¾ per cent were sufficient to achieve an accounting profit on most sovereign loans. During the 1970s, when many bankers agreed with the doctrine that 'countries cannot go bankrupt' (attributed to Mr Walter Wriston of Citibank), only a small extra premium was deemed appropriate to reflect risk. In view of the historical record the Wriston doctrine may seem rather whimsical or, as Keynes might put it, an expression of bankers' lifelong romanticism. Wriston justified it on the grounds that 'Bankruptcy is a procedure developed in Western law to forgive the obligations of a person or company that owes more than it has. Any country, however badly off, will "own" more than it "owes".'[14] Implicit here is the belief that the geographical areas which nations occupy cannot vanish and that every government will recognize a responsibility for the financial obligations of its predecessors. However, a deep knowledge of the twentieth century is not required to appreciate that the size, shape, form and attitudes of political entities can be changed radically by warfare and revolution. The bankers seem to have assumed that the territorial boundaries and international political structures of the 1970s were sufficiently fixed that they should not feel anxious about these old sources of instability. Again, they placed their trust in the continuation of the *Pax Americana*. After the 25 years of rapid growth worldwide after the Second World War this was not a silly idea. It seemed to receive confirmation from the presence of airports, Sheraton hotels, Coca-Cola tins and other imagery of market capitalism in the most backward Third World countries. In one area of the world, Latin America, it was also supported by the absence of significant intra-regional military conflict for many decades and the pervasiveness of the USA's influence.

III

Rates of return on capital are usually higher, and profitable investment opportunities more numerous, in developing countries than in developed countries. In a logical, businesslike and peaceful world, capital should flow to nations in the Third World from savers in the First World. The most sympathetic interpretation of the sovereign lending boom of the 1970s is that it was an aspect of this benign process of capital transfer. It assisted economic advance by enabling the borrowing countries to purchase machinery, expertise and technology which would not otherwise have been within their reach.

Indeed, the evidence is that in the early stages of the lending boom developing countries which borrowed tended to raise their investment rates. According to analysis by World Bank economists, the positive relationship between borrowing and investment was statistically significant for the periods 1965–72 and 1973–8. However, high investment does not always translate into high growth. The relationship between borrowing and growth was less convincing. Although most countries which borrowed also enjoyed better-than-average growth, it is not clear that the superior growth performance was attributable to their extra indebtedness.[15] The danger is that credit can be extended not to buy more capital goods but to finance balance-of-payments deficits due to excessive government expenditure and consumption.

At any rate, because of the favourable combination of interest rates and export growth rates, borrowing nations in the 1970s could and did run primary payments deficits without suffering a serious deterioriation in their key debt ratios. There were net resource transfers to the Third World. It has been estimated, for example, that the cumulative net transfer to Latin America between 1976 and 1981 was almost $106b.[16] Most Latin American countries had trade deficits and imported substantial and increasing quantities of capital goods.[17] Brazil, for example, had an enormous trade gap in the mid-1970s. In 1975 its imports of $12,050m exceeded its exports of $8,502m by over 40 per cent. In the six years to 1981 its cumulative trade deficit was almost $10½b but, happily, this debt incurral did not seem excessive because exports were also growing swiftly. It has been estimated that the debt/ export ratio of eight important Latin American countries was slightly under 200 per cent in 1975, rose to exceed 200 per cent in 1978, but then fell back to under 200 per cent in 1980. In Brazil's case external debt went up by 24.4 per cent a year between 1976 and 1980 and exports by 18.7 per cent.[18]

The boom in sovereign lending was under control until 1979, the year of the second oil shock. Some of the closely monitored ratios, such as the debt service ratio, were deteriorating, but the debt/export ratio had not changed much in most of the indebted nations, while conspicuous borrowers such as Brazil and Mexico appeared to be in a healthy economic condition. In the southern cone of Latin America Argentina, Chile and Uruguay had made impressive recoveries from desperate financial straits in the mid-1970s and seemed to deserve further infusions of bank credit. For example, Chile's exports boomed at 28.0 per cent a year from 1976 to 1980, far outpacing the 16.2 per cent annual increase in debt. Even Peru – traditionally one of the most hapless debtors – increased its exports by 22.9 per cent a year in the same period, while its debt rose by only 8.0 per cent a year.[19] In 1983 Rimmer de Vries, chief international economist of Morgan Guaranty Trust Company, could argue in evidence to the Senate Foreign Relations Committee that the modest rise in debt/export ratios in the late 1970s 'reflected borrowings to build up foreign exchange reserves, which climbed from $33 billion at year-end 1975 to over $75 billion at year-end 1979. In sum, recycling after the first oil shock proceeded much more smoothly than even the optimists had expected. By financing LDC current account deficits banks, together with official institutions, played an enormously constructive role in preventing the 1974–75 recession from becoming more widespread and prolonged.'[20]

However, two events in 1979 upset all the calculations. The first was the second oil shock which followed the overthrow of the Shah of Iran. The official price for Saudi light oil rose from $12.70 per barrel in 1978 to $28.67 in 1980, causing another drastic disturbance to the pattern of international payments. The current account of oil-exporting developing countries moved from a very small deficit of $0.7b in 1978 to a massive surplus of $100.1b in 1980. The subsequent sequence of events was similar to that which occurred after the first oil shock. The industrial countries moved into substantial deficit, but then baulked at the possibility of continually incurring debt to the oil exporters and took corrective action. The only remaining candidates to assume the deficit were again the oil-importing developing nations. Their combined deficit, which had been $25.1b in 1977 and $35.5b in 1978, soared to $53.8b in 1979, $77.5b in 1980 and $91.0b in 1981. Some of these nations had avoided borrowing after the first oil shock and once more they were careful not to borrow after the second. The position of the indebted developing countries was worse, with their deficit soaring from $36.9b in 1977 to $112.6b in 1981.[21] If the recycling process was to work as smoothly on this occasion, the banks would have to provide larger loans than in the mid-1970s.

The wisdom of continued recycling after the second oil shock does seem very doubtful in retrospect. Perhaps even at the time there should have been a wider recognition that the borrowing countries were building up a debt-servicing obligation with which they would be unlikely to cope. Lomax, chief economic adviser of the Nationl Westminster Bank, judged that in the new conditions massive recycling was 'positively damaging'.[22] Indeed, it has been argued that the job of recycling should never have been handled by the private commercial banks in the first place. It may have been true that debt/export ratios were not much different in 1980 from those in 1975, but, according to some commentators, this was no reason for complacency. Lord Lever and

Christopher Huhne claim in their *Debt and Danger* that 'The similarity of the conventional creditworthiness ratios at the beginning and end of the period merely disguises a much more fundamental change in the structure of the outstanding debt. The advanced countries had thrown a single vulnerable section of their economies, the banking system, into a task which it could not bear without official support.'[23] In their view there is a definite contrast between loans from governments, who can 'afford to roll over interest and capital obligations as circumstances require', and loans from banks, who cannot do so without 'embroiling themselves in a dynamic of increasing incredibility'. They point out that the share of outstanding commercial debt in total loans rose from 11.6 per cent in 1973 to 37.5 per cent in 1982, making debtors more susceptible to 'the disintegration of market confidence'. In the case of Latin America the shift towards bank finance was more pronounced and, if one agrees with the Lever and Huhne diagnosis, more alarming. Banks accounted for 16.4 per cent of Latin America's external public debt in both 1960 and 1970, but for 56.1 per cent in 1980.[24]

The views presented by Lomax, and by Lever and Huhne, are cogent and persuasive. But they should not be accepted uncritically. It needs to be repeated that debt/export ratios for most developing nations were no worse in 1980 than a decade earlier, that countries which had borrowed in the 1970s had on the whole enjoyed higher investment and faster growth than those which had not, and that a case could be argued that the flow of finance to the Third World was contributing to a more complete assimilation with the economies of the First World. An important insight here is that international lending is ultimately deferred trade, because the debts can be serviced and repaid only by receipts from exports.[25] Bankers were not being altogether fatuous when they congratulated themselves at dinners and conferences for not only creating a new and apparently profitable line of business, but also for helping the cause of international economic integration. Even Volcker, commenting in March 1980, could argue that recycling 'has not yet pushed exposures of either borrowers or lenders to an unsustainable point in the aggregate'. He admitted that 'problem cases exist now and will no doubt continue to show up'.[26]

In fact, it was the second shock of 1979 – the change in American monetary control procedures initiated by Volcker himself – which was to transform the manageable debt situation of 1980 into the unmanageable debt crisis of 1982. We have seen that debtor nations in Latin America and elsewhere had no great difficulty keeping their borrowings under control while dollar interest rates were beneath their export growth rates in dollar terms. However, when the Federal Reserve's actions in October 1979 led to sharp increases in dollar interest rates, the debt problems of the commodity-exporting developing countries became inevitable. As the loans extended in the 1970s were at variable interest rates, higher interest rates implied more substantial interest charges on these existing debts. If the Latin American nations were to enjoy the same resource transfer as in earlier years of the decade, they would have to run up debts at a faster rate because the increase in indebtedness would now have to compensate for the larger interest charges. Both the bankers and the borrowing countries should have had reservations about an accelerated incurral of debt. But, in 1979 and 1980, they were not sure how to interpret the more onerous interest burden. Previous episodes of monetary restraint had been transient, with the Federal Reserve unable to maintain a rigorous anti-inflation stand against hostile political forces within the USA. After October 1979 debt growth in the major Latin American countries was more rapid than the increase in exports and output, but bankers could initially justify this on the grounds that they were performing their usual function of assisting customers through periods of temporary difficulty. They did not quickly appreciate, nor indeed did anyone else know for certain, that October 1979 was ultimately to prove a watershed in international financial history.

The change in American monetary policy and the associated increase in real interest rates, and not the irresponsibility of the banks, were the prime causes of the debt crisis. The Lever and Huhne analysis does not adequately recognize the significance of the altered macroeconomic stance in the USA. Neither the banks nor the debtor countries were involved in 'a dynamic of increasing incredibility' while real interest rates were low or negative. Indeed, it requires a strenous imaginative effort to see how they could have been. As long as interest rates were less than the rate of increase in commodity prices, commodity exporters could have accumulated excessive debt only through remarkable extravagance. But, once interest rates were above commodity inflation, debt growth acquired its own familiar momentum. We have already seen in our previous discussions of debt dynamics that the situation can indeed slide into 'increasing incredibility' if nothing is done.

Lever and Huhne argue that serious problems would not have arisen if the developing countries had borrowed from governments and public agencies rather than from banks. But the designation of the lender does not change the logic of the debt trap. It remains indisputable that borrowers would have had trouble servicing their debts once interest rates exceeded commodity inflation. Of course, if the loans had been granted at much beneath market rates and if, in consequence, the interest burden had not increased intolerably after 1979, their argument would be valid. But the banks extended credit predominantly to middle-income countries who were not eligible for concessional, low-interest finance. They avoided the low-income developing countries partly because these countries were in receipt of substantial concessional finance from public agencies anyway and partly because they took a jaundiced view of the creditworthiness of the poorest nations. Their scepticism has been amply justified, as debt arrears in the low-income developing countries have been far worse than in Latin America. Of course, there are some very poor countries in Latin America, notably Peru and Bolivia, but it is significant that they received much less attention from the banks than the large, middle-income nations. Indeed, the geography of default and debt arrears in the 1980s suggests that the banks were not foolish in the choice of destinations for their loans in the 1970s. On the whole, the hopeless cases – countries such as Sudan, Guyana, Chad, Tanzania and the like – never attracted bank finance, except where it was for trade purposes and had a guarantee from an official export credit agency in a developed country.

This is not to say that the banks were irreproachably astute. The sovereign lending boom was for them an apprenticeship in a new kind of business rather than an extension of routine practices which had been tried and proved successful in industrial countries. To some extent their executives lived in a Potemkin world where the governments of the borrowing countries put on a performance, with glittering stage props and false scenery, to persuade them to lend money. The location of the joint annual meeting of the World Bank and the IMF rotated between Washington and other capitals, perhaps to mark the leadership role assumed by the USA in an increasingly closely knit world economy. At dozens of cocktail parties, crammed together in only a few days, bankers, economic journalists, finance ministers and civil servants from all over the globe could meet informally and discover their common needs and interests. The occasion became almost a rite of passage for up-and-coming international bankers. But that was not all. 'It was an exciting period for many young and middle-aged men who were introduced to jets, first class hotels and exotic places. Promotional visits took place by City of London missions to far-flung places like Seoul, Teheran, Mexico City, São Paulo, Bahrain and many others.'[27] Like all apprentices, the banks had to learn by trial and error and they made mistakes.

These mistakes were harmful for the borrowers as well as for them. The World Bank economists who found a positive relationship between debt and investment in the 1965–72 and 1973–8 periods also identified a negative relationship between changes in the ratio of external debt to GDP and the growth of GDP in the 1979–83 period.[28] The boom in sovereign lending had a number of unfavourable effects on the structure of the debtor nations' economies. It is to these effects that we must now turn. Emphasis will be placed on the key point that the debtor countries' difficulties were containable until 1979 and were aggravated to the point of unmangeability only in 1980 and 1981. The break is undoubtedly related to the change in the relationship between interest rates and commodity inflation which occurred in these years.

IV

Among the most important of the unfavourable effects was a weakening of financial self-reliance. Foreign borrowing came to be regarded not as a temporary luxury, but as a permanent habit. Some less-developed countries, particularly in Latin America, failed to realize that the newly permissive financial environment was due to the accidental conjunction of favourable but transient developments in global payments flows. They thought that instead it was a durable change in the international financial system. They adjusted domestic savings patterns too readily in the optimistic assumption that the new ease of borrowing would continue. External savings were allowed to finance a higher share of total investment. The surplus on the capital account of the Latin American region's balance of payments represented 8.8 per cent of its total capital formation in 1965–70, 15.5 per cent in 1971–3 and 22.3 per cent in 1976–80.[29] There was nothing unhealthy about this as long as external savings were additional to domestic savings, as was true for most of the 1970s. However, towards the end of the decade a disturbing tendency emerged in a number of countries. External savings began to substitute for instead of supplement domestic savings, and domestic savings contracted.

The drop in domestic savings was largely due to a sharp rise in the financial deficits incurred by the public sector. During the 1950s and 1960s Latin American governments, unlike their counterparts in the developed countries, incurred budget deficits for most of the time, but – except in the often grossly misgoverned countries of the southern cone (Argentina, Chile and Uruguay) – these deficits were reasonably modest and could be absorbed without much difficulty by domestic savings. In 1970 the public sector deficit in Brazil was 2.5 per cent of GDP, in Mexico 1.8 per cent, in Venezuela 2.6 per cent and even in feckless Argentina 1.1 per cent. In the course of the 1970s the position deteriorated. By 1980 the public sector financial deficit in Brazil was 9.1 per cent, in Mexico 7.9 per cent, in Venezuela 13.5 per cent and in Argentina 4.3 per cent.[30] The main reason, or rather the standard rationalization, for this slide into deficit was that the nations concerned lacked adequate infrastructure and could therefore claim to have a variety of public sector projects which would generate high social returns. Because of the inadequacy of domestic savings, it was judged sensible to tap the international capital markets.

In fact, many of the public sector projects were seriously misconceived and did not earn a satisfactory rate of return. The trouble was undoubtedly related to two characteristics of the 1970s lending boom, low real interest rates and the vigorous marketing efforts of the lending banks, which allowed governments to become cavalier in their assessment of investment projects. With their exports in dollar terms rising at 15–20 per cent a year, their economies typically growing at rates of 5 per cent or more a year, dollar interest rates of under 10 per cent and a widespread belief that this favourable constellation of economic variables would persist, Latin American governments were not nervous about their ultimate ability to repay. This financial self-confidence may have been not unreasonable in macro terms, but the increasing sloppiness of investment appraisal at the micro level was difficult to excuse. The low quality of investment was particularly obvious in countries which received large and sudden windfalls from sharp increases in the prices of their major commodity exports, were immediately granted another windfall in the form of abundant loans from impressionable and over-enthusiastic international bankers, and were then unable to put the influx of money to good use. Oil-exporting nations were most susceptible to these excesses. An analysis of a sample of 1,600 projects in seven oil-exporting countries found frequent cost escalations, completion delays and postponements or suspensions. In general, the larger the project, the greater the waste: 47 per cent of the projects of over $1b went wrong in one way or another, with the average cost escalation being 109 per cent. Even when they were completed, the schemes were often of doubtful economic validity. A sugar project in Trinidad is estimated in 1983 to have had production costs that were 'five times those of efficient world-scale producers, despite the fact that some of the latter, notably in Australia, had unit labour costs several times higher'.[31]

Mexico was both among the most active borrowers and one of the most careless in its use of the funds. It should be said, in mitigation, that few countries were given stronger temptations to participate in the sovereign lending boom. One observer has recounted how, at the Palace Hotel in Madrid in 1981, during the annual meeting of the Inter-American Development Bank, he 'saw bankers queuing up to offer their banks' services to Angel Gurria, the man in charge of Mexico's borrowing, who was reclining in an armchair'.[32] It is perhaps not surprising that Mexico's public sector financial deficit climbed from 7.9

per cent of GDP in 1980 to 14.5 per cent in 1981 and 17.6 per cent in 1982.[33]

The trend towards wider budget deficits and inefficient public sector investment projects was unsound. It was obvious in official aggregate data and should, by itself, have caused bankers to have second thoughts. But even clearer warnings were being given by more detailed evidence, such as symptoms of resource misallocation between industries. The increased predilection of Latin American governments for grandiose public sector projects not only bloated budget deficits and led to higher external indebtedness. It also increased the demand for labour and capital, which put pressure on domestic resources, added to inflation and contributed to a continent-wide appreciation of real exchange rates. In 1982 the Inter-American Development Bank (IDB) conducted a study which showed that for the region as a whole the revaluation of the real exchange rate average 2.30 per cent a year between 1971 and 1980.[34] This had disturbing implications in both the short and the long run. In the short run, the higher real exchange rate reduced exports, increased imports, widened the payments gap and so made the debtor nations even more dependent on external funds. In the long run, the overvaluation of exchange rates was even more dangerous because it deterred investment in exporting and import-substitution industries. But Latin America would eventually need to export much more in order to service its debts. The imperative of debt control, that the rate of export growth should at least match the rate of interest, was being ignored. If interest rates were rising (as they evidently were in the late 1970s), a higher rate of export growth would be needed sooner or later. But underinvestment in export industries foreshadowed a probable export slow-down or severe adjustment strains if an export drive were to become necessary.

It may well be asked why this pattern was allowed to emerge and continue. The structure of development in some countries became increasingly lop-sided, with the proceeds of foreign loans being invested in offices, shopping malls, apartment blocks and hotels instead of the vital export industries. Arguably, the banks made one of their worst errors by watching macroeconomic indicators of solvency rather than the specific uses to which their loans were being put. The phase of most blatant overvaluation was in the three years 1979 to 1981 just as the boom in sovereign lending was reaching its peak. In 1979 and 1980 Brazil was able to negotiate massive jumbo loans the proceeds of which were added to reserves to finance future payments imbalances. Loans of this kind perpetuated and exaggerated unrealistic exchange rates, further deterring the growth of export-oriented industries. The IDB study estimated that over half of the exchange rate appreciation in Latin

America in the 1970s could be attributed to the inflow of external capital, with the rest due to improved terms of trade. But in 1980 and 1981 taken by themselves the flood of sovereign loans must have been the dominant influence. The IDB has calculated that in 1980 the Argentine exchange rate had appreciated by 170 per cent in real terms compared with 1975, obviously ridiculous and unsustainable and the principal reason for the massive deterioration in its trade position. The Mexican exchange rate, which was fully competitive in the mid-1970s, appreciated in real terms by 40 per cent between 1977 and 1981, hampering the development of tourism and export-oriented manu-facturing and thereby increasing dependence on oil production.[35]

Within Latin America the inappropriateness of the exchange rates ruling in 1980 and 1981 was widely understood. It contributed to one of the most destructive aspects of the sovereign lending boom. To the people of Latin America, who have long experience of financially untrustworthy governments, the prediction and anticipation of devalu-ations are national pastimes comparable, in the intensity of the passions aroused, with the forecasting of international football results. But, whereas Latin Americans have deep loyalty to their football teams, they have none to their currencies. The overvaluations of the late 1970s, 1980 and 1981 provoked massive capital outflows. Virtually all the money was destined for financial centres in the developed countries. There was an unhappy irony in this. While Latin American governments borrowed supposedly to improve their development prospects, their citizens sent their savings abroad to avoid currency devaluation. Implicitly, govern-ments and citizens had different assessments of the viability of the borrowing on which their countries had embarked. A World Bank analysis shows that in one case, Venezuela, capital flight actually *exceeded* gross capital inflows. In two other cases – Mexico and Argentina – the outflows were extremely large in relation to the inflows. The estimates for these and five other countries are given in table 10.[36]

Most of the capital outflow was conducted openly. Mexico had several decades of exchange freedom until 1982, while Argentina had a fairly liberal exchange control regime between 1976 and 1981. There was nothing improper about transferring dollars from bank accounts in Mexico City and Buenos Aires to bank accounts in Miami, London or Switzerland. But this does not mean that the dollars had necessarily been acquired legitimately in the first place.

The scope for misappropriation arose largely because of the sovereign character of the borrowing. As we have seen, most loans to Latin America in the 1970s had a government or central bank guarantee. The involvement of the state lulled the banks into a false sense of security, because they did not doubt a government's preparedness to honour its

Table 10   The problem of capital flight in five Latin American countries, 1979–1982

	Capital flight ($b)	Gross capital inflows ($b)	Capital flight as percentage of gross capital inflows
Venezuela	22.0	16.1	136.6
Argentina	19.2	29.5	65.1
Mexico	26.5	55.4	47.8
Uruguay	0.6	2.2	27.3
Brazil	3.5	43.9	8.0

For definitions and methods, see source.

Source: *World Development Report 1985* (New York: Oxford University Press, 1985), p. 64

financial commitments and they did not have to worry about the particular uses to which loan proceeds were put. In fact, the loan proceeds wee not infrequently channelled to the personal benefit of a small number of well-connected individuals. We may outline a sequence of transactions to give insight into the possibilities. The story is, of course, fictitious, but it bears a resemblance to actual events. It is most easily related in the present tense, although most of the misdemeanours occurred in 1980 and 1981.

A syndicate of banks in London assembles a $100m loan to a bank in Buenos Aires, with the risk being assumed by the Argentine government. In theory, the $100m is now to be lent to promising industrial and agricultural companies, all of whom are profitable, generate dollar earnings and repay the bank in Buenos Aires on time, and the bank in Buenos Aires then repays the syndicate on time as well. In practice, matters are very different. The management of the bank sets up a consultancy company and hires it to provide advice to the bank for $1m. As the consultancy company is 100 per cent owned by the managers, they are credited with $1m in their personal bank accounts. The balance of the $100m is lent to a variety of good causes. Relatives of the management are deemed to be particularly deserving. They also establish bogus companies (so-called *empresas de papel* or paper enterprises) and receive loans of perhaps $20m which they have no intention of repaying. The bank does not demand security, but instead accepts the personal guarantees of the borrowing individuals. When these individuals switch the money to an account in Miami and take the next plane there, there is nothing the bank can do to retrieve the loans. Next on the list of beneficiaries are old cronies, who find that in the new environment property speculation is remarkably profitable. The banks' senior executives lend them $10m to buy an office block in central Buenos Aires. Once the deal is completed, the bank contacts a property company and indicates that it is prepared to lend $15m for the acquisition of the same office block. If the proposal is accepted, the old cronies pocket $5m. An attraction of this transaction from the viewpoint of the bank's management is that there appears to have been a genuine loan repayment. This helps to pacify the accountants who might otherwise have objected to the absence of arm's length transactions on transparently commercial terms. If the accountants, lawyers, central bank regulators and other professional parties really do complain, the answer is to persuade them to establish their own *empresas de papel*. These *empresas*, despite the lack of any trading record, are accorded a high credit standing by the bank and quickly receive a significant loan. It is recognized and understood that such loans might, after a short lag, find their way − like so much else of the initial proceeds of the syndicated credit − into an account in Miami.

The last paragraph should not be misinterpreted. It is an exaggeration. Most of the billions of dollars which flowed into Latin America in the late 1970s, 1980 and 1981 were invested productively. But our account of the virtual disappearance of $100m is neither fantasy nor caricature. A distressingly high proportion of the so-called 'capital inflows' into Latin America were destined to become capital outflows into developed countries, with bank accounts and real estate in Florida being the favourite final resting place. Perhaps the most sickening aspect of the whole business is that the fly-by-night rascals who effectively stole the proceeds of syndicated loans did not have to carry the burden of debt service. Some time after the departure of their managements from Mexico, Argentina or Venezuela the self-styled 'banks' would be declared insolvent. They were therefore unable to repay the syndicated credits which had made their transgressions possible. But part of the original arrangement was that the loans were guaranteed by the government or central bank of the country concerned.[37] Although the 'banks' and their managements no longer had to worry about servicing the debts, the government − and so the nation as whole − certainly did have that task. It fell on the general body of taxpayers, not the jet-setting fraudsters, to meet the demands of the international bankers.

The capital flight which accompanied the concluding phase of the sovereign lending boom was very substantial only in Mexico, Argentina and Venezuela. Nevertheless, various kinds of corruption, fraud and embezzlement were commonplace in business and politics throughout Latin America. In Chile exchange controls hindered massive outward movements of funds, but loan proceeds were still grossly misdirected. Large conglomerates known as *grupos* had banking subsidiaries which borrowed from the international banking system. These subsidiaries then channelled the dollars to other parts of the conglomerate, often contrary to business logic and purely to serve the directors' interests. A report prepared by the Chilean Superintendent of Banks and Financial Institutions in 1982 showed that loans to companies connected with owners of financial institutions averaged 15.4 per cent of all bank assets and were frequently in excees of 20 per cent.[38]

It is not trivialization to blame the misdeeds on long-standing institutional characteristics of the debtor nations as well as aspects of the Latin American temperament and outlook. First, the long traditions of banking practice and professional ethics, which are found in the advanced industrial countries, were lacking. These deficiencies were largely responsible for the backwardness of financial systems and the inadequacy of domestic saving which provided the original justification for external borrowing. As we shall see in chapter 5, one outcome of the sovereign lending boom was to exacerbate the weaknesses of Latin American financial systems. In this respect, the long-run effect of the boom was extremely detrimental.

Secondly, and perhaps more controversially, the elites of Latin American nations do not have the well-developed sense of public responsibility which distinguishes their counterparts in countries like the USA and the UK. The East Coast establishment and the British public official class may not be as overtly moralistic as they were 50 years ago, but they do recognize ethical responsibilities in many areas of public life, are generally free from corruption and frequently subordinate their own short-term material advantage to the service of a wider social good. In Conrad's *Nostromo* Charles Gould, the English mine-owner in the apocryphal (but not unrealistic) Latin American Republic of Costaguana, is said to have a political ideal no more profound than to defend 'the commonest decencies of organised society', but he is mocked by the adventurer Decoud. 'But, then, don't you see, he's an Englishman. . . . He could not believe his own motives if he did not make them first a part of some fairy tale.'[39] Latin Americans, by contrast, live in countries with long and depressing records of political instability, and do not have the same commitment to the preservation of an ordered society with certain recognized values.

Broadly the same point has been made by the Mexican intellectual Octavio Paz in a recent interview. In his view, the economic failure of Latin America stems from its political failure and, in particular, from a pernicious political conception inherited from its Spanish and Portuguese colonial masters. This is the idea of a 'patrimonial state' in which 'the Prince governs with his servants, his slaves and his family – in other words, where he regards the realm as his personal property'. It follows

Table 11 The growth of the patrimonial state in Latin America, 1970, 1975 and 1980–1982

	Public sector expenditure as a percentage of GDP				
	1970	*1975*	*1980*	*1981*	*1982*
Argentina	32.8	37.8	40.2	41.9	35.2
Brazil	28.4	28.4	32.4	34.9	31.6
Chile	40.6	33.6	32.0	35.9	36.2
Colombia	25.9	27.6	29.4	30.1	n.a.
Mexico	20.6	32.7	36.3	42.3	47.5
Peru	24.6	45.9	60.8	56.8	n.a.
Venezuela	31.6	59.9	66.0	67.9	65.8

For definitions, see source.

Source: *External Debt and Economic Development in Latin America* (Washington: Inter-American Development Bank, 1984), p. 28

that 'the administrative and economic privileges of the Mexican bureaucracy are political in origin, and spring from the political monopoly enjoyed by the ruling party'.[40] It is not too far-fetched to see a connection between these remarks and the undoubted fact that in 1980 and 1981 many Mexican bureaucrats did treat the proceeds of sovereign loans as their private property.

International bankers may have had idealistic visions of dispensing loans to help Latin American nations escape their patrimonial past and become more fully integrated with the market economies of the industrialized world. If so, it has to be said that they were curiously blind to what their clients were doing with the money. A good case can be argued that the sovereign lending boom actually strengthened the patrimonial state. By directing the funds in the first instance to governments or their agencies, the lending boom expanded the economic power of political leaders and bureaucracies. By facilitating public sector investment, it contributed to an increase in the share of government expenditure to GDP in most countries. The relevant figures are given in table 11. It is striking that in Mexico the ratio of public expenditure to GDP more than doubled between 1970 and 1981, hardly a good advertisement for the bankers' claims to be strengthening the free market system.

V

We can bring the strands of the argument together and draw some conclusions. The sovereign lending boom was motivated by the belief that the future would be like the past. Since the end of the Second World War no government had failed to honour its debts, while during the 1970s the exports of the major borrowing nations consistently rose at a higher rate than the rate of interest on their debts. The absence of sovereign defaults for a generation gave ample justification for expecting that there would be none during the envisaged terms of the new loans; the favourable relationship between export growth and interest rates suggested that a net resource transfer to Third World debtors could be reconciled with reasonable financial stability and the preservation of creditworthiness. It was not, either at the time or even in retrospect, clearly imprudent and misguided for major international banks to start lending to the governments of developing countries in the mid-1970s. A strong case can also be argued that, until 1979, the effects of the sovereign lending boom had been largely benign and that the behaviour of the critical debt ratios did not suggest that the situation was unsustainable.

The change in American monetary policy in October 1979 and the second oil shock altered the debt outlook radically. Most importantly, the sharp increase in dollar interest rates resulted in an adverse relationship between them and the rate of growth of exports. While interest rates remained above export growth rates, net resource transfers to developing countries could continue only if they were accompanied by increases in the ratio of debt to exports. But increases in the debt/export ratio could not be allowed to continue indefinitely. Before 1979 the sovereign lending boom was sustainable; after 1979 it became unsustainable. Sooner or later the main participants would have to call a halt.

The most powerful criticism of the banks is that they did not react to the events of 1979 by restricting credit immediately. Although there are several alternative ways of measuring the growth of developing country debt, they all show that 1981 was the peak year for lending. This is particularly clear in Latin America, where the increase in net external debt, $25.9b in 1979 and $32.6b in 1980, reached $47.8b in 1981 (see table 12). On the face of it, the banks' response to the changed monetary environment was at best eccentric and at worst downright foolish. The higher level of dollar interest rates would obviously make it more difficult for the debtor nations to repay. But the banks appeared to be lending them more money, not less. In fact, as we shall see in the next chapter, appearances are deceptive. When allowance is made for the impact of higher interest charges on debt growth, the banks did start to trim their lending in 1981.

Nevertheless, the banks' behaviour was, at least to some extent, perverse. This perversity is strongly evidenced by the rush of flight

Table 12 The balance of payments of the seven largest Latin American nations, 1974–1984

	Change in net external debt ($b)	Direct investment ($b)	Change in international reserves ($b)	Misc. capital, errors ($b)	Current account balance ($b)
1974	12.5	1.5	−3.9	−4.6	−5.5
1975	12.0	1.9	−0.2	−1.7	−12.0
1976	13.5	0.5	−4.1	−0.5	−9.4
1977	15.3	1.4	−4.7	−3.0	−9.0
1978	24.7	2.0	−7.0	−5.7	−14.0
1979	25.9	3.0	−9.1	−2.9	−16.9
1980	32.6	3.4	−2.0	−8.5	−25.5
1981	47.8	4.5	1.1	−17.4	−36.0
1982	35.5	2.8	17.0	−22.6	−32.7
1983	16.3	2.0	4.7	−19.3	−3.7
1984	16.9	2.7	−10.4	−7.3	1.9

A minus sign in the reserves column indicates an increase in the reserves. A minus sign in the current account column indicates a deficit. Current account balance is equal to sum of previous four columns, with sign reversed.

Source: *Economic and Social Progress in Latin America: External Debt, Crisis and Adjustment* (Washington: Inter-American Development Bank, 1985), p. 22

money out of Latin America, partly driven by fears of currency devaluation. There was a definite contrast in perception between the managements of the international banks and the populations of the debtor nations. This contrast may be explicable by greater local awareness of the widespread misuse of the dollars being made available to political figures, bureaucrats and leading businessmen. Perhaps visiting bankers should have paid more attention to the detailed allocation of their money and not concentrated so exclusively on the macroeconomic data. They may also have been duped by the conspicuous prosperity of several Latin American nations in the 1979–82 period, much of which reflected a boom in construction activity and increased consumption of imported luxuries. These signs of economic buoyancy were bogus. They depended on the continuation of foreign loans and the foreign loans depended on the money being invested in export promotion rather than squandered on apartment buildings, Japanese consumer electronics, Swiss perfumes and the like. Nevertheless, growth rates in much of Latin America in the late 1970s, 1980 and 1981 were exceptionally good, even if somewhat artificial. Bankers may have extrapolated these growth rates, and the rates of increase in export value achieved in the 1970s, into the indefinite future.

On the far from foolish assumption that dollar interest rates would fall from the unprecedented levels which followed the October 1979 measures, it was not difficult to prepare reassuring projections of debt/ export, debt interest/export and debt/GDP ratios into the 1980s. In short, heavy sovereign lending was unsustainable after the events of 1979, but no one knew in 1980 or 1981 how long the condition of unsustainability would last. It was possible that real interest rates would return in the mid-1980s to the levels of the mid-1970s, in which case debtor nations would be in a viable situation once again. Indeed, who could have said for certain in 1980 or 1981 that Volcker's actions in October 1979 would mark a decisive turning-point in international monetary affairs? Had not previous displays of toughness by the Federal Reserve evaporated under political pressure? In an otherwise appre- hensive analysis in its September 1980 *World Financial Markets* publication, Morgan Guaranty was still able to forecast an optimistic case in which 12 major oil-importing LDCs performed satisfactorily in the mid-1980s. Increases of only 8.5 per cent a year in their external bank debt between 1983 and 1985 could be reconciled with growth of their GDPs at 5 per cent a year.[41]

In any case, the bankers could console themselves with the selfish thought that, if the debtor nations did slip into financial difficulties and threaten repudiation, the governments of the USA and other leading industrial nations, in association with the IMF, would coerce delinquents into payment. This complacency about the effectiveness of the USA as an international policeman was based on its success in the small number of previous post-war episodes with recalcitrant debtor nations. So far the bankers' confidence has also proved largely justified in practice. When it became obvious in 1982 that high real interest rates would persist, and when the bankers consequently wanted to limit their exposure, the debt crisis began in earnest. But as yet none of the large Latin American debtors has refused outright to pay. On the contrary, they have all made remarkable sacrifices in order to honour their debt obligations as fully as possible. Their sacrifices are evidenced most spectacularly in the emergence of large trade surpluses and consequent net resource *outflows* to the developed nations, an achievement which has led some observers to regard the situation as sustainable. The mistake here – as we shall see in the next chapter – is to overlook the domestic consequences within the developing countries of their im- pressive record on the external front. Even if their balance-of-payments situations are now sustainable, the domestic financial conditions of many Latin American countries are not.

5

The Bust in Sovereign Lending

I

The beginning of the debt crisis is usually dated as 18 August 1982 when Mexico announced it could not service its foreign currency debt. More exactly, it could not raise new loans sufficient to repay the old debts which were coming due. Talks about a rescue package started immediately with the International Monetary Fund (IMF), the Bank for International Settlements (BIS) and the commercial banks. There was little advance preparation by either Mexico or its creditors. When asked who orchestrated the Mexican rescue, Donald Regan, then Secretary to the US Treasury, replied, 'There was no Toscanini. There was no Beethoven. It was more like Arnold Schoenberg, improvising as he composed.'[1] Although a $925m loan was made available by the BIS straightaway, a 90–day moratorium on all principal repayments on the public foreign debt was announced on 20 August.

The Mexican news was regarded, correctly, as the harbinger of debt difficulties in other countries. However, it is misleading to think that there was an abrupt change in the financial circumstances of the developing world. We have argued in this book that the antecedents of the debt crisis are to be sought in American monetary policy in the late 1970s, particularly in the change in monetary control procedures in October 1979, and the subsequent sharp rise in real interest rates. Awareness that the high level of real interest rates was not a freak, but would last for some years, spread gradually. As bankers came to understand the implications, they reappraised their approach to sovereign lending. This reappraisal was conducted throughout 1981 and early 1982, not suddenly in the course of one month.

The deliberateness of the banks' change of view was reflected in two developments *before* August 1982. First, lending became increasingly short term. The tendency towards shorter maturities had been apparent as early as the mid-1970s and was the main reason that the ratios of debt service to exports rose even though debt/export ratios were generally stable. But it was much more pronounced in 1981 and 1982. An analysis by American Express Bank reveals the extent of the change. It proposes the concept of 'excess short-term debt', defined as the amount by which short-term debt exceeds immediate trade financing requirements (taken to be the value of imports over the next six months). In the frenzy of the oil boom, Mexico was particularly slapdash in its management of the short-term position. Its excess short-term debt, nil in the middle of 1980, soared to over $6b in the middle of 1981 and then to over $23b just before the moratorium announcement. Argentina was also running into trouble some time before the complete suspension of new credits. Between the middle of 1979 and the middle of 1981 its total short-term debts more than doubled from $4.5b to $10.4b. Its excess short-term debt is estimated to have climbed over the same period from only $502m to $6.2b. On the whole, Brazil paid more attention to the maturity profile of its debt than other Latin American countries. Even so its bankers were so diffident about extending medium-term credits that, over the three years to early 1982, medium-term debt rose by 43.3 per cent from $26.6b to $38.3b whereas its short-term debt climbed by 129.1 per cent from $6.2b to $14.2b.[2]

The banks' motive for shifting towards short-term maturities was the belief that, in the event of serious trouble, they could withdraw more easily if a loan was due to be repaid soon than if it was due to be repaid at a distant date. In other words, short-term finance is more cowardly than medium-term lending. In practice, this line of thinking proved fallacious because after the crisis broke all banks were obliged to maintain their exposure, irrespective of the original maturity of their loans. For the borrowing countries, greater dependence on short-term money was unwelcome because it increased their vulnerability to sharp changes in banks' assessment of their creditworthiness.

The second sign that bank attitudes were being revised before August 1982 is that, although the total amount of bank lending to the Third World peaked in 1981, the net resource flow and the amount of voluntary new money to some countries fell after 1980. Here we see the crucial importance of the rise in dollar interest rates in late 1979 and 1980. As we have emphasized before, the growth of debt has two components – new lending and the addition of interest to old loan principals. With the jump in interest rates, the total growth of debt had to increase in 1980 and 1981 if the debtor nations were to receive the same amount of new lending. Obviously, when banks lend to countries in order that the countries can pay interest back to the banks, they are not extending genuine new credit at all. Instead there is just an elaborate and apparently circular game of pass the parcel, with the right hand (the banks) giving to the left hand (the debtor countries) in order that the left can return to the right what the right hand was already owed. There was much activity of this kind in the early 1980s, with a distinction being drawn between 'spontaneous lending' (new lending, not intended to compensate for the repayment of interest or principal on old loans) and 'concerted lending' (lending made to enable debtor countries to meet their obligations on old loans). The term 'concerted lending' reflected the role central banks in the industrial countries played in forcing commercial banks – many of whom wanted to withdraw from the international debt game altogether – to maintain their involvement.

The purpose of all this relabelling and reshuffling was to preserve the facade that money had been repaid on the due date. This may seem futile and rather silly, but it was – and remains – very important in the accounting approach to bank profits. If the formalities of repayment and new lending have been complied with, the interest on old loans is deemed to contribute to bank profits; if they have not been, the loan is classified as in some way unsatisfactory. (Loans can be put into various categories, such as 'substandard', 'non-performing' and 'value-impaired'.) The gap between form and substance may seem narrow, but – as we saw in the Introduction – banks can have genuine difficulties in knowing at what point a bad loan becomes definitely bad. A loan which appears hopeless one year may be perfectly sound two or three years later. Bankers may have felt in the early 1980s that lending to the Third World, like theatre-going, would depend for its eventual success on a prolonged suspension of disbelief.

At any rate, the net resource flow to a developing country is best measured – from an economic rather than as accounting standpoint – by the excess of the increase in debt over interest charges. Even this idea suffers from ambiguities. An argument can be made that a reduction in unused credit facilities should be regarded as equivalent to a cut in new lending, since they both limit a borrowing country's potential ability to import. Moreover, a distinction should be drawn between credit extended by banks and finance from the IMF and other public bodies to help meet obligations to banks (and others). If the change in unused credit commitments is taken into account, and if the figures are restricted to the banks, the American Express analysis shows that a net outflow began in 1981 for half of the 24 countries it considers.[3] This conclusion undermines the criticisms directed against the banks, and given some support in chapter 4, for maintaining lending to countries like Argentina and Mexico in 1980 and 1981.

Other studies reach different results. For example, the Inter-American Development Bank (IDB) suggests in its 1986 *Annual Report* that the positive net resource transfer to Latin America peaked in 1981, became negative in 1982 and heavily negative in 1983. The IDB data are reproduced in table 13. The contrast between the American Express and IDB conclusions reflects differences in coverage and definitions. There is ample scope for discussion about which data set and what definition is appropriate. Perhaps it is not surprising that there is a debate about whether the banks were foolish to remain involved in sovereign lending in this period. Perhaps it is also rather naive to expect anyone to reach a simple verdict of guilt or innocence about their behaviour.

But all analyses agree on two points. First, interest payments rose very sharply because of the increase in dollar interest rates in 1980. Interest on the external debt of the seven largest Latin American debtors jumped from $14.2b in 1979 to $30.7b in 1981, reflecting a change in the London inter-bank offered dollar rate from an average of 12.2 per cent to 16.6 per cent.[4] Their interest bills in 1974 and 1975, $3.7b and $4.6b respectively, look trifling by comparison. Secondly, whatever the uncertainties about 1981 and the precise scale of the phenomenon, the net resource flow – from both Latin America and

Table 13 The net resource transfer to and from Latin America, and levels of gross domestic investment

	Net resource transfer ($)[a]	Gross domestic investment ($)[a]	NRT/GDP (%)	GDI/GDP (%)
1970	2,541	83,596	0.7	22.7
1971	4,389	90,283	1.1	23.0
1972	6,709	93,904	1.6	22.3
1973	9,212	106,300	2.0	23.4
1974	15,384	124,432	3.2	25.6
1975	19,015	131,020	3.8	25.9
1976	19,852	134,328	3.7	25.1
1977	11,104	143,179	2.0	25.4
1978	20,271	147,252	3.4	25.0
1979	17,040	151,180	2.7	24.2
1980	20,636	168,003	3.1	25.5
1981	24,424	166,622	3.7	24.9
1982	−10,044	143,454	−1.5	21.7
1983	−30,189	115,847	−4.7	18.1
1984	−25,963	117,649	−3.9	17.8
1985	−29,089	122,771	−4.2	17.9

[a] 1984 US dollars.

Source: Statistics prepared by Inter-American Development Bank in Washington and supplied to author by Mr Hector Luisi, IDB representative in London

other developing countries – became negative in 1982 and has remained so ever since.

Of course, these developments are related. When banks saw that their customers faced disagreeably higher interest rates, they became more reluctant to meet future loan applications. The net resource flow to the Third World was therefore hit in two ways, by a rise in the interest burden and by a drop, indeed a virtual cessation, in 'new money' or 'spontaneous' lending.

II

The emergence of net resource transfers out of Latin America was profoundly damaging to the economies of the region. In view of the sharply higher level of interest rates, they had to increase the underlying growth rates of their economies, and so of their exports, if they were to keep debt/export ratios under control. But negative resource transfers hit growth prospects in two ways. The first, and more obvious, is that they implied a need for reductions in domestic expenditure if external payments were to remain viable. This need to reduce domestic expenditure could be satisfied through curbing consumption or investment. In most countries the decline in investment was appreciably greater in percentage terms than the decline in consumption. Lower investment has resulted in slower growth of the capital stock and so in a poorer long-term growth outlook. Secondly, the withdrawal of foreign finance obliged Latin American governments to cover their borrowing needs from domestic sources, which invariably implied higher money supply growth and faster inflation. Faster inflation in turn impaired the efficiency and coherence of financial systems, dislocating the mechanisms of savings and investment, and further reducing long-run growth potential. Through their impact on the structure of Latin American economies, these developments made the eventual resolution of the debt problem even more difficult and remote. The first of these two processes is discussed in the remainder of this section, and the second in the next section.

The arithmetical effect of the cut in resource transfers on investment is the more straightforward to document. According to the IDB (in the figures reproduced in table 13), Latin America's net resource transfer swung from a positive $21.3b in 1981 to a negative $9.2b in 1982 and a heavily negative $28.8b in 1983. It remained at roughly the 1983 level in 1984 and 1985. In other words, the Latin American nations were deprived between 1981 and 1983 of about $50b of resources that would otherwise have been available for their use. The loss of resources was equivalent to over 8 per cent of the continent's GDP. This drastic assault on their well-being was immediately registered in the national accounts of the countries affected. The relative size of exports and imports changed radically, with imports declining abruptly and the net export position becoming much stronger. The domestic counterpart to this swing on the external items were falls in the ratios of consumption and investment to GDP.

The IDB has estimated that, for the continent as a whole, the ratio of gross investment to GDP tumbled from 25.5 per cent in 1980 and 24.9 per cent in 1981 to 21.7 per cent in 1982 and 18.1 per cent in 1983.[5] The drop in the investment/GDP ratio therefore amounted to almost 6 per cent in the two years from 1981, accounting for the greater part of the deterioration in the net resource flows. The continent-wide investment/GDP ratio stabilized at about 18 per cent in 1984 and 1985, but has shown further signs of weakness in 1986 and 1987. Emphasis should be placed on the inadequacy of an investment/GDP ratio of 18 per cent by Latin America's own past standards, as the corresponding figure in the 1970s was slightly more than 24 per cent. Indeed, one of the most ironic and pathetic aspects of the debt crisis is that heavy external borrowing in the 1970s did not support an increase in investment in later years, but acted to reduce it. What should have been a health-giving transfusion of capital from the advanced countries proved instead to lead to a constant haemorrhage of badly needed resources. Although this may seem paradoxical, the outcome is inherent in the logic of the debt trap. In a high-interest environment a borrowing nation soon faces a mounting interest bill on past debts which encroaches on the discretionary incomes remaining in the hands of its citizens and limits their ability to support new investment.

That the sovereign lending boom was primarily responsible for the slide in investment can be demonstrated in another way. As a general rule, the fall in investment was greatest in those countries which had relied most heavily on foreign finance. Perhaps the starkest example was Chile which had enjoyed a positive net resource transfer equivalent to 13 per cent of GDP in 1980 and 16 per cent in 1981, much higher than for Latin America as a whole. When new bank credits came to an end in 1982, investment – particularly investment in stocks – crashed by 65 per cent and national output by a traumatic 14.3 per cent. This cyclical slump was the worst in Latin America.

But at least Chile has seen a worthwhile recovery in investment since 1982. Other countries have not been so fortunate. For example, Argentina suffered a continuous fall in investment in the early 1980s, with its investment/GDP ratio down from 22.9 per cent in 1980 to only 10.9 per cent in 1985. At a level as low as this investment is not sufficient to match depreciation on old machinery, plant and buildings, and the capital stock is contracting. The implication is not just that Argentina will have a lower trend rate of growth than before the debt crisis, but that national output may be on a declining path for several years. If so, Argentina's chances of escaping from its debt troubles are negligible. As the interest rate on its debts will undoubtedly remain positive and must therefore exceed the growth rate of its national output (and, probably, its exports), its debt/export ratio will worsen remorselessly.

The only country in Latin America not to have experienced a large fall in investment is Colombia. The share of investment in its GNP was 19.2 per cent in 1980 and very similar at 19.4 per cent in 1984. This immunity to the continent-wide collapse in investment is very significant. The key to understanding its fortunate position is that Colombia – uniquely in Latin America – abstained from the sovereign lending boom. In consequence, when dollar interest rates rose sharply after 1979 Colombia was not faced with a large and sharply higher external interest bill. Its national output remained, more or less, as fully under the control of its own citizens as before and could be channelled into investment on the same scale. Thus, in 1981 net factor payments abroad, consisting predominantly of interest payments, were a mere 0.5 per cent of Colombia's GNP whereas they amounted to 4.0 per cent of Argentina's and Brazil's and 4.3 per cent of Chile's.[6] The relative success of the Colombian economy, at least on this particular criterion, is instructive. It bears witness both to the wisdom of its policy-makers in not participating in the borrowing boom and to the destructive impact on the rest of Latin America of the jump in dollar interest rates in 1979.

III

The connection between the net resource outflow from Latin America and the fall in investment is direct and easy to understand, but this should not be allowed to disguise the importance of the second mechanism at work. We saw in chapter 4 that the ready access to external loans which characterized the 1970s encouraged Latin American governments to become rather casual in the management of their own finances. Budget deficits widened throughout the region. (Interestingly, Colombia is again an exception, with its public sector deficit *lower* in 1980 at 1.3 per cent of GDP than in 1970 when it was 4.0 per cent of GDP.[7]) The sudden curtailment of foreign credit in 1982 therefore presented them with an unpleasant fiscal dilemma.

They had two options. Either they could curb their deficits by raising taxes and lowering expenditure or they could try to finance the deficits to a greater degree from domestic sources. Fiscal retrenchment was undoubtedly the textbook prescription. It was advocated repeatedly, and with ever-increasing unpopularity, by the IMF in its discussions with the political leaderships of the debtor countries. The main drawback was that attempts to narrow budget deficits on the revenue side were hampered by the substantial declines in sales and output, and so in the tax base, which typified Latin American economies in 1982 and 1983. The alternative approach, to attack the expenditure side, involved cut-backs in politically sensitive items of public spending just as most Latin American countries were moving from military dictatorship to demo-cracy. Because of these pressures programmes of fiscal austerity were, in the majority of cases, incomplete and unconvincing.

The relevant data are given in table 14. It shows that, with the exception of Venezuela, the major nations of Latin America had a larger budget deficit – expressed as a share of GDP – in 1984 than in the late 1970s. Moreover, most were unable to prevent an increase in the budget deficit/GDP ratio between 1982 and 1984 even after the onset of the debt crisis had signalled the need for fiscal restraint. It should be said, in partial mitigation, that this policy failure was not entirely due to a lack of will or of political courage. In some countries, notably Brazil, governments managed both to curb expenditure and to introduce tax increases, but were unable to control budget deficits because of enormous increases in the servicing costs on domestic debt. Their problem was that savers in their own countries demanded real interest rates yet higher than those required by foreign bankers. They became

Table 14 Public sector deficits in Latin America, 1977–1984

	Public sector deficit as percentage of GDP		
	Average 1977–80	1982	1984
Argentina	−7.4[a]	−17.7	−12.0
Brazil	−7.6[a]	−15.8	−23.5
Chile	3.0	−3.4	−3.9
Ecuador	3.0	−6.7	−0.4
Mexico	−7.2	−17.6	−7.6
Peru	−5.4	−9.1	−7.6
Venezuela	1.2[a]	−12.9	3.5

[a] 1970–80.

Minus sign indicates deficits.

Source: Morgan Guaranty, *World Financial Markets*, September/October 1985

caught in an internal debt trap just as vicious as the external debt trap caused by the sharp increase in dollar interest rates.

As new money was no longer available from foreign sources, governments had to finance their budget deficits to a much increased extent from domestic savings and to borrow more heavily from their local financial systems. But this shift was difficult to implement. There is a significant contrast between the financial machinery of a typical developed nation and that of a less-developed nation. Because savers in developed societies attach some credibility to official promises to honour their debts whereas in most less-developed societies they attach very little, the ratios of public sector debt to GDP are characteristically much lower in less-developed countries than in developed countries. Indeed, in many less-developed countries a meaningful market in public debt does not exist. Governments are therefore forced to cover their borrowing needs from the banking system. This adds to the money supply and fuels inflation.

The process is most dangerous when governments borrow from the central bank and the central bank issues new bank notes to meet the government's requirements, a form of behaviour which is commonly described as 'printing money'. The consequent expansion of the central bank's balance sheet usually injects new liquidity into the commercial banks and so provides them with the raw material for further, and still more inflationary, growth in credit to the private sector. In short, the domestic financing of budget deficits is far more likely to generate inflationary pressures in a less-developed country than in Europe or North America. These remarks apply with particular force to Latin American countries because of their lamentable records of fiscal irresponsibility and the reluctance of their citizens to accumulate long-term public debt. The situation can be summarized by saying that the cessation of foreign loans to Latin American governments in the early 1980s obliged them, because of their persisting excessive budget deficits, to resort to the printing presses. They could not, like Italy or Belgium, rely on a rise in the ratio of public debt to national income to avoid early inflationary damage.

The scale of the shift to domestic financing varied between countries. We saw in chapter 4 that Mexico indulged in a particularly adventurous fiscal policy in 1980 and 1981. It was successful, by abandoning some of the more ill-conceived mega-projects of the boom years, in cutting the public sector deficit from 17.6 per cent of GDP in 1982 to 7.6 per cent in 1984.[8] But, whereas in 1980 and 1981 external sources had financed 46 per cent of the deficit, they covered only 8 per cent of it in 1984 and 1985.[9] Greater dependence on domestic sources implied, unavoidably, faster growth of the money supply and higher inflation. Consumer prices, which has risen by only 18.2 per cent in 1979 and 26.4 per cent in 1980, increased by 101.9 per cent in 1983 and 65.5 per cent in 1984. In Brazil, by contrast, there was little change in the proportion of the deficit financed domestically. But, because the deficit itself soared as a share of GDP from 7.6 per cent in 1979 and 1980 to 23.5 per cent in 1984, the public sector's finances had a much stronger inflationary punch. The rise in consumer prices, which had usually been under 40 per cent a year in the 1960s and early 1970s, stood at 95.2 per cent at the end of 1981 just before the debt crisis broke. It then climbed steadily, reaching 164 per cent in 1983 and 209 per cent in 1984, and touched a record of 234 per cent at the end of 1985.

The Brazilian case is interesting because the difficulties in eradicating inflation could be attributed to its unusually comprehensive system of indexation. Under this system the government had to pay monetary correction to holders of government debt to compensate them for inflation. Although the ratio of public debt to national income was a meagre 10 per cent, inflation at 200 per cent implied that the cost of monetary correction would be 20 per cent of national income. As this was the dominant element in the public sector deficit, it is understandable that indexation was interpreted as the primary cause of a self-fulfilling inflationary process. Indexation resulted in a massive bill for monetary correction, which caused the excessive budget deficit, which caused a highly inflationary rate of money supply growth, which in turn caused a massive bill for monetary correction and so on.

Evidently there was considerable variety in the precise mechanisms by which the debt crisis initiated more severe domestic inflationary problems in Latin America. Nevertheless, the deterioration in inflation was continent-wide and had a common root in the external shock of higher dollar interest rates. The pervasiveness of the trend emerges in table 15, which suggests a connection between the scale of the increase in inflation and the burden of interest payments on foreign debt. The only exception is Venezuela, where inflation was slightly lower in 1985 than in the early 1980s, an achievement consistent with its uniquely tight fiscal control in this period. The most extreme inflationary episode occurred in Bolivia. The inflation rate soared wildly from 123.5 per cent in 1982 to 275.6 per cent in 1983, 1,281.3 per cent in 1984 and 11,749.6 per cent in 1985. For a short period in early 1985 Bolivia suffered a frank hyperinflation, a condition defined in the textbooks as an increase of 50 per cent or more in prices per month. At the peak in February prices rose by 183 per cent, equivalent to an annual rate of over 25 million per cent. The ultimate absurdity was reached when the currency's loss of value was so complete that in some circumstances it was no longer worthwhile to count units. *The Wall Street Journal* of 8 February 1985

included a story about how the Banco Boliviano Americano no longer
bothered to check the number of notes deposited with it, but merely
weighed them by the sackful to assess their value. 'The 1,000–peso bill,
the most common one, costs more to print than it purchases. It buys one
bag of tea. To buy an average-sized television set with 1,000 peso bills
takes more than 68 pounds of money.'[10]

Inflation at such rates, or even at the more modest 100 per cent a year
level which was more typical of the continent, is extremely disruptive of
normal financial business. The difficulty, in a nutshell, is that interest
and capital payments become indistinguishable. They are both overwhelmed by the sums that borrowers must pay to lenders to adjust for
inflation. More specifically, the cash-flow strain on borrowers is severe
if they are expected, shortly after having received the proceeds of a
loan, to repay the lender an amount – whether it be called interest,
capital, monetary correction or whatever – which matches an inflation
rate of 100 per cent or more.

A vivid illustration is given by the Brazilian middle classes who
virtually stopped servicing their mortgages in 1984 and 1985 because,
with inflation at over 200 per cent, the annual cost of the mortgage
exceeded the original loan. The problem, that cumulating inflation-
related payments soon smother any other sums involved in credit
transactions, is quite general. A common reaction is for governments to
intervene by high-handedly imposing a maximum figure for the nominal
interest rate. For example, in 1984 Argentina implemented a programme
of so-called *concertación* between employers and unions in which

Table 15 Debt servicing and inflation

	Interest payments as percentage of exports, 1985	Debt/ export ratio, 1985	Inflation rate (%)	
			1981	*Mid–1985*
Argentina	55	5.9	105	1,130
Brazil	44	4.0	106	217
Chile	47	5.3	20	35
Colombia	23	2.7	27	28
Ecuador	25	2.6	13	30
Mexico	37	4.5	28	53
Peru	35	4.5	75	169
Uruguay	36	5.6	34	70
Venezeula	23	2.1	16	13

Source: Balassa et al. (eds), *Toward Renewed Economic Growth in Latin America*, 1986,
p. 70

interest rates were set each month at a level slightly lower than in the previous month. The aim was to enforce a, gradual moderation of inflation expectations. In the event inflation accelerated because of lax fiscal and monetary control. One result of *concertación* was therefore heavily to erode the real value of savings once the inflation rate started to increase.

Indeed, in conditions of rampant inflation, the imposition of interest rate ceilings invariably leads to negative real interest rates. This deters saving and so reduces the quantity of resources available for investment. Here we see the link between the jump in inflation which followed the debt crisis and the decline in investment. The fall in saving can be blamed on the destruction of the incentive to hold financial assets in an inflationary environment; it can be regarded as the consequence of the disruption of the traditional financial relationships which, in more settled conditions, bring borrowers and lenders together. Although low savings and malfunctioning capital markets are long-standing attributes of many Latin American countries, they were seriously aggravated after the debt crisis.

It should be strongly emphasized that the loss of investment resources due to lower domestic savings is additional to that caused by the swing from positive resource transfers in the late 1970s to negative resource transfers in the mid-1980s. With less money available for investment, the underlying growth rates of both output and exports will be lower than would otherwise have been the case. Of course, the lower is the growth rate of exports, the harder it will be to narrow the gap between it and interest rates. As a result, the debt crisis has moved even further away from a solution. Moreover, the shock to domestic financial confidence will have lasting effects. Higher inflation and the disruption of financial systems will jaundice savers' attitudes for decades to come. This internally imposed constraint on the growth of the capital stock, and so on the scope for increasing exports, will persist even if a change in the relationship between interest rates and commodity inflation eventually allows a resumption of resource inflows from abroad.

The extent of the fall in domestic savings has been conditioned by the circumstances of each individual country. There are some problems of evaluation because a nation's savings have two components, saving by government and saving by the private sector. Negative real interest rates and the breakdown of financial intermediation should have an adverse effect only on the private sector element. Differentiation between the public and private sectors is particularly important for Chile, which recorded the biggest collapse in national saving, from a ratio of 14.3 per cent of GNP in 1980 to a mere 1.4 per cent in 1982. On closer examination this collapse is almost fully explained by a drastic change in government finances, from a surplus of 6.4 per cent of GNP in 1980 to a deficit of 5.0 per cent in 1982. Private sector savings, in fact, were roughly stable between 1980 and 1982, and then rose sharply to 11.9 per cent of GNP in 1983, contrary to the pattern in other countries.[11] This commendable performance reflects the continuation of positive real interest rates in Chile, possible because inflation never rose to the stratospheric levels common elsewhere in Latin America but typically stayed in a 15–30 per cent range. Nevertheless, Chile suffered badly from mismanagement, incompetence and fraud in its financial system.[12]

The largest decline in private saving was in Venezuela, where it more than halved as a share of GNP from 22.0 per cent in 1980 to 8.5 per cent in 1982, a change probably connected with the timing of capital flight. But perhaps the most ominous was in Argentina. In the 1950s and 1960s Argentina has a reasonably good financial system which was successful in mobilizing savings and directing them to worthwhile investments. Despite many misguided policies, such as industrial protectionism and excessive state involvement in the economy, domestic savings were sufficiently sizeable in scale and appropriate enough in direction to support a reasonable rate of economic growth of about 4 per cent a year. When bankers considered Argentina as a destination for loans in the late 1970s they regarded this as the minimum likely growth rate in future and factored it into their calculations of the probable debt/export and debt/income ratios. Instead, private savings went down from 18.2 per cent of GNP in 1980 to 13.8 per cent in 1984, a slide which largely accounts for the contemporaneous drop in investment and Argentina's current inability to replace its capital stock. As we have already noted, with its capital stock declining year by year its ability to produce, both for the home market and for export, is being reduced. The inescapable conclusion must be that its chances of honouring its debt commitments in full have vanished.

The financial systems of most Latin American countries, never the strongest parts of their economies, have been crippled by the increase in inflation which followed the debt crisis. When inflation exceeds 50 per cent a year signals about the relative profitability of long-term investments become confusing and opaque. Bankers find it increasingly difficult to discriminate between sense and nonsense in loan proposals, as calculations about the impact of inflation overshadow calculations about the true economic viability of a project. The seriousness of the damage cannot be over-estimated. It is the task of financial systems to channel domestic savings into investment, and a high level of savings and an efficient allocation of investment resources are essential to the achievement of strong economic growth. The American economist Professor Ronald McKinnon has complained that the growth of Latin

America has long been held back by what he terms 'financial repression', which is to be understood as the inefficient and retarded patterns of financial intermediation found throughout the continent.[13] Through its effect on inflation, the debt crisis has exacerbated financial repression.

Indeed, there must be concern that the wounds to financial confidence will never heal properly. Heavy capital flight from Latin America in 1980 and 1981 symptomized the lack of trust savers had in their own countries, largely the result of fears that inflation would wipe out the real value of their financial assets. These fears, based on long memories of economic mismanagement by governments, will now be more deeply entrenched than ever. The problem of stimulating domestic savings and using them to generate self-sustaining economic growth will be that much harder in future.

IV

In 1985 and 1986 several governments in Latin America realized that inflation was having a highly destructive effect on their economies. Two of them therefore embarked on ambitious and wide-ranging anti-inflation programmes. On 14 June 1985 the Argentine government announced the Austral Plan to counter an inflationary process which had culminated in consumer prices that were 1,100 per cent higher than a year earlier, while on 27 February 1986 the Brazilian government introduced the Cruzado Plan after inflation, again on a 12-month basis, had exceeded 400 per cent. These two Plans have been much discussed in the international press, with many of the assessments being approving or even laudatory. In the word of Morgan Guaranty's *World Financial Markets*, 'Enthusiasm for Brazil . . . has surged since it adopted the Cruzado Plan. . . . The rave notices contrast sharply with the negativism pervading much international commentary on Mexico and other Latin American countries.'[14] In fact, both the Austral and Cruzado Plans were misconceived in certain crucial respects. Arguably, their long-term effect has been to worsen the financial plight of these two very important debtor nations.

There were differences between the two Plans. In Argentina emphasis was placed on the government's determination to curb the budget deficit and to avoid the printing of money at the central bank, whereas in Brazil these standard features of an orthodox stabilization package were absent. Instead the main measure of budgetary control in Brazil was the elimination of indexation. The logic of the Brazilian step should be obvious from our earlier discussion. It was in a *Catch-22* situation where monetary correction due to indexation for past inflation was the dominant element in a budget deficit which determined future inflation. But the two Plans also shared certain characteristics. New monetary units, which gave their names to the Plans, were introduced in both. More fundamentally, they had in common a reliance on direct wage and price controls, and an attempt to limit the budget deficit by tax increases. It is in these characteristics that the explanation for the Plans' long-term detrimental effects is to be sought.

In Argentina the Austral Plan was successful in cutting the budget deficit, a step correctly seen as a prerequisite to effective inflation restraint. However, the main contribution to deficit reduction came from tax increases which fell inequitably on large businesses (particularly multinationals), rural landowners (whose land represents a tax base which is impossible to hide) and arable farmers.[15] The concentration of the extra tax burden on agriculture proved extremely harmful. It caused farmers to take land out of production and lowered grain production. The wheat harvest in 1986 was 8.5m tonnes, a startling decline compared with 15.0m tonnes in 1984. Since arable crops and their by-products account for two-thirds of Argentina's exports, the fall in production has disturbing implications for the external payments position over the medium term. Exports in 1986 were 18 per cent lower than in 1985, while the trade surplus was almost halved from $4.6b to $2.6b.[16] In effect, the Austral Plan led to a slow-down in inflation at the expense of a deterioration in the balance of payments.

The debt/export ratio, which had been stable at about 4¾ between 1982 and 1985, rose sharply to just over 6 at the end of 1986 and could well approach 10 at the end of 1987. Against this background it seems strange that a large number of foreign banks and other creditors were prepared in August 1987 to roll over $30 of old debt and extend a loan of almost $2b to replace maturities of about the same size. The assumption has to be that the creditors, knowing that they will have to write off a high proportion of their loans, decided to lend a bit more to discourage a total repudiation in which they would have to write off everything. Their behaviour is made all the more quixotic by the fading of any benefits the Austral Plan had for inflation. Retail prices in the month of July 1987 rose by 10.1 per cent (equivalent to an annual rate of 220 per cent).[17]

The intensification of Argentina's economic problems has not been accompanied by an amelioration of its business ethics. On 19 September 1986 Dr Machinea, the president of the central bank, announced at a press conference that the central bank had uncovered a fraud by its previous administrators, involving $110m in export credits arranged by a small provincial bank called Banco Alas. (The central bank had a scheme which gave preferential low-interest loans to banks granting export finance.) It was discovered that 'only $300,000 of the $110 million in letters of export credits could be verified. Investigation showed that 16 of the 20 companies on the list of exporters to whom Banco Alas said it had extended credits did not exist, and the four others denied any business relationship with the bank.' Police searched through the directors' homes and 'turned up a number of Swiss and American bank accounts in the names of bank officials'.[18] The Banco Alas scandal was only one of a number of financial crimes exposed by the Argentine authorities in late 1986 and early 1987. Indeed, in October 1986 the entire former board of the central bank was accused of fraud by the state prosecutor. It has to be emphasized, even if it cannot be strictly proved, that the misdeeds were on a more extensive scale at the height of the sovereign lending boom in 1980 and 1981. Jet-setting fraudsters have stolen large sums from Argentina while it has been a democracy under President Alfonsin, but they stole much more while it was a military dictatorship.

Brazil has never suffered to the same extent as Argentina from dishonesty and corruption in its financial system. Nevertheless, the Cruzado Plan was similar in character and effect to the Austral Plan. It cut inflation, but only by inflicting long-term structural damage. It relied, for its initial effectiveness, on a strict freeze on prices. This eroded profit margins, particularly on those products which had the misfortune not to have had price increases shortly before the freeze was imposed. The arbitrariness of the profit losses undermined business-men's confidence and reduced their willingness to invest. At the same time the removal of indexation eroded the public's confidence that, if money was left with a financial institution, it would retain its real value. Uncertainties about the real value of bank deposits and other financial assets were intensified by blatant official tampering with price indices. As a result, savings contracted and the financial system's ability to finance new capital spending declined. The simultaneous alienation of business confidence and savers' trust helps to explain why firms refused to invest more in late 1986, even though a furious boom in consumption led to some of the highest rates of capacity utilization ever seen in Brazilian industry. Instead gross capital formation, which was already down from 21½ per cent of GDP during 1980–2 to 16½ per cent during 1983–5, fell once more.

The decline in investment argues that the Cruzado Plan, like the Austral Plan, bought a short-term gain in inflation at the expense of long-term losses on efficiency and growth. Moreover, balance-of-payments weakness emerged after a lag of only a few months. The buoyancy of domestic demand, much of it motivated by a desire to buy goods before the artificial price controls broke down, attracted increased imports. Towards the end of 1986 the trade surplus, which had run at $13.1b in 1984 and $12.5b in 1985, almost disappeared. To counter the deterioration an austerity package on 21 November included tax increases equivalent to 4 per cent of national income. There was also more interference with the consumer price index, which no longer has any credibility with the general public. Although early 1987 saw a strong improvement in the balance of payments, every other indicator of economic performance – inflation, growth and employment – went from bad to worse. On 20 February Brazil announced a moratorium on interest payments on its external debt. A bitter domestic debate has subsequently erupted about the political acceptability of the IMF deal which is now (August 1987) needed to mollify the international banks.

The passage of events invites a critical interpretation of the Austral and Cruzado Plans. After the initial interest rate shock and commodity price declines of 1980, 1981, and 1982 the most compelling issue facing Argentina and Brazil, like other Latin American countries, was to correct their balance-of-payments deficits. A massive deflection of resources from the satisfaction of domestic demand to the improvement of the external balance was the task of 1983 and 1984. It was achieved not by eliminating budget deficits but by substantial devaluations. These devaluations raised the price level and enabled governments to finance their deficits by levying the inflation tax on holders of money balances. But by 1985 and early 1986 inflation had risen so sharply that it had become intolerable. The Austral and Cruzado Plans were therefore brought in to curb inflation. They attained this end, but only by renewing the original imbalance on the external accounts. In effects, there was merely a rotation of problems. Nothing was solved. Even worse, the Austral and Cruzado Plans involved new inefficiencies, distortions and uncertainties which will reduce the long-run growth rates of Argentine and Brazilian exports.

V

Enough has been said to demonstrate the point made at the end of chapter 4. However impressive the efforts made by Latin American countries to strengthen their external payments, their internal financial circumstances have worsened drastically since the debt crisis and are now, in many cases, unsustainable. They are unsustainable because rapid inflation has destroyed and is continuing to destroy traditional patterns of saving and investment. In some countries the process has been taken so far that domestic savings are no longer adequate to support the capital stock and output is in long-term decline.

The argument is sufficiently powerful in itself to cast doubt on the widely held view that 'the debt crisis is over'. But what about the state of Latin America's balance of payments? We have already noted that the region accomplished a remarkable transformation in its external payments between 1981 and 1984. Its current account deficit, \$39.9b in 1981, had been trimmed to \$2.1b three years later. But does this performance constitute a conclusive refutation of the widespread scepticism about Latin America's ability to honour its debts?

We suggested earlier that one criterion for saying that a country had a sustainable payments position was that its debt/export ratio should be stable through time. This idea was refined by Cohen in a paper on the evaluation of sovereign debt in the November 1985 issue of *Economic Policy*. His view, which has some similarity with the central thesis of this book, is that no problem could arise when the real interest rate is lower than an economy's growth rate. But, when the real interest rate exceeds the growth rate, the optimal strategy is to run a current account surplus equivalent to a fixed fraction of its export receipts. The level of this fraction should be set to ensure that the debt increases at the same rate as exports. His finding is that Latin America needs to devote only 13 per cent of exports to repaying its debt. As its trade surplus in recent years has commonly been rather higher than that, his conclusion is that the overwhelming majority of debtor countries are solvent.[19] Similar complacency, based on a related analytical framework, has been expressed by Blanchard in a paper concentrating on Brazil's position.[20] Indeed, a relatively relaxed attitude towards the debt problem has been common in academic circles in recent years.

The trouble is that, whatever the academic niceties of the matter, debt/export ratios are still not behaving properly. Latin American nations have made great efforts to reduce their payments deficits, but they have done so by import compression rather than export expansion. In fact, the continent's exports were lower in 1985 at \$95.6b than in 1981 when they were \$100.7b. Because interest payments are so heavy, the achievement of massive trade surpluses has not been sufficient to eliminate current account deficits altogether and most countries' external debt continues to rise year by year. Obviously, the implication of stagnant exports and mounting debts is further increases in debt/export ratios.

Some of the relevant numbers are set out in table 16, which gives information on the developing countries as a whole and so enables us to extend the discussion beyond Latin America. Most of Latin America comes under the heading 'Other middle-income oil importers', where

Table 16 The continuing increase in debt/export ratios in the Third World

	Debt/export ratio (%)					
	1970	*1980*	*1981*	*1982*	*1983*	*1984*
All developing countries	108.9	89.8	96.8	115.0	130.8	135.4
Major exporters of manufactures	91.5	77.3	81.7	97.1	105.2	109.1
Other middle-income oil importers	111.0	120.7	136.4	155.4	175.5	183.9
Low-income Africa	75.2	175.8	216.5	260.6	279.5	278.1

Source: World Bank *World Development Report 1985*, p. 24.

	Debt/export ratio (%)				
	1982	*1983*	*1984*	*1985*	*1986*
Argentina	405	454	473	474	537
Brazil	339	366	322	352	350
Chile	333	377	402	428	427
Mexico	299	316	293	325	420
Venezuela	169	216	177	217	333
Nigeria	85	166	165	153	261
Phillipines	270	295	312	319	313

Some of the figures need to be revised in the light of later information. The UN Economic Commission for Latin America (ECLAC) estimates Argentina's debt/export ratio in 1984, 1985 and 1986 as 488, 481 and 606 respectively.

Source: Morgan Guaranty *World Financial Markets, September/October* 1985 and September 1986

we can see that, after a long period of approximate stability in the 1970s, the debt/export ratio rose steeply from 120.7 per cent in 1980 to 183.9 per cent in 1984. But the plight of these nations was less grave than that of low-income Africa, whose debt/export ratio in 1984 was much higher than any other group's and almost four times the level in 1970. The statistics on seven particularly indebted countries emphasize that the slide continued in 1985 and 1986. The deterioration was most pronounced in the case of the three oil exporters, Mexico, Venezuela and Nigeria, following the breakdown of the Organization of Petroleum Exporting Countries (OPEC) cartel in December 1985.

The message must be that in most of the Third World the debt problem is still worsening. Not only are the majority of indebted countries suffering from internal decay, but also their external positions continue to weaken. It is puzzling that some academic authorities appear to believe that the worst of the difficulties have been overcome. It is also rather strange that newspapers in the creditor industrial nations should pay less attention to the debt problem now than in 1982 or 1983. The explanation for this relative indifference today may be that, in many cases, negotiations on the rescheduling of debts have been completed. Although the total amount of debt has not been reduced, the next payment may be quite small and several quarters away.

But by itself rescheduling is not an answer. As long as interest is being added to old debts at a faster rate than national output or exports are growing, the underlying situation is unsatisfactory and becoming more so as the years go by. Rescheduling bears comparison with the anaesthetic applied at an operation to treat a terminal condition. It may take away the pain and, for a period, put the patient in a better frame of mind for surgery. But it is certainly not a substitute for surgery and its effects wear away in due course. The debtor nations, just like a patient returning to his senses to discover that nothing has been done, will find to their dismay that – when they are eventually obliged to consider repayment – their external obligations are larger than ever.

VI

If our analysis so far is accepted, the outlook for many of the debtor nations is hopeless. Because of the wide gap between the interest rate on their debts and the rate of increase of their exports, they must export more goods to the creditor nations than they import. This reverse transfer drains them of resources which might otherwise be used for domestic investment, restricting their economic growth and impairing their ability to raise exports. But, without renewed growth and higher exports, they will never be able to service their debts again. What can they do?

The crudest response would be to repudiate the external debt. Indeed, there is an argument that – as soon as the resource transfer becomes negative – repudiation is the most natural course of action.[21] The borrowing nation has received as much benefit as it can from the inflow of resources from abroad and, by refusing to send anything back, it incurs none of the costs of repayment. This highly cynical view may seem rational, but it has to be qualified. First, creditors can impose sanctions, some of which may prove very disagreeable to the debtor. Secondly, and perhaps more fundamentally, international financial markets have memories. A country's record in honouring its past debts affects its creditworthiness in seeking new loans in future. Of course, the lower its credit rating, the more expensive will such loans be.

Whether the costs of sanctions and reduced creditworthiness are sufficient to deter repudiation depends on circumstances. But it is clear that creditors have strong incentives to let debtors know that repudiation will be punished so harshly that it would have been less expensive for them to have honoured the debts in full. The trouble is that debt repudiation is like a contagious disease. Unless it is stamped out as soon as it appears, it is liable to spread uncontrollably. If the industrialized creditor nations allow one or two financial invalids in the Third World to miss payments and no measures are taken against them, every debtor has a temptation to miss payments as well. It makes no difference to the need to retaliate whether the bad debtors are feigning illness or are genuinely sick. The imperative to discourage imitators remains. Not surprisingly, American spokesmen have been belligerent in their warnings about the consequences of unilateral repudiation. According to Mr R. T. McNamar, speaking as Deputy Secretary to the US Treasury on 12 October 1983, 'Under such circumstances, the foreign assets of a country would be attached by creditors throughout the world; its exports would be seized by creditors at each dock where they landed; its national airlines would be unable to operate; and its sources of desperately needed capital goods and spare parts virtually eliminated. . . . Hardly a pleasant scenario.'[22]

The scenario certainly is not pleasant, but perhaps it is not altogether convincing either. In recent years a few countries have, in effect, repudiated their debts and they continue to participate in international trade. For example, on 31 May 1984 Bolivia repudiated its debt by explicit presidential announcement. Its plunge into hyperinflation nine months later is hardly a strong recommendation for this policy action, but the USA has subsequently given special assistance to strengthen the chances of a return to economic viability. Much depends on the willingness of the country concerned to put its own house in order and on the tone of its defiance of international financial etiquette. In July 1986 Venezuela declared that it did not intend to service $6.9b of private sector debt properly and would instead give creditors 15-year bonds carrying a 5 per cent interest rate. It took this step unilaterally and provocatively, without reference to its creditors, giving as justification that much of the money received by the private sector had not been borrowed but stolen. (We have discussed some of the relevant mechanisms in the Argentine context.) But the banks were not prepared to accept this as a legitimate pretext and began withdrawing lines of trade credit. Venezuela must have been frightened, because it quickly backtracked and tried to reach a more conventional accommodation with its creditors.

There may be a half-way house between aggressive, bad-tempered outright default and attempts to reach whole-hearted agreement with creditors. Kaletsky has proposed the concept of 'conciliatory default'. A 'conciliatory defaulter would continue servicing debts owed to official foreign creditors, such as the IMF, World Bank, and foreign governments . . . and would probably make a point of maintaining the service of short-term debt in the hope of renewing trade credits'.[23] Peru initially chose a strategy along these lines with the announcement by President Garcia on 28 July 1985 that debt service payments would be limited to 10 per cent of exports. It continued to pay back World Bank and IDB loans in full and on time, while US aid agencies and other governments also received payments with some degree of regularity. But in the middle of 1987 the World Bank and the IDB were also cut off. President Garcia has made it plain that none of Peru's creditors can expect any improvement in their treatment for the foreseeable future.

The banks have retaliated against Peru in the same way that they threatened against Venezuela, by withdrawing trade credit. Moreover, the IMF has made its displeasure clear by ruling that Peru is ineligible for any Fund facilities. Ultimately Peru may suffer severely. Its reserves are now negligible, at little more than $1b, and a complete suspension of trade credit would force it to match every import purchase by an export sale. But, for the time being, the virtual repudiation of commercial bank debt has not been obviously ruinous. Similarly, in mid-1986 Costa Rica announced that it wanted to cut its interest payments to commercial banks by two-thirds of the amount due. So far (August 1987), there has not been a single court action in retaliation, although the banks have rejected both this proposal and a subsequent less ambitious request that Costa Rica be granted the same favourable terms as Mexico in its 1986 rescheduling. (See the next section for details.) There is a definite contrast with a previous case in 1981, when Cost Rica's refusal to honour interest in full caused several bank syndicates to take the country to court and their action obliged the government to resume normal interest payments.[24] It does not seem exaggerated to say that recent reactions to debt repudiation have been so light that they are unlikely to deter potential delinquents.

If so, the debt situation will enter a new and more problematic phase. Unless creditors punish repudiating sovereign borrowers with conspicuous harshness, they should not be surprised if the number of repudiations multiplies. Instead of the virus being easy to isolate and confined to such marginal borrowers as Peru, Bolivia and Costa Rica, it could infect the large so-called 'MBA' nations (Mexico, Brazil and

Argentina). In such circumstances the most effective strategy for the creditor nations will be to give preferential terms to the more well-behaved debtors and so try to separate them from the less well behaved. It will be much easier to handle repudiation if the debtor nations announce the bad news one by one than if they all act simultaneously.

Indeed, the formation of the Cartagena group, which was immediately christened the 'debtors' cartel', could be interpreted as an attempt to anticipate this strategy. It stemmed from a public letter, urging a reduction in international interest rates, signed by the Presidents of Brazil, Argentina, Colombia and Mexico on 19 May 1984, but eventually its members came to include 11 Latin American states. By presenting joint demands the Latin American debtor nations wanted to give an impression of seeking strength in numbers; they appeared to be presenting an open challenge to the case-by-case approach favoured by most Western governments.

In practice, however, the USA has always – at least, until now – been able to enforce a policy of divide and rule over the major debtors, while the international banks have acted with a surprising degree of cohesion. Instead of the debtors' cartel envisaged by the Cartagena agreement, there has effectively been a cartel of creditors. There has been a particular eagerness to help Mexico, perhaps because of its geographical proximity and consequent strategic importance to the USA. Arguably, this favouritism amounts to precisely that kind of discrimination which the post-1945 international economic order was supposed to eliminate. At any rate, until now no important borrowing nation has openly repudiated its debts, either in full or in part. (The Brazilian moratorium on interest payments – while it may evolve into repudiation – is *not* equivalent to a blank refusal to recognize or repay debt.)

VII

But are creditor banks and governments fully satisfied with the way the debt crisis is developing? Surely, they realize that present trends are unsustainable and at some point are liable to become counter-productive. They must see that the negative resource transfers from Latin America are draining it of the finance it needs to improve its economic prospects. Moreover, creditor banks have an important motive, in terms of balance sheet structure, for wanting to end the long saga of debt renegotiation. At present, when a loan to a developing country is about to be repaid, the lending banks are press-ganged by officialdom in their own countries into providing money for a new loan (the so-called 'concerted lending') of the same or greater size. The continual expansion of debt through the addition of interest charges increases the banks' exposure and prevents them from seeking more promising uses of their funds.

Debt foreclosure would seem to have obvious attractions for creditor nations and institutions. Within national frontiers it is commonplace for creditors, after possibly a long period of propping up financially imperilled companies, to withdraw support. They stop the compounding of interest on past debts and seize the assets of insolvent organizations, not from a benevolent wish to administer financial euthanasia, but because it is the best option available to them. At least, after the disposal of assets, they have got something back. Many international banks, who regard their Latin American loans as beyond recovery, would welcome a similar kind of arrangement between debtors and creditors across national frontiers. The problem is that bankruptcy proceedings cannot be applied to sovereign governments. Ironically, it was Mr Walter Wriston himself who proclaimed this as part of his doctrine and asserted that it did not matter because any country will always ' "own" more than it "owes" '. He apparently never envisaged the possibility that debts might indefinitely rise faster than national income. Nor did he explain how creditor banks might attach some part of what a nation 'owns'.

An alternative to foreclosure is debt forgiveness. It might seems sensible for banks to agree with an over-borrowed nation, whose inability to service its loans is self-evident, that the face value of its debts should be reduced. The actual amount of forgiveness would be determined by negotiation, but with creditors not intending to impose sanctions. The hope would be that it could service the remnant of the loans on time, without undue stress and, most importantly, without the creditors having to increase their exposure. The objection to this simple and straightforward suggestion, which makes such a strong appeal to common sense, is the same as with debt repudiation. It creates a precedent. If one debtor nation is given easier terms, every debtor nation will want easier terms. This problem could be overcome only if debt relief were accompanied by sanctions of some kind. But such sanctions might damage the debtor nation's economic health, again reducing its ability to service debt and so acting against the creditors' interests.

The same drawback applies with any form of debt relief, including the relaxation of repayment terms and an easing of the conditions attached to loans. As soon as one country is granted special terms, every other country will want similar concessions. The best example of this tendency came after the agreement between Mexico and the IMF on 22 July 1986. The agreement made the level of new bank loans dependent on oil prices, with more money being made available the lower were prices. By implication, a country is entitled to borrow more money the lower are the prices of the products it exports. As the dangers in this counter-intuitive principle hardly need to be spelt out, perhaps it is not surprising that many commercial banks were reluctant to participate in the Mexican deal. At any rate, Brazil indicated shortly afterwards that it also would seek some easing of its debt terms, with annual debt servicing payments restricted to 2–2.5 per cent of GDP compared with a prevailing level of 4.6 per cent.[25] A logical extension of the Mexican deal would be for countries whose exports are dominated by coffee, including Costa Rica and Colombia, to try to reach agreements on a link between 'new money' lending and coffee prices. Particularly risky, from the creditors' standpoint, would be to grant the greatest concessions to the most embarrassed debtor. It would give debtors every incentive to mismanage their finances in order to increase their eligibility for concessions. Clearly, in a system where the most over-indebted receive the greatest debt forgiveness, it is desirable to be over-indebted.

The Baker Plan, proposed in September 1985 by the US Secretary of the Treasury at the annual meeting of the IMF and the World Bank, tried to overcome this sort of problem by making debt concessions contingent on changes in domestic economic policy. The function of the new credit facilities promised by the Plan was to bribe debtor nations into adopting more free-market policies, with the idea that such policies would strengthen their ability to produce and, hence, to meet their financial commitments. This supply-side approach has the merit of turning the focus away from the debt numbers themselves and back towards the internal condition of the borrowing nations. But its impact within the developing world has been limited so far. Of the major debtors, only Mexico has responded positively and, as we have seen, its deal had a number of controversial features. Indeed, in one respect the Baker Plan was overtly discriminatory. It designated 15 countries as prospective candidates for assistance, including such notorious mis-creants as Peru and Venezuela. By contrast, South Korea, which has both substantial debts and an impressive supply-side performance, was excluded. The South Korean government might reasonably complain that its good behaviour was penalized, whereas Peru's bad behaviour was rewarded.

Despite the considerable attention paid to the Baker Plan in the media, it is a distraction from the key issue. The root cause of the Third World debt problem, as we have emphasized repeatedly, is the gap between interest rates and the rate of increase in commodity prices. By implying that a few well-designed institutional changes can radically alter this situation, the Baker Plan promises far more than it can deliver.

VIII

We can now bring the threads of the argument together. Despite great efforts to correct their external payments deficits since the onset of the debt crisis in 1982, most Third World countries have still not been able to prevent an increase in their debt/export ratios. On this widely recognized criterion of the seriousness of nations' financial difficulties, the debt problem continues to worsen. The chances of eventual improvement have been weakened by declines in investment, notably in Latin America, because of the reduced availability of both foreign and domestic savings. The reduction in foreign savings reflects the swing from positive to negative resource flows after the move to very high real interest rates in the industrial countries in the early 1980s; the reduction in domestic savings is due to the disruption of financial systems which was an unfortunate by-product of the balance-of-payments adjustments made by most debtor countries. The fall in investment is one of the most worrying aspects of the contemporary debt problem, as it implies a long-term deterioration in growth prospects, including the growth prospects for exports.

Both debt repudiation and debt forgiveness are ruled out for the same reason. They destroy the obligations between borrower and lender on which any enduring system of international credit has to be based. If a country repudiates and is not punished severely by its creditors, all other countries have an incentive to repudiate. If a country is forgiven its debts and suffers no penalty, all other countries have an incentive to press their creditors for forgiveness.

So, we are forced to asked in some desperation, is there any solution to the Third World debt problem? Or is it destined to worsen year by year and to culminate in the bankruptcy of country after country, in the *bolivianización* of whole continents? The main conclusion of this chapter is that, without a change in the relationship betweeen dollar interest rates and the rate of increase in commodity prices, the Third World debt problem is insoluble. Indeed, the obstinacy of the problem is a large part of the reason why we warned in the Introduction about the possible disintegration of the international financial system. The breakdown of the international financial system would imperil a number of major banking institutions, whose loan losses would come to exceed their capital. But perhaps yet more important it would pose a threat to the multilateral, non-discriminatory trading and payments arrangements which the world has enjoyed for over a generation.

A catastrophe like this must be averted. It seems obvious, if the argument of this chapter is accepted, that the governments and central banks of the main industrial nations, and particularly the US government and the Federal Reserve, would be justified in altering the macro-economic policies of the early 1980s. Most critically, they must engineer a change in the relationship between interest rates and the rate of increase in commodity prices. It is clear that this change must be effected in dollar terms, because most Third World debt is denominated in dollars. Nevertheless, in view of the interdependence between interest rates in the major currencies, policy adjustments in the USA should be supported by appropriate action in Japan, West Germany and the other important nations.

But what would be the implications of a change in the relationship between interest rates and the increase in commodity prices? In the six years from 1981 to 1986 prime rates were, on average, almost 15 per cent a year higher than the change in US crude material prices (in the official producer price index) and 20 per cent a year or more higher than the change in most commodity price indices. It is the financial strain of this period that has burdened commodity-exporting Third World nations with debts that they are unable to service properly. It seems reasonable to expect that their debts would again become manageable if there were a five- or six-year period in which the increase in commodity prices was 20 per cent or more a year above prime rates.

But what, then, would happen to inflation? Interest rates cannot go negative in nominal times. Realistically, the lowest level at which they could be held is 2 or 3 per cent. So, a 20 per cent differential between interest rates and the rate of commodity inflation implies that commodity inflation would have to reach almost 25 per cent a year. At present most commodities are in excess supply and price falls remain common. It will take some years of above-trend growth in the world economy, perhaps putting pressure on capacity, before this excess supply can be removed. To foment commodity inflation of 20 per cent or more will therefore probably involve shortages of many finished products, driving up their prices. But, if the prices of finished products are increasing in conjunction with rapid rises in commodity prices, a severe generalized inflation must develop.

So, on this line of reasoning, the Third World debt problem can be solved only by a return to rapid inflation. This outcome would be depressingly ironic. We have argued that the debt crisis was the sequel to, and in one sense a result of, the US Federal Reserve's anti-inflation programme after October 1979; we now see that the abandonment and reversal of that programme seems to be one way, perhaps the only way, to end the debt crisis. Because of the high real interest rates of the early 1980s and the debt build-up associated with them, low inflation cannot be reconciled with a simple resolution of the Third World debt problem. We shall pick up this theme and develop it in the final chapter.

The pessimism of our conclusion is so radical that we must ask whether it needs to be toned down in any way. There are, in fact, three caveats which need to be mentioned. Regrettably, although they are all the constant subject matter of political meetings and international conferences, they do not promise any substantive improvement. They give international financial bureaucrats something to chatter about and excuses for the much-quoted 'cautious optimism', but they cannot change the remorseless compounding of interest on old debts which is the source of the debt problem.

IX

The first caveat to our pessimistic conclusion is that it may be possible, to some extent, to replace high-interest loans from the commercial banks by concessionary finance from the multilateral organizations and the governments of the industrial creditor nations. By reducing the average interest rate on debt, such substitution would narrow the all-important gap between interest rates and commodity inflation. The Baker Plan could be interpreted as a step in this direction, as it envisages an enlarged role for World Bank lending which is less expensive (although not to a great degree) than that from the banks. (IMF balance-of-payments assistance is appreciably cheaper.) Lord Lever has suggested, more ambitiously, that export credit agencies in the industrial countries should insure the export of capital to the Third World, just as they currently insure the export of goods.[26] The insurance would apply to accumulating interest on existing debt and so might enable the lenders to offer less demanding terms.

A shift to concessionary finance has some merit, not least because it is a sign of preparedness to act by the creditor nations, but it also has limitations. It resembles debt forgiveness, which we have already seen is a risky course to pursue. It also has a direct monetary cost to the governments of creditor nations. In view of the seriousness of their own fiscal constraints, they are unlikely to allow concessionary finance to become particularly large. The message must be that a move towards low-interest official lending away from high-interest private lending may achieve some marginal alleviation of the debt problem, but it cannot by itself be a solution.

The second possibility is for debtor countries to diversify their exports, so that these are no longer dominated by one or two commodities but include a wide range of products including manu-

factured goods. We have seen that the harshness of the financial pressures on the Third World is the result not merely of high real interest
rates, but also of the particularly wide gap between interest rates and
the rate of change of commodity prices. By moving into manufactured
goods a developing country reduces its vulnerability to terms-of-trade
shocks over which it has little control. Indeed, the success of South
Korea in escaping from its debt problems can be regarded as partly due
to the very high proportion of industrial products in its export total.
Although little attention is paid to the fact in the press, South Korea has
an external debt of $40b, the fourth highest among developing
countries. But such has been its rate of export growth that few bankers
lose sleep about its ability to meet its obligations.

Unfortunately, it requires a major structural adjustment for any
economy to boost the ratio of manufactured to total exports. It takes
time and investment to encourage internationally competitive manu-
facturing. But, because they are caught in the debt trap, time and
investment resources are exactly what developing countries do not have.
Perhaps the best approach is trade liberalization by developing
countries themselves. A considerable body of evidence from several
countries suggests that the unilateral removal of trade barriers leads to
rapid growth of both imports and exports, but with the higher level of
exports invariably associated with a greater variety of products sold
abroad.[27] The objection to this idea, and the reason why it cannot
constitute a comprehensive answer to the debt crisis, is that rapid
growth of Third World manufactured exports is almost certain to
provoke increased protectionism in the already industrialized creditor
nations. Some of the most vexed issues in international trade and
finance intersect at this point, emphasizing the need for the governments
of the leading nations to coordinate policies for both areas.

We come, finally, to the third potential escape route. The last two
chapters have brought out, on a number of occasions, that sovereign
debt is quite different from commercial debt contracted between private
parties in a single country. Specifically, in the 1970s international banks
did not seek collateral for sovereign debt, not least because they would
have had no simple legal remedy for attaching it in the event of
repudiation. They have not had the option to declare foreign countries
insolvent and seize assets. Instead, if they want to trim their exposure,
all they can do is to sell the loans in an informal market in Third World
debt which has grown up in recent years. These sales have resulted in
the loans being traded at a discount, determined by the market's
perception of the creditworthiness (or lack of it) of the various
countries. Thus, in May 1987 Brazilian loans could be bought at 63 per
cent of their face value, Argentine 60 per cent, Mexican 60 per cent and

Peruvian a mere 16 per cent. The gap between market price and face value creates an opportunity for governments and investors to reach mutually advantageous deals. These deals, known as debt/equity swaps, reduce Third World debt.[28]

The precise mechanics can become very intricate, but one common sequence of transactions is straightforward. Investors purchase loans at a discount with dollars, deliver the loan documents to the central bank of the less-developed country concerned and receive in return the face value of the loans in local currency. The local currency can then be used to purchase assets within the country and these typically take the form of equity investments. At the end of the debt/equity swap the government has rid itself of unwanted floating-rate dollar debt, the international bank has taken a bad loan off its balance sheet (at a loss, but probably less than expected) and the investor has bought cut-price assets which may eventually yield a healthy stream of profits. Everyone appears to gain – and the debt burden has undoubtedly been eased.

Debt/equity swaps are best considered as a device for enabling the parties involved to overcome the key drawback of sovereign debt, that creditors cannot take possession of collateral when a loan goes sour. As such they are imaginative and interesting, and they will go some way to mitigating the debt problem. But they must be kept in perspective. Only in one case, that of Chile, have they so far made much difference to the overall debt position. (In 1986 $1b of Chile's external debt of $21b was converted into equity.)[29] In most countries an even lower fraction of total debt has been involved and the implications for ultimate solvency are trivial. The same deterrents to conventional direct investment in debtor countries – such as restrictions on profit repatriation, the threat of nationalization, discrimination by government in favour of local competition – apply to equity interests obtained through swap procedures.

X

Low-interest finance reduces the rate of interest on debt; export diversification and the promotion of manufactured exports increase the rate of growth of exports; and debt-equity swaps lower outstanding debt totals. All three ideas therefore attack the root cause of the Third World debt problem, as they narrow the gap between interest rates and the rate of growth of exports from less-developed countries. But none of them is significant enough to alter our main conclusion. They do not really constitute grounds for 'cautious optimism', not matter how many statements to that effect come from the World Bank, the IMF and the

American government. The interesting question is rather how soon the pessimists will be proved right.

As with the problem of domestic public debt in nations such as Italy, there will be no single Day of Judgement. Instead there will be a cat-and-mouse game between the major debtors on the one hand and the international banks and the IMF on the other. The debtors will not pay interest on time because of dissatisfaction with some of the bankers' conditions. Sanctions will be threatened but not applied. The debtors will then slip behind on capital repayments, while negotiations continue. Sanctions will once more be threatened but not applied. The bankers and debtors will agree on conditions, accepting that the overdue interest and capital can be rescheduled. The conditions will be broken. Again no sanctions will be applied. Even after the rescheduling, the debtors will again fail to pay interest. And so it will go on. The final act in the soap opera will involve meetings, which will continue for months and months, between bank managements, bank auditors and government regulators in the major industrial nations to discuss the precise definition of national insolvency.

No one will declare openly that debt repudiation has happened or is happening. But, without a drastic change in the relationship between interest rates and commodity inflation, there must be no doubt that it will happen.

PART III

The Debt Threat to the American Private Sector

6

'Some of them hated the mathematics'

I

The American people enjoyed running into debt in the 1970s. For a number of reasons – notably the tax system and the low level of real interest rates – it made good financial sense for individuals and companies to borrow. By the mid-1980s people had become more nervous about incurring debt because of the much higher level of real interest rates. But credit was more freely available than ever and in any case it was difficult to stop the growth of debt through the constant addition of interest charges to old loans. Meanwhile, under the influence of supply-side economics, the government began to run large budget deficits and the public sector's appetite for debt reinforced the private sector's. As a result the ratio of debt to national income, which had been stable for 30 years until 1981, started to rise rapidly. The consequent deterioration in balance sheets has been termed the 'leveraging of America'.[1]

We have already discussed several aspects of this process. In the Introduction we gave some statistics on the increase in the USA's debt/income ratio, since it constituted one of the clearest real-world applications of our analytical framework. In chapters 1 and 2 we considered the record of budgetary control in the USA, pointing out how the long tradition of fiscal responsibility broke down after the Eisenhower Presidency. In chapter 3 we explained why the private sector's eagerness to borrow in the 1970s contributed to the abrupt increase in real interest rates after 1979.

There is much more to say. This chapter and the next will focus on the growth of private sector debt in the USA, picking up some of the idea introduced in chapter 3. The first task is to relate our analytical framework to the subject of private sector debt. We shall then discuss the growth of debt, and changing attitudes towards it, between the 1930s and 1980s. Finally, we shall see how the financial system has responded to the shock of high real interest rates in the last few years. Lurking in the background throughout the discussion is the question, 'Could the 1930s be repeated?'.

II

In the first part of the book our analytical ideas were put to work to explain the behaviour of public debt in the major industrial economies; in the second part they were used to diagnose the causes of the growth in developing countries' external debt. The same ideas are readily extended to the case of a private sector borrower in the USA. To exemplify the argument – which is identical in structure to that in the opening sections of chapters 1 and 4 – we can consider the position of a real estate developer who depends on bank credit.

The developer intends to build an office block on a plot of land at a cost of $10m. Suppose that he is not prepared to put up any money of his own and so makes no investment in the development, even though he intends to own the equity in it outright. He therefore borrows the full $10m from a bank. Suppose that the rent on the building is $1m a year, that annual management expenses are nil and that, with interest rates of 10 per cent, interest charges each year are also $1m. (This is all rather unrealistic, but we are illustrating a point.)

Now, using the same terminology as before, it is clear that the developer's primary balance – the difference between his rent income and his non-interest expenses – is $1m. He may, like many characters in the real estate business, be a flamboyant, high-spending individual. So he takes the $1m away for his own consumption. As he does not apply it to servicing the debt, the bank adds the $1m interest to the original loan, which becomes $11m after the first year. Will the bank protest about the developer's failure to service his debt? The answer, which may seem surprising, is 'not necessarily'. What the bank needs, as we emphasized in our original discussion of this subject in the Introduction, is an assurance that its loan is backed up by collateral. It must be confident that, if it calls for repayment, the borrower can sell the asset for a price equal to or above the value of the loan. If the price of the office building is rising by 10 per cent a year, it is worth $11m at the end of the first year. It remains exactly equal to the loan, just as at the beginning of the transaction. If the bank was happy then, it should still be happy now.

The real estate developer is, of course, even happier. Without putting up any funds of his own, he takes an income of $1m from the building. If rents increase consistently by 10 per cent a year, supporting the same rate of appreciation in office prices, his income also grows steadily. It is obvious that – in this stable environment of 10 per cent interest rates and 10 per cent a year rental growth – both the developer's debt/income ratio and the ratio of debt to the bank's collateral are constant. The situation can continue indefinitely, to the satisfaction of all the parties involved.

Now consider the implications of changing the balance between interest rates and the growth rate of rental income. Let the change be drastic, with interest rates increasing to 15 per cent and the annual growth rate of rental income slowing to 5 per cent. Suppose that the same developer goes ahead, helped by another bank loan, with a new office building also costing $10m and suppose that, as before, he is not prepared to service the debt from the rental income.

At the end of the first year the debt has become $11.5m, while the developer's prospective income is $1.05m and (assuming that the building appreciates in line with rents) the value of the building is $10.5m. At the end of the second year the debt is $13.225m, prospective income $1.1025m and the value of the building $11.025m. It is quite clear that the developer is bust. His debts exceed his assets by over $2m, and – even if he radically alters his life-style and devotes all the rental income to servicing the loan – he will never be able to eliminate the deficiency. As long as interest rates exceed the growth rate of rents, the bank is in an equally helpless position. It may step in, take control of the building and insist that the rental income be used to service the debt. But the arithmetic is remorseless. At the end of the third year, prospective rents of little more than $1.15m remain altogether inadequate to bridge the gap between the value of the building, which will move towards $11.6m over the next 12 months, and the loan of over $15m. Moreover, just as the developer had to pay interest to the bank, so the bank has to pay interest to its depositors. If its interest costs exceed its interest receipts, it may quickly find itself in the same predicament as the developer.

The implications of this example are easy to summarize. If the rate of interest is equal to the rate of growth of rental income and the real estate developer sets aside none of his primary balance (i.e. the difference between rents and non-interest expenditure) to service his debt, his debt/income ratio is constant through time. But, if the rate of interest exceeds the rate of growth of rental income and he still makes no effort to service the debt, the debt/income ratio increases without limit. Conversely, if the rate of interest is beneath the growth rate of rental income, the debt/income ratio declines continuously.

Although the example has focused on a real estate developer, it could equally well have related to a farmer, an individual or a company.

Instead of rental growth, we would have talked in terms of increases in farm income, wages and salaries, or profits. At the level of the economy as a whole, the totality of private incomes is relevant. The argument about the behaviour of private debt works in exactly the same way as our earlier analysis of public debt in the developed countries and of Third World debt. However, it is the relationship between the interest rate and the growth rate of private sector incomes, rather than that between the real interest rate and the economy's growth rate or between the interest rate and the growth rate of exports, which is critical.

Moreover, by considering a real estate developer's circumstances, we have been reminded of some interesting differences in assessing the sustainability of private, as opposed to public, borrowing. In our example the $10m loan was equal, at the beginning of the development, to the value of the building. In practice, no bank manager would expose his institution to such a high degree of risk. He would instead require that the developer put up some capital of his own to protect the bank against potential difficulties. The bank might also ask for a charge on some of the developer's other assets so that, if the developer's equity interest had been wiped out, it still had means of avoiding loss.

The viability of the loan therefore depends not only on the relationship between interest rates and rental growth, but also on the adequacy of the bank's 'margin' of collateral and the strength of the debtor's other assets. (As we saw in the Introduction, Keynes assigned great importance to these variables in his analysis of the banking crisis of the 1930s.) These considerations do not arise with either the domestic debt of industrial countries' governments or the external debt of developing countries. In both cases no formal collateral is offered when the debt is incurred. Debt/equity swaps in the Third World may be attempts to establish collateral for sovereign bank debt, but the possibility that they might be needed was not entertained when the loans were initially signed.

Clearly, the behaviour of asset prices, as well as the relationship between interest rates and the growth rate of incomes, is important to understanding the dynamics of private debt in the USA. The key assets in this context are the various forms of real estate. Because they have the great advantage from the lender's viewpoint that they are highly visible and physically stuck in a particular location, land, buildings and houses are used as collateral in loans taken out for a great variety of purposes, not just in those for real estate development. Unlike share certificates, they cannot be removed by a borrower if he decides to quit the country.

III

To understand the significance of the rise in the debt/income ratio in the USA since 1981 it needs to be put in its historical context. The starting point has to be the Depression of the 1930s, undoubtedly the most traumatic event in American economic history. The Depression was far more brutal in impact in the USA than in most European countries. Not only was the financial disintegration on a more extensive scale, with 40 per cent of the country's banks failing, but also it was in more abrupt contrast to the prosperity of the 1920s. The recital of macroeconomic data is frightening enough. GNP fell continuously from 1929 to 1933, by 9.5 per cent in 1930, 7.7 per cent in 1931, 13.8 per cent in 1932 and 2.6 per cent in 1933. (It may help to give perspective to note that the largest decline in GNP in the last 40 years was 2.6 per cent in 1982 and that a 'recession' is now defined as two successive quarters of falling GNP.) But the macro numbers do not say anything directly about the many individual humiliations and hardships inflicted on millions of people by mass unemployment. It has been aptly said that few Americans who lived through those years did not bear some sort of 'invisible scar' from their experiences.[2]

The Depression disturbed all parts of the economy, but the shock was most severe in regions dependent on commodity production. The reason was that, as in nearly all business down-turns, commodity prices fell by more than the overall price level. Farming was the worst-hit activity, with the price of farm products in 1933 less than half the level of 1929.[3] Many farmers who had bought their land on borrowed money found that they could not meet their mortgage payments. At one stage in 1932 20,000 farms were being foreclosed each month. But the banks who took possession of the properties could do nothing except sell the land and buildings, as they needed to have funds to meet deposit withdrawals. Their forced selling drove down land prices even further, destroying the collateral for other bank loans and aggravating the breakdown of rural credit. The turmoil of the American Midwest in this period provoked John Steinbeck to write his novel *The Grapes of Wrath*. Published in 1939, it described the migration of the Joad family from Oklahoma to California in a constant hunt for work.

One of the most graphic passages describes the emotions of 'the owner men' as they came to dispossess the tenant farmers. In Steinbeck's words, they were caught in a mathematics 'larger than themselves'. They worked for banks and finance companies which 'don't breathe air, don't eat side-meat' but instead 'breathe profits' and 'eat the interest on money'. The owner men, no less than the farmers, could not escape the mathematics.

Some of them hated the mathematics that drove them, and some were afraid, and some worshipped the mathematics because it provided a refuge from thought and from feeling. If a bank or a finance company owned the land, the owner man said, the Bank – or the Company – needs – wants – insists – must have – as though the Bank or the Company were a monster, with thought and feeling, which had ensnared them.[4]

More prosaically, the Joads were prey to the debt trap and the impersonal arithmetic of compound interest. Although their plight was to be immortalized in one of the greatest works of American fiction, they were only one example among many. In 1935 there were an estimated two million homeless people, the so-called 'Okies' and 'Arkies', travelling on roads and railways in search of a job.

The financial system was condemned as the culprit for these and other miseries. Popular anger was directed against banks which had lent money in the late 1920s to support rampant share speculation, often to their own employees and sometimes dishonestly. The Senate Committee on Banking and Currency in 1931 and 1932 discovered many instances of misconduct. Albert H. Wiggin, president of the Chase National Bank, was found to have been selling the stock of his own company short at a time when he was urging other bank executives to invest in it; Ivar Kreuger, whose Swedish Match Company had relied on $250m borrowed in the USA, was shown to have put up as collateral a forged issue of Italian bonds; and Charles E. Mitchell, president of the National City Bank, was found guilty of tax evasion.[5] But, in truth, banks were victims as well as culprits. Many of them did their best to assess loans carefully, but events were outside their control. In the final settlement the banks which failed were able to repay nearly three-quarters of the deposits they had owed. Friedman and Schwartz have pointed out that the $2.5b of losses from bank failures between 1930 and 1933 was trivial compared with the slump of $85b in the value of preferred and common stock in the same period.[6]

Whatever the rights and wrongs of the Depression era, it had a profound impact on attitudes, behaviour and policy over the next generation. The 25 years to 1929 were marked by ever-increasing optimism about economic prospects and growing preparedness in the financial system to take risks; the 25 years after it were characterized by persistent doubts about the resumption and durability of growth, and by extreme caution towards the extension of credit at financial institutions. This caution was partly due to the regulatory response to bank failures and collapsing share prices. In 1933 the Federal Deposit Insurance Corporation was established to ensure that bank customers received the full value of their deposits. The aim, which was largely achieved, was to dissuade people from unnecessarily and harmfully withdrawing funds from sound institutions. In the same year the Glass–Steagall Act, one of the landmarks in US financial regulation, strengthened the Federal Reserve System, imposed restrictions on the amount of lending for securities trading its member banks could make and required investment banking (issuing securities) to be separated from commercial banking (making loans). The restrictions on securities lending were specifically designed to prevent the undue use of bank loans for the speculative carrying of securities. The rise in stockbrokers' loans from $1,767m to 1926 to $8,549m in 1929 had been widely blamed for the unjustified surge in share prices before the Great Crash.[7]

The reluctance to take risks also stemmed from fear that the trials and tribulations of the 1930s might return. No bank officer who had experienced and survived the financial holocaust of those years would ever again readily contemplate lending to financiers and speculators. Indeed, after the trauma that had hit farming, many financial institutions were diffident about granting mortgages to farmers against the collateral of prime agricultural land, an asset which would normally be regarded as excellent support for a loan. With beliefs such as these being very widely held and a common perception that technological opportunities had been largely exhausted, an influential school of economists suggested in the late 1930s that the USA faced many years of slow or negligible growth. This prospect, which they termed 'secular stagnation', remained a fashionable talking point until the 1950s. It reinforced the general hesitation about running up large debts to invest in either financial or tangible assets. Instead companies preferred to purchase capital assets from retained profits and to keep debt low in relation to equity, while individuals channelled their savings into safe investment vehicles, such as bank deposits, and avoided borrowing.

Behaviour of this kind would have led, in any event, to a strengthening of private sector balance sheets. But the Second World War reinforced the trend. The government ran large budget deficits to finance military expenditure, causing rapid monetary expansion. This improved the financial situation of companies and individuals in two ways. It led to a substantial increase in prices, reducing the real value of debts incurred in the past, and it boosted holdings of bank deposits. By the mid-1940s the American private sector was exceptionally under-borrowed. In 1946 all debt owed by businesses and households amounted to only 45.4 per cent of GNP, while the assets they owned were a multiple (perhaps four or five times) of GNP. Household debt was particularly modest, only 16 per cent of GNP. Business debt, which had been 123 per cent of GNP in 1932, was a mere 29 per cent in 1946.[8]

It was understandable, against this background, that debt would rise faster than incomes in the late 1940s and 1950s. The increase in debt could be interpreted as one aspect of the return to peacetime normality. There were no excesses. Consumer credit expanded swiftly in the late 1950s, but it remained tiny in relation to personal wealth and was in any case the logical financial counterpart to increased ownership of cars and consumer durables. Company borrowing was kept under tight control. As late as 1960 it was equivalent to only 30.5 per cent of GNP, far less than 30 years earlier. Kaufman has subsequently blessed this period as one of 'economic moderation', with low levels of indebtedness being associated with 'moderate growth, moderate unemployment, some unused physical resources, and price stability'. In his view, the nearest the USA came to an optimum investment climate was in the early 1960s.[9]

One feature of the economic moderation of the 1950s and early 1960s deserves special emphasis, because it highlights the contrast between this period on the one hand and both the 1930s and the most recent decade on the other. Financial institutions, particularly banks, were careful to maintain rock-solid balance sheets. Their prudence and restraint were expressed in high ratios of capital to assets, of safe assets (such as government bonds) to total assets and of liquid assets to deposit liabilities. The abundance of capital in relation to assets was to ensure that, if some of the assets became worthless or dropped in value, banks would still be solvent; the large holdings of government bonds were designed to prevent such falls ever becoming significant in relation to total assets; and the strength of liquid resources was intended to buttress customers' confidence that banks could meet runs on deposits. By this means the banking system constructed a series of balance sheet fortifications to protect itself against another assault of the kind it had suffered in the early 1930s. The underlying philosophy was that it was better to be safe than sorry.

IV

A more casual attitude towards debt emerged gradually as memories of the Depression faded. As with American fiscal policy, the early 1960s were the years of transition between the financial caution of the post-Depression period and the permissiveness of recent decades. In part the change was generational, as people who could remember the arbitrary cruelties of the 1930s retired from positions of authority and were replaced by successors whose business experience was confined to the safe, predictable and gentle 1950s. In part the greater eagerness to borrow was motivated by the relationships between the relevant economic variables, such as interest rates and the inflation rate. Most important of all was the relationship between interest rates and the expected rate of change in the prices of assets, like houses, real estate and farmland, which could be bought with borrowed money.

Mortgage borrowing grew quickly in the 1950s, reflecting a backlog of demand for housing after the War. Nearly all of it was done at fixed rates of interest, of between 4 and 6 per cent, for a long term (often in excess of 25 years). Savings and loan associations (also known as 'thrifts'), which had been exempted from some of the more restrictive anti-bank legislation of the 1930s and benefited from preferential tax treatment, dominated the mortgage boom. Their assets climbed from under $10b in 1945 to nearly $130b in 1960.[10] In the prosperous environment of the 1950s and 1960s very few mortgage borrowers were unable to meet their commitments. There were occasional 'credit crunches', enforced when the Federal Reserve became anxious that monetary conditions were too loose, but their characteristic was that the supply of funds to prospective borrowers dried up, not that the cost of funds to existing borrowers rose sharply. As a result monetary tightening did not lead to a significantly worse incidence of mortgage delinquencies. Commercial banks, resenting the rapid growth enjoyed by the savings and loan associations, sought and achieved more equal tax treatment. By the late 1960s and 1970s they also were actively seeking to expand into mortgage finance.

The influx of new credit was a strong force behind a persistent upward creep in house prices. Between 1963 and 1973 the median selling price of new one-family homes rose by 6.1 per cent a year, noticeably more than the 3.8 per cent a year increase in consumer prices recorded over the same period.[11] People began to regard their houses not just as homes but as investments. Anyone who had borrowed mortgage money at a fixed rate of 5 per cent in the 1950s saw the value of his house steadily rising more than his interest bill. The calculation became more favourable still if allowance was made for the deductibility of interest from taxable income. By the early 1970s the American public had a growing demand for mortgage debt, which financial institutions were increasingly keen to meet. Mortgage borrowing therefore expanded more quickly than ever, fuelling a yet higher rate of house price increases and encouraging optimism about continuing inflation of house prices in future. In the five years to 1978 the price of new one-family homes went up by 11.4 per cent a year, while the pre-tax cost of mortgage money remained in single figures and the post-tax cost for many highly paid individuals was less than half as high.

Residential real estate values are fundamental to understanding financial psychology because, for most people, their home is the most valuable single asset they own. The advantageous gap between interest rates and the rate of increase in house prices was important not only as a stimulant to mortgage credit, but also as a catalyst for other borrowing decisions. With people's equity in their own homes becoming more valuable, they could offer better security for other kinds of consumer credit. The house price boom of the mid-1970s was therefore accompanied by buoyant credit for the purchase of cars and consumer durables. Consumer credit of all kinds expanded by 9.4 per cent a year in the ten years to 1973, when it represented just over 18 per cent of personal income. In the next six years it went up even more quickly, by 11.1 per cent a year, and continued to outpace the growth of personal incomes.

Companies' demand for credit also strengthened in the 1960s and 1970s. Business corporations' debt, which had been only 22.4 per cent of GNP at the end of 1946, was 30.5 per cent in 1960 and 37.7 per cent in 1978.[12] As much of this debt must have been incurred by companies in robust financial health, and it remained modest (relative to turnover) compared with the late 1920s, perhaps it does not deserve much attention. However, increasing corporate indebtedness symptomized, if not to an alarming degree, the decay of the strict standards of financial discipline instilled by the Depression. It was in the 1960s and 1970s that the leveraging of corporate America began. It was also in these years that financial operators and risk arbitrageurs, who became notorious in the 1980s, learnt their techniques.

As we explained in chapter 3, throughout the 1970s rising inflation and continued appreciation of asset values, combined with the tax advantages of borrowing and the impact of 'bracket creep', led many Americans to believe that the straightest path to self-enrichment was to fall heavily into debt. This kind of thinking was particularly persuasive in the most dynamic regions, notably California and the 'Sun Belt' of the South and Southwest, where it encouraged the speculative construction of large office blocks and other buildings. Just as the financial logic for individuals to borrow for house purchase was compelling while the rate of increase in house prices exceeded the mortgage rate, so real estate developers could not go wrong in areas where the rate of rental growth was above the rate of interest they had to pay on loans. In California and the Sun Belt rental growth throughout the 1960s and 1970s was fast enough to outweigh the increase in the interest burden.

By the end of the 1970s the debt aversion of the immediate post-Depression years had been largely forgotten. Whereas in the 1940s common prudence and recent memories obliged people to accumulate financial assets in order to avoid bankruptcy, in the late 1970s the fashion was to borrow heavily, acquire rapidly appreciating assets and profit from inflation. Residential and commercial real estate were the classic channels for this kind of activity, but other assets soon emerged both as hedges against inflation and vehicles for speculative credit growth. Items which are tangible, durable and easy to collect, such as postage stamps and Chinese porcelain, became favoured investments. Perhaps more ominously in view of the historical record, investors began to regard farmland with new enthusiasm. They believed that a worldwide shortage of food, widely forecast to be permanent and almost ineradicable because of high population growth, guaranteed rapid increases in farm rents into the indefinite future.

Investment in farmland by outsiders may have been part of the explanation why its value rose by 14.4 per cent a year between 1972 and 1981, while farm prices instead went up by only 8.1 per cent a year.[13] But it cannot have been the whole story. Farmers themselves were also borrowing heavily. Indeed, the figures show that debt owed by farmers expanded more than the increase in farmland value. While the farm sector's real estate holdings are estimated to have gone up from $267.4b in 1972 to $846.7b in 1981 (or by 3.17 times), its debt climbed from $59.6b to $202.1b (or by 3.39 times).[14] The plight of the American farmer in the 1930s was remembered, if at all, only as a historical aberration. After 40 years of uninterrupted prosperity, a catastrophe on the same scale was unthinkable.

Houses, office buildings, farmland and collectables are known, along with precious metals and commodities, as 'hard assets' to distinguish them from financial assets such as bonds and stocks. By the late 1970s the habit of borrowing to acquire such hard assets had become pervasive and deeply rooted, and the ratio of private sector debt to GNP had risen substantially compared with the late 1940s. (The overall debt/income ratio was stable because of the decline in the ratio of public sector debt to GNP.) It would have been logical to expect, against this background, that individuals and companies would have had more difficulties servicing their debts. But that was not the case.

On the contrary, bad debt experience in the late 1970s was unusually favourable. The number of business failures in 1978, which could be regarded as the peak year of the debt habit for most Americans, was the lowest since 1948. The failure rate (i.e. the number of failures per 10,000 listed enterprises) was a mere 23.9, much less than in the tranquil late 1950s and early 1960s when it had typically been over 50. The farm sector shared in the satisfactory debt experience of the rest of the economy. As a legacy from the Depression period, farmers in the USA are entitled to borrow at favourable rates from a group of institutions which have an implicit Federal guarantee. The Farm Credit System,

privately owned but supervised and examined by an agency of the
government, is the most important of these. Among other responsibilities, it oversees the operations of 390 Federal Land Banks. In 1977
and 1978 the percentage of delinquent loans (i.e loans where payments
are late) at these banks was under 0.5 per cent, while actual loan losses
were negligible.[15]

As loan loss experience was so good, banks and other financial
institutions were prepared to take on more risks than in the 1940s and
1950s. In the unusually peaceful financial conditions of the 1960s and
1970s, they dismantled some of the fortifications they had built after the
Depression to defend their balance sheets against economic trouble.
This trend was evidenced most obviously in a decline in the ratio of
capital to assets. Banks need capital, which consists of equity belonging
to the shareholders and a variety of other liabilities, to protect their
depositors if loans are not repaid. If loan losses are expected to be
minimal, it is good business strategy to reduce the capital/asset ratio and
earn a higher rate of return for shareholders. The tendency to trim
capital/asset ratios was most pronounced at the largest institutions. In
1960 all commercial banks in the USA maintained a ratio of equity to
assets of 8.1 per cent, while the money centre bank holding companies –
traditionally regarded as the core of the banking system – had a ratio of
9.0 per cent. In principle, the extra equity gave them added resilience
and justified their reputations for solidity and trustworthiness. However,
over the next 20 years the average equity/asset ratio of all commercial
banks fell to 5.8 per cent, whereas at the money centre banks it tumbled
to 3.6 per cent. On the face of it, the large banks had become the most
vulnerable.

It is important, before we proceed, to understand what a 3.6 per cent
equity/asset ratio means. When a bank lends money it takes on the risk
that some of the money will not be repaid. If loan losses amount to 2 per
cent of assets and equity amounts to 9 per cent of assets, it is in no
difficulty. It has a cushion of 7 per cent left. Moreover, the profits on the
good 98 per cent of its assets can be retained, constantly replenishing
capital. But suppose loan losses amount to 4 per cent of assets and
equity is only 3.6 per cent of assets. The bank is then effectively
insolvent, with its survival dependent on the goodwill of depositors. In
the late 1970s loan losses had been negligible for almost 40 years, with
the typical annual loan loss provision for the whole banking system at
less than 0.3 per cent. Unlike their counterparts in the 1940s and 1950s,
banks' executive officers had no experience of loan loss ratios
amounting to 2, 3 or 4 per cent in a single year, and they took a relaxed
view of capital requirements. Their viewpoint was understandable, but
the contrast with attitudes 20 or 30 years earlier could hardly have been

more complete. It showed not only how thoroughly memories of the Crash and the Depression had been erased, but also how dependent the banks had become on the continuation of the fair-weather conditions of the post-war period.

The latent problem was that, just as the Crash and the Depression were exceptional historical accidents, so the calm and stability of the 1960s and 1970s might eventually prove to be exceptional historical blessings. There was certainly a paradox in the highest ratio of private debt to GNP since the War being reconciled with a low rate of business failures and favourable loan loss experience. The key to explaining the paradox was – as our analytical framework would have suggested – that interest rates were low in relation both to the inflation rate and, more critically, to the rate of increase in the prices of hard assets. This situation, so reassuring for the many financial institutions which saw the collateral for their loans appreciating in value every year, was inherently unsustainable. As we saw in chapter 3, it encouraged ever-stronger credit demand from the private sector and led to accelerating monetary expansion. Sooner or later a macroeconomic antidote, in the form of a large rise in interest rates and a prolonged period of interest rates exceeding the rate of change in hard asset prices, would be essential.

7

The Leveraging of America

I

We are now in a better position to understand the full significance of Volcker's adoption of reserve targetting on 6 October 1979. As we saw in chapter 3, it was followed by a sharp increase in real interest rates, with the move to dear money made more pronounced because Volcker's anti-inflationary monetary policy coincided with financial deregulation and the supply-siders' tax cuts of 1981. The change from low or negative real interest rates in the 1970s to high real interest rates in the 1980s radically altered the environment for borrowers and lenders. It forced all economic agents to reconsider their financial behaviour.

Change came quickly to the housing market. Savings and loans associations which had lent out money at 5 or 6 per cent 15 years earlier had to pay interest rates of 15 per cent or more on their deposits. It was unrealistic to expect them to find new high-yielding mortgages as suddenly as their cost of funds had increased. In 1978 the yield on all mortgages (i.e. new and old) held by mutual savings banks was 7.94 per cent, while the interest rate on their new mortgages was 9.54 per cent; in 1981 the yield on all mortgages was up to 8.97 per cent, but the interest rate on new mortgages had soared to 14.74 per cent.[1] The difference between the two interest rates – one reflecting the past record of lending and the other determined by current market conditions – was an indication of the savings and loans associations' unprofitability. Net operating income of insured savings and loans associations fell from $5.7b in 1978 to $0.8b in 1980 and then became negative in 1981 (minus $7.1b) and 1982 (minus $5.9b). Many of them lacked the capital to survive an extended period of loss-making, while the figures for net operating income did not include the much larger unbooked losses incurred on old mortgage holdings. The General Accounting Office, which carries out financial scrutinies for Congress, estimated that at the end of September 1985 1,294 of the 3,180 federally insured savings institutions had net worth equal to or less than 3 per cent of liabilities.

Out of this total 461, with assets of $113b, had negative or zero net worth and were thus insolvent.[2]

The crisis in mortgage finance was associated with a drastic reappraisal of the economics of home ownership. In the 40 years to 1979 it had always been worthwhile to borrow to buy a home because the rate of house price appreciation consistently exceeded the post-tax interest rate. By contrast, in the five years after 1979 post-tax interest rates far exceeded the rate of house price change. New home prices went up by under 5 per cent a year, while the price of old homes was broadly stable. In some parts of the country, notably California, the value of residential property fell heavily, as a reaction to a speculative boom in the late 1970s. Meanwhile the interest rate on new mortgages mirrored the fluctuations in prime rate. From 9.54 per cent on average in 1978, it soared to 12.66 per cent in 1980 and 15.12 per cent in 1982, and remained as high as 12.36 per cent in 1984. A small but increasing proportion of home owners found that they could not service their mortgages on time and had no choice but to default.

Despite rising deliquency rates, financial institutions invented new and more elaborate ways for people to incur debt. Mortgages in the USA have traditionally been at fixed interest rates, perhaps because of the greater certainty about the size of their debt burden this gives to borrowers. The fixed rate pattern suited the savings and loans associations, which frequently have to adjust interest rates on their deposits in line with prevailing market conditions, as long as interest rate fluctuations were small. But, in the topsy-turvy conditions of the early 1980s with interest rates varying from 10 to 20 per cent in relatively short periods, they would have been better placed if the return on their mortgage debt also changed with market conditions. The savings and loans associations therefore started offering adjustable rate mortgages.

Kaufman has criticized this and similar developments in commercial banking on the grounds that 'variable rates free the institutional lender from interest-rate risk in lending and encourage him to speed ahead with spread banking, a now well-known process of borrowing funds and investing them at a fixed rate over costs'. In Kaufman's view, because spread banking insulates credit transactions from interest rate changes, 'rising interest rates no longer impede the innovative institutional lender from increasing asset size'.[3] This criticism seems rather forced, since it is surely sensible for financial institutions to develop business practices which enable them to achieve their objectives with less risk. But of course it is true that the more financial institutions lend, the higher is the amount of debt that people owe. In that sense the switch to adjustable rate mortgages and spread banking was an important aspect of the leveraging of America.

Mortgages account for the majority of personal debt in the USA. However, the early 1980s also saw proliferation and rapid growth in other types of debt. The greater diversity of debt instruments was both a tribute to the inventiveness of banks and other intermediaries, and a sign of their customers' financial myopia. Symptomatic was a sharp increase in borrowing on credit cards. As most people regard credit cards as a marginal and temporary source of finance, they are relatively indifferent to the interest rate. Credit card companies are able to charge a very wide margin – perhaps of 10 per cent or more – over the cost of funds. As long as borrowers are able to repay, they are an extremely profitable branch of financial business. With profits in more conventional activities under pressure, financial institutions engaged in intense competition to supply cards to an ever wider range of customers. These came to include many people with little financial sophistication and few assets. Credit quality declined as debt growth accelerated. By 1986 credit card defaults amounted to 4.2 per cent of charges outstanding, twice as high as in 1985. The increased incidence of default reflected a greater number of personal bankruptcies. In 1982 bankruptcies accounted for 10 per cent of credit card defaults; in 1986 they were responsible for 45 per cent.[4]

The irresponsible extension of fringe forms of personal credit aggravated the problems facing the mortgage industry. Savings and loans associations had serious enough difficulties in the 1980s from the high costs of servicing deposits without having to worry also about borrowers' reduced ability to maintain mortgage payments. The more personal bankruptcies there were, the fewer were the number of borrowers who could keep up to date on their mortgages. Losses continued to be incurred by many savings and loans associations in the mid-1980s despite a substantial reduction in interest rates. Theoretically, the safety of deposits as savings and loan associations is protected by the Federal Savings and Loan Insurance Corporation (FSLIC), which has a fund to compensate for failures in individual institutions. (The FSLIC is similar in structure to the Federal Deposit Insurance Corporation (FDIC). The fund has been accumulated from insurance premiums paid by thrifts in the past.) But such have been the drains on the FSLIC in recent years that the fund is almost exhausted. At the end of 1986 the FSLIC's usable reserve was down to $1.9b, compared with $4.5b at the end of 1985. Since there were contingent liabilities of $8b from propping up 60 'virtually failed' thrifts, it seems that the FSLIC was actually in the red.[5]

In 1987 Congress debated a number of plans to introduce new capital into the organization, with the administration's favoured option a five-year plan which would cost the taxpayer $25b but require thrifts to increase the insurance premiums they pay. We see here the beginning of a new phase of the domestic American debt problem. Although it began because of rapid and unsustainable growth in private sector debt, it is now being tackled by the injection of public money into supposedly private financial institutions in order to maintain an appearance of solvency and normality. While mortgage rates remain above the rate of increase in home owners' incomes, there are no good reasons for expecting an early improvement in the FSLIC's fortunes; and while the average interest rate on deposits stays higher than the average return on mortgage books which date back to the low interest rate environment of the 1950s and 1960s, hundreds of savings and loan associations will be on the brink of closure. More concisely, high real interest rates have crippled, and will continue to cripple, the American housing finance industry.

The impact of the post-1979 move to high real interest rates on office and commercial real estate was longer delayed than that on residential real estate. We have seen that during the 1970s there had been almost uninterrupted excess demand for office space in most regions of the USA, particularly so in the economically dynamic regions of the Sun Belt and California. In 1979 and 1980 there was still a backlog of excess demand. Although construction activity was strong, an office vacancy index compiled by Coldwell Banker, a Chicago-based real estate service, was at very low levels. In 1980 and early 1981 less than 4 per cent of office space was available for letting over the nation as a whole and rental growth was expected to remain good in the next few years. These expectations would have encouraged more office construction in any event, but a further stimulus was received from the 1981 Economic Recovery Tax Act. As explained in chapter 3, the Act made yet more indulgent the already highly favourable tax treatment afforded to the real estate industry.

Office construction continued rising in 1982, despite its being a recession year for the US economy. There was a small dip in 1983, but then further and more rapid growth in 1984 and early 1985. The result of the boom was that, by the second quarter of 1985, new office building work was virtually three times higher in value than five years earlier. More space was coming onto the market than ever before. Unfortunately, the demand for space did not stay in line. As a survey on investing in US real estate in *The Wall Street Journal* of 7 April 1986 soberly remarked, because growth in the employment of office workers slowed in 1985 to 2 per cent from 4.5 per cent in 1984 and the profits of office-based service industries had deteriorated, the supply of newly completed office space had come to exceed demand by a factor of about 30 per cent.[6] Coldwell Banker's office vacancy index rose from 5 per cent in early 1982 to 11.7 per cent in 1983, 13.9 per cent in 1984 and 16.1 per cent in 1985.

Inevitably, rental growth stopped. Indeed, in many regions effective rents declined, with developers offering one-year rent holidays in order to encourage new tenants to take space. The investment arithmetic for real estate speculation had been totally transformed. Instead of the high rental growth and low interest rates of the 1970s, the early and mid-1980s were characterized by zero or negative rental growth and high interest rates. Our discussion in the opening section of chapter 6 points to the likely consequences of the changed relationship between rental growth and interest rates. In contrast with the effortless fortune-seeking of the 1970s, when any highly geared owner of equity in office buildings became steadily richer just by sitting on his stake, in the 1980s it was difficult for developers to extricate themselves from an ever-worsening financial plight. Every year that rental growth was less than the interest rate on their debt, their ability to meet their commitments deteriorated. If they tried to sell their buildings, repay their loans and so anticipate pressure from the banks, they were liable to depress real estate values, eroding the collateral on which the banks depended. The problems in the real estate industry ineluctably spread to the banking system.

Although the linkage between real estate problems and banking difficulties was evident in all parts of the USA, it was most vivid in certain regions. The recession of 1981 and 1982 followed the usual cyclical pattern, causing sharper falls in commodity prices than in the prices of industrial products or services. Real estate in regions of the USA which specialized in primary commodities was therefore most vulnerable to the changed relationship between rental growth and interest rates. It was particularly unfortunate that the commodity-producing areas also tended to be those which had enjoyed the greatest economic dynamism and the most exuberant real estate markets in the 1970s. In Texas, for example, many fortunes had been made from a combination of oil development and real estate speculation. When the oil price fell in 1982, the state's economy was exposed in two ways. Not only were there the direct repercussions of the lower price on its industries, but also a slow-down in the demand for office space coincided with record levels of office building activity.

Houston, the fourth largest city in the USA, was the most conspicuous casualty. In July 1981 over 94 per cent of the city's office space was leased. This condition of virtual full occupancy stimulated unprecedented construction activity, with 60m square feet of new space being added between 1981 and 1984, much of it financed by bank credit. But absorption dropped beneath the 10m and 11m square feet levels achieved in 1980 and 1981 at the peak of the oil boom. By mid-1984 only

71 per cent of office space was occupied. Not surprisingly, developers had to offer extended free rent periods or special fit-up payments to induce new tenants to take up space.[7] But oversupply remained obstinate, and both rentals and the market value of buildings declined.

As the number of corporate and personal insolvencies rose, banks were caught by the inability of their customers to service their debts. The first significant example was the failure of the Penn Square Bank in July 1982, mainly because of bad loans to Texan and Oklahoman energy companies. Continental Illinois, a large money centre bank headquartered in Chicago which had lent to Penn Square, was heavily involved and found difficulty maintaining its creditworthiness in the inter-bank market. In May 1984 the FDIC was obliged to guarantee all of Continental Illionis's liabilities to prevent it from going out of business. With $30b of deposits at stake, it was the largest banking rescue in American history.

Within Texas itself, the catalogue of bank failures lengthened during the mid-1980s. In 1986 26 banks failed and to the first four months of 1987 a further 17 went under. Texas today (August 1987) is facing so many economic pressures that it has started to lose population to other states for the first time in the 150 years since it gained independence.[8] It is quite likely that a future rise in the oil price will ease the troubles in the energy sector, but the unceasing addition of interest charges to old real estate loans will hobble the banks, developers and construction companies for years to come.

While Texas suffered in the mid-1980s from the fall in the oil price, the Midwest was hit by the decline in food prices. Although in both cases the dependence on commodity production seemed to be largely to blame, high real interest rates were more directly responsible for the turmoil in regional financial systems. Their impact in the Midwest was rather different from that in Texas. Whereas in Texas and, indeed, the rest of the Sun Belt, the most obviously affected asset was office real estate, in the Midwest it was farmland. As the value of farmland fell, banks had no alternative to foreclosure for thousands of small farmers unable to maintain payments on their debts. At times people worried whether the Depression years were being replayed. Farmers could be excused for thinking that the prosperous 1970s, just as much as the grim 1930s, were a historical aberration.

Hard times began quite soon after the adoption of reserve targetting in October 1979. The sharply higher level of interest rates caused an appreciation of the dollar on the foreign exchanges, which undermined the international competitiveness of US farm exports. The rise in farm prices decelerated markedly from the 8.1 per cent annual rate enjoyed between 1972 and 1981. In 1982 and 1985 they actually fell. Farmland values reflected the change in market conditions. They continued to advance through sheer momentum in 1980 and 1981, but in 1981 – for the first time in over a decade – they increased at less than the rate of interest. Clearly, farmland had dwindling attractions to non-farm investors. From being heavy net buyers in the late 1970s, they became net sellers in the early 1980s. In 1982 farmland prices reported their first fall since the 1930s. It was only a trifling drop of less than 1 per cent, but it gave the signal for more disinvestment. In 1983 the value of farmland went down by 6 per cent, in 1984 by 1 per cent and in 1985 by 12½ per cent. With prime rates remaining at over 10 per cent until the summer of 1985, any farmer who had borrowed heavily against land collateral was in an impossible financial position.[9] The change between the 1970s and early 1980s in the relationship between interest rates and farmland prices mirrored that in the relationship between interest rates and rental growth; and, just as the crisis in real estate hurt the banks who had supported real estate development in the 1970s, so the financial stress in farming damaged the credit institutions which specialized in the rural sector.

At the end of 1985 total farm debt stood at $212b. As with debt in so many other contexts, it had continued to rise after the initial onset of trouble not because there were willing borrowers and lenders, but because of the addition of interest charges to old loans. In the brave words of Mr Cornelius Gallagher, the Bank of America's vice-president in charge of agricultural lending in California's San Joaquin Valley, 'We're not about to walk away from the farmers. We're resisting foreclosures and we intend to keep right on lending based on sound, basic principles.'[10] Of the $212b total, commercial banks held about $51b, the Farm Credit System $74b and the Farmers Home Administration – regarded as the 'lender of last resort' to farmers in need of emergency assistance – held a further $27b. All three categories of institution subsequently had major difficulties. Farm banks accounted for more than half of all the bank failures in the USA in 1985 and 1986, while by mid-1986 the Farm Credit System had become virtually bankrupt after massive write-downs on its loans and almost a quarter of the Farm Home Administration's borrowers were delinquent.[11]

In early 1987 there were some signs of improvement. The fall in the dollar in the previous two years had been followed by an upturn in food prices, while lower interest rates helped farmers limit the growth of their debt. However, it needs to be emphasized that – as in the mortgage industry – government help had contributed much to the better mood. In September 1984 the Federal government set up a $650m fund to enable the Farm Home Administration to write off 10 per cent of loans and forgive five years of interest for farmers considered good long-term customers;[12] the Food Security Act of 1985 greatly expanded federal assistance to farmers, with government support of $25.8b in 1986 more than six times higher than five years earlier;[13] and in May 1987 the Farm Credit System was in negotiations with Congress over a $6b credit line to help it restore its depleted reserves and stay in business. Farming has not been restored to full financial health as long as it depends on bail-outs at the taxpayers' expense.

The American government has traditionally been far less susceptible to lobbying for financial help from Big Business than from farming. It is therefore fortunate that the post-1979 rise in interest rates was followed by prudent financial management in the majority of American companies. There is little evidence that, at the aggregate level, the balance sheet strength of Corporate America declined in the early and mid-1980s. True enough, company borrowing rose faster than national income and so the ratio of business corporations' debt to GNP increased from the 37.7 per cent recorded in 1978. But it was never remotely comparable to the 123 per cent of 1932, while on some of the standard measures the corporate financial situation was stable.

A company's vulnerability to unforeseen adversity depends largely on the ratio of equity to debt. If for any reason cash flow suddenly weakens and turns negative, it has to continue to service its debt until the position improves. If it cannot service the debt, it has to close down. The purpose of equity is to give it the resources to see it through such periods of negative cash flow. Equity therefore acts as a buffer against shocks; the lower the ratio of debt to equity, the greater is the corporate sector's resilience when confronted by untoward economic fluctuations. 'The capacity to borrow rests on the foundation of equity capital. Without sufficient equity, private money and bond markets could not function.'[14]

Debt/equity ratios can be measured in several ways. But perhaps the most logical approach is to compare the total of bank loans and bond issues with the stock market value of equity, as the stock market attempts to make an unbiased assessment of what companies are really worth. Using this method the debt/equity ratio of US companies was broadly similar in the mid-1970s and the mid-1980s. There was no obvious tendency to deterioration after the jump in interest rates in 1979 and 1980.[15]

But it would be wrong to conclude from this that the balance sheet of Corporate America is unblemished. Although the aggregate numbers are satisfactory, there have been many individual cases of financial adventurism which have resulted in an excessive build-up of debt. Financial deregulation in the early 1980s encouraged a rash of innovative practices in venture capital and the financing of mergers and acquisitions. Their purpose was to increase the potential reward to the players involved, but their drawback was that they involved more debt and more risk. The leveraged buy-out was one of the best examples of the new techniques. Typically, a venture capital company would lend a large sum of money to a group of individuals, often former management, to buy up and run the subsidiary of a large industrial company. The loan would be repaid from future profits, leaving ownership in the hands of the management. In other words, by assuming the potentially ruinous risk of being unable to repay the debt, management gained the opportunity to enjoy the full rewards of a business which had previously been owned by other people.

Arguably, leveraged buy-outs illustrate all that is best about American finance and entrepreneurship. They clearly enhance incentive, encourage effort and stimulate good management. But they also lead to an increase in the ratio of debt to income. It is difficult to be so enthusiastic about another innovation of the 1980s, the use of 'junk bonds' to finance take-overs. A skilful manoeuvre with junk bonds is the financial, although not perhaps the moral, equivalent of the contest between David and Goliath. A second-ranking company, whose paper is not recognized by the rating agencies as 'investment grade', has to issue debt at a higher rate of interest than the well-recognized top companies. The proceeds from the issue of such 'junk' can nevertheless be used to buy up any quoted company. A favourite tactic of take-over raiders in the mid-1980s was therefore to issue junk bonds on a sufficient scale to pay for stakes in large and allegedly undervalued companies. By this means an individual with limited resources could come to influence the destiny of the mega-corporations.

Like leveraged buy-outs, the activities of the corporate raiders are undoubtedly a spur to good management. But they are perhaps less admirable since it is far from clear that raiders are necessarily better managers than executives in companies threatened by take-over. In the notorious and well-publicized case of Ivan Boesky it now seems that his only distinctive management expertise was an astuteness in collecting inside information. Moreover, junk bond issuance creates particularly onerous debt. There are many junk bonds in existence with coupons of 14, 15 or 16 per cent.[16] It is hardly credible that, in an economy with an inflation rate of under 5 per cent, industrial profits can rise at this rate for any extended period of time. So we have another instance of an interest rate on debt much in excess of the rate of growth of borrowers' income. Indeed, the reluctance of American companies to incur junk bond liabilities before the 1980s may be seen as an expression of the innate financial conservatism of previous decades, while the sudden fashion for them in recent years – often for motives of frank opportunism – signals a slide into risky, perhaps irresponsible and certainly unsustainable financial practices. It is worrying that the number of defaults on junk bonds, only two a year on average between 1972 and 1981, was 17 with a value of $100m in 1985 and 30 with a value of $3.1b in 1986.[17]

The banking system has facilitated some of the most imaginative manoeuvres of the take-over raiders, risk arbitrageurs and venture capitalists of the 1980s. As the Bank Credit Analyst, the Montreal-based forecasting organization, has warned, 'Drawn by profit, bankers are channelling their limited liquidity into high-risk areas of the financial sector which offer higher yields. Never in the course of monetary history has there been a scheme which attracted lenders into economically non-productive enterprises at rates of return in excess of prevailing market rates that has not come to a bad end.'[18] For them, the rush of money into speculative finance is part of 'the paranoia found in financial manias'. The language may seem exaggerated, but it has to be said that some of the bank-financed stock manipulations of recent years bear comparison to those in the late 1920s which preceded the Great Crash. It is inconceivable that in the 1950s and 1960s, the heyday of economic moderation, bank executives would have sanctioned $750m in loans to an individual like Ivan Boesky for the explicit purpose of 'playing the market'.

In truth, the banks had changed their standards in all areas of lending over the 40 or so years of low or moderate real interest rates to 1979. It was this change in attitude, this constant erosion of bankers' traditional caution in credit appraisal, which – more than any other factor – had been responsible for the fall in commercial banks' equity/asset ratio from 8.1 per cent in 1960 to 5.8 per cent in 1980. In addition, as the Bank Credit Analyst has shown, the quality of bank assets had deteriorated. The ratio of risk assets (total assets less government securities and cash) to all US bank assets, which had been in the 70–80 per cent range in the 1920s and had fallen to 20 per cent in 1945, was back up to 50 per cent by 1960 and stood at about 75 per cent in the late 1970s.[19]

In consequence, the financial difficulties in real estate, farming and energy, as well as the more exotic areas of high finance, came just as the banking system was at its most vulnerable for two generations. The thick balance sheet fortifications of the immediate post-war years had been largely dismantled. We have already seen that bank failures rose sharply in the Farm Belt, Texas and other so-called Oil Patch states after the 1979 jump in interest rates. But these were only the most spectacular illustrations of a general theme. The problem was national, and not merely regional, in scope.

The business failure rate, so low in 1978, increased abruptly as the economy tried to adjust to the higher level of real interest rates after 1979. From a figure of 23.9 (per 10,000 listed enterprises), it climbed to 27.8 in 1979, 42.1 in 1980 and then 61.3 in 1981, the first year that real interest rates went above 10 per cent. The number of business failures, only 6,600 in 1978, rose to 17,000 in 1981, and 88,300 in 1984, as the long period of high real interest rates – and of the associated gap between nominal rates and the rate of growth of borrowers' income – took its toll. The banks, which inevitably had more bad customers and worsening records of loan repayment, were bound to suffer reduced profitability. Loan losses, which had been a meagre 0.25 per cent of bank assets in 1980, had risen to 0.56 per cent in 1984. This may not seem dramatic, but it was significant in relation to the slim margins earned by banks in the extremely competitive environment of the early 1980s.[20]

Weakening profitability undermined banks' ability to cope with reductions in the value of loan collateral and was associated with occasional difficulty in renewing deposits. Bank failures, which along with mass unemployment symbolized the Depression for many Americans, again became a topic for newspaper comment. In 1978 there had been seven bank failures out of a total US bank population of almost 15,000. As late as 1981 there were still only ten, but thereafter the number rose rapidly, reaching 42 in 1982, 48 in 1983, 79 in 1984, 120 in 1985 and 138 in 1986. It is not coincidence that this increase began as real dollar interest rates were established at the 10 per cent level. Nor should there be any surprise that, with real interest rates still very high by historical standards, 1987 is likely to see more than 200 banks – the highest number since the 1930s – go out of business.

II

In the Introduction it was argued that, if a nation's debt/income ratio rose by more than 1 or 2 per cent a year, its financial situation was unsustainable. The observation applied with particular force to advanced industrial countries with a financial interrelations ratio greater than unity, because a financial interrelations ratio at this level indicated that most tangible assets had already been matched by a debt instrument or financial claim of some sort. The USA today is clearly in an unsustainable position of this kind. Its financial interrelations ratio is greater than unity, while the debt/income ratio has been increasing by much more than 2 per cent a year since 1981.

The last section gives a better idea of how unsustainability manifests itself in the private sector. It adds substance to the warning in the Introduction that the American financial system faces 'continuing and potentially drastic upheaval' until the debt/income ratio stops rising. The rash of bank failures is the most telling sign that the behaviour of the debt/income ratio is unacceptable. There are obvious similarities, in form if not in extent, to the pattern of financial breakdown in the 1930s. Some economists have cast doubt on the seriousness of the bank failures by saying that nearly all of them have occurred in small institutions, typically with liabilities of under $10m, which have importance only to a few localities. But the increasing number of problem banks reflects the increasing number of personal and corporate bankruptcies. As such, it is symptomatic of a large, general and nation-wide threat to the American economy. Moreover, although the elimination of problem banks may at present be an orderly and gradual process, the incidence of bank failures cannot be allowed to rise indefinitely. It is ominous that every year in the 1980s has seen more bank failures than the year before.

We return to our central point. While real interest rates remain significantly above the long-run growth rate of American GNP, the debt/income ratio will keep on rising and the rot in the financial system will spread. Indeed, two standard responses to recent financial strains carry particular dangers for the future integrity and efficiency of the institutions involved. The first of these – the injection of public funds to shore up the capital of insolvent private sector organizations – has been adopted in farming and the savings and loan industry, and will undoubtedly become more widespread if the debt/income ratio continues to climb.

Although perhaps suitable as a stop-gap response, it could be very harmful if maintained for any length of time. If farmers, the housing finance industry and other government-aided producer groups come to believe that public money will always be avilable to compensate for managerial inadequacies, the discipline of market forces – which is essential to the success of a capitalist economy – will be devalued. The attenuation of market forces will probably be accompanied, at least in part, by arbitrariness and corruption in the distribution of public money to particular private sector organizations. Moreover, nothing will have been done to remove the basic cause of the problem, the excessive level of real interest rates. On the contrary, the increase in farm subsidies, the bail-out of the Farm Credit System and support for the FSLIC will all increase the budget deficit, and so tend to raise real interest rates further. There is a risk that the USA could go down the same perverse route as Italy in the 1970s. The larger budget deficit will drive up real interest rates; high real interest rates will further cripple private sector borrowers; private sector borrowers will demand and receive more subsidies from government; the government will find that the cost of the subsidies increases the budget deficit, which again drives up real interest rates; and so on. In short, it is counter-productive for the government – when it has put privately owned banks out of business by foolish macroeconomic policies – to assume the responsibilities of a 'hidden banker' on the Italian model.

The second approach is to promote the introduction of new private sector capital to financial intermediaries in difficulty. The FDIC and FSLIC have favoured this method in recent years, notably by arranging for many undercapitalized or insolvent institutions to be taken over by more successful rivals. On the whole, the recapitalization of failed or failing financial companies is an excellent idea, and the FDIC's and FSLIC's work has undoubtedly done much good. As the addition of new equity should remove deficiencies in capital due to the mistakes of previous management, it enables the core activities of financial institutions to survive without interruption. If these core activities are basically sound, there are benefits to existing customers, the new shareholders and society at large. However, there is a dark side to the financial marriage-broking performed by the FDIC and FSLIC In the 1980s.

Critical to the outcome of any financial restructuring is the viability of the core activities. In some cases banks and thrifts may be quite beyond recovery, with an ineradicable loss-making gap between the rate of return on mortgage assets and the rate of interest on deposits. As reputable financial organizations are therefore unlikely to provide support, the right answer is to close the condemned institutions down and repay the depositors with FDIC or FSLIC funds. Regrettably, because the FDIC and FSLIC have only limited resources, they may be tempted to relax their regulatory standards and induce disreputable operations to assume control of the insolvent organizations. This option may be less expensive to them in the short run but it is potentially very expensive to the community.

The danger is that the management of quite large deposit-taking institutions may fall into the hands of financial buccaneers with little sense of public accountability. They may use the deposits for their own private purposes, regardless of fiduciary responsibilities. One classic fraud is for a bank to sanction a loan for the purchase of real estate at an improperly inflated price, usually from someone connected with its own management. We have already mentioned this possibility in our discussion of how Argentine banks misused funds borrowed from the international financial system. Similar misconduct is beginning to be found in the USA.

Business Week reported, in its 13 July 1987 issue, on the activities of a real estate operator called Thomas Gaubert. In January 1983 he bought 51 per cent of a Texas thrift, Citizens Savings & Loan Assn, for $10.5m and renamed it Independent American. A year or two later he proposed buying up unfinished apartments belonging to Empire Savings & Loan, another insolvent thrift based in Texas. Bank examiners heard of his plan and investigated. They 'unearthed a daisy chain of "land flips" in which developers would buy land, then quickly sell it to someone else at a much higher price – repeatedly, until the bubble burst, leaving Empire with a host of bad loans'. Further enquiries identified more anomalies. In March 1986 Independent American came under the informal control of the regulators at the Federal Home Loan Bank Board. A company specializing in problem loans was called in to inspect the portfolio. It found 'a large number of complex, unorthodox and "screwy" deals', according to a preliminary report obtained by *Business Week*.[21]

This tale may seem unimportant, just an isolated instance of a form of financial malpractice which every business community suffers from time to time. In fact, it is more ominous. It demonstrates that, as long as real interest rates remain so high, the obligation of the FDIC and FSLIC to prevent depositors suffering loss must involve increased Federal assistance. To sell insolvent thrifts to private entrepreneurs is foolish if the insolvency is chronic and irremediable. No one should be surprised that the purchasers turn out to be crooks and that, eventually, yet more public money is needed. Until real interest rates return to normal, pre-1979 levels, the stresses within the American financial system due to growing private sector debt and insolvency will worsen.

None of this is to deny that the American financial system has enormous flexibility and versatility. In the next chapter we shall consider the most promising answer to the threat of ever growing private sector debt, the attempt to change debt into equity (or other tradable instruments) and so securitize financial flows. But securitization will never be a complete solution. The weaknesses of deposit-taking institutions will remain, enfeebling the whole American financial system. As banks and thrifts are overwhelmed by mounting interest on bad loans made in the past, their ability to extend credit for profitable and worthwhile new business ventures will be impaired. The financial system will become both less successful in allocating resources and more vulnerable to political intervention. In this sense, high real interest rates are profoundly subversive of such basic characteristics of the American economy as private property and free markets.

Indeed, we have here another irony of supply-side economics. Because of the effect of fiscal deficits on real interest rates, the problems of private and public debt intersect. In principle, the supply-siders are strong defenders of market capitalism. In practice, they have favoured macroeconomic policies which have increased real interest rates and so made it more difficult for market capitalism to work effectively. Supply-side economies has proved to be an intellectual curse, not only on the American political process, but also on the American private sector.

PART IV

The Debt Dilemma: a Global Perspective

8

The Challenge to Market Capitalism

I

The three areas of debt growth in the late 1970s and the 1980s have not been independent. The increase in public debt in the developed countries, by weakening investor confidence in governments' long-run commitment to sound money, was instrumental in causing a rise in real interest rates. The rise in real interest rates then recoiled on policy-makers by aggravating the difficulties of fiscal management and undermining the solvency of other debtors, both in the private sector and abroad. This deterioration in solvency was harshest in its impact on dollar debtors, reflecting the exceptional sharpness of the increase in real dollar interest rates between the late 1970s and early 1980s. It has hit both sovereign borrowers in the Third World and private sector borrowers within the USA. The mismanagement of the public household in developed countries, the boom and bust in sovereign lending, and the leveraging of the American private sector are closely related variants of a common theme.

The closeness of their relationship is suggested by the proximity of certain key dates. We suggested in chapter 3 that Volcker's move to reserve targetting on 6 October 1979 was the watershed between the low-real-interest-rate, rising-inflation 1970s and the high-real-interest-rate, falling-inflation 1980s. Dollar interest rates in real terms, as measured by the difference between prime rate and the increase in the producer price index, reached 10 per cent shortly afterwards in 1981. It is striking that 1981 was the year that the USA's debt/income ratio, which had been stable for decades, first began to edge upwards, while the sequence of subsequent events quickly reflected the change in the interest rate environment.

In November 1981 *The Atlantic Monthly* published an interview with budget director Stockman in which he warned that the Reagan administration had failed to restrict government expenditure. The interview was the first sign of anxiety about the state of American public finances which has continued to the present. In July 1982 Penn Square Bank failed. Apart from an exceptional case in 1974, it was the first significant bank failure since the 1930s and marked the beginning of a still unchecked rise in the number of US problem banks. In August 1982 Mexico announced that it could not service its foreign currency debt. The news inaugurated the Third World debt crisis, since it was followed by a batch of similar announcements from other developing countries' governments. Clearly, the three forms of debt problem examine in this book started more or less simultaneously. Their conjunction in late 1981 and 1982 was not an accident, but must instead be attributed to the shared impact of very high real dollar interest rates.

It could be argued that common timing does not necessarily imply common causality. However, there is another important reason for regarding the three apparently distinct classes of debt difficulty as aspects of a single debt problem. It is that the debtors' plight had a similar structure in every one of the countries affected. In the Introduction we highlighted the contrast between the real interest rates facing a 'representative' dollar borrower and those confronting an indebted commodity producer. The representative borrower had to pay an average of 9.6 per cent a year between 1981 and 1986, which – although a heavy burden by all past standards – could nevertheless be viewed as compensation for the years of low or negative real rates in the 1970s. But commodity producers had a much tougher time. For them the average real interest rate over the same period was 14.1 per cent.

A corollary of the more severe interest burden on commodity producers was that they experienced relatively greater strain in servicing debt. In the developing countries it was the commodity-exporting nations, particularly those dependent on a single export (oil, as in the case of Mexico or Venezuela) or a limited range of exports (farm products in Argentina, copper and other minerals in Chile), which ran into most trouble. Countries such as Brazil and South Korea, with a diversified mixture of export products and a high proportion of manufactured to total exports, were generally more successful. Similarly, within the USA it was the commodity-producing regions which experienced the toughest financial conditions. Roughly speaking, the central areas (the Farm Belt of the Midwest, the Oil Patch in the Southwest, the states with large mining industries in the Rockies) were depressed, while the two coasts (the East Coast with its wide range of manufacturing industries, financial services and high-tech, and the West Coast also with diversified manufacturing and high-tech) remained prosperous. These patterns are not coincidental. The government of

Argentina faced essentially the same hostile forces, in terms of high interest rates and weak food prices, as farmers in the Midwest; the Chilean government had to grapple with the financial consequences of low copper and molybdenum prices in much the same way as did such major US mining companies as Phelps Dodge and Amax; Mexican businessmen were nervous about the collapse in oil prices in 1986 for essentially the same reasons as Texan real estate developers.

The parallels between the financial traumas confronting highly borrowed commodity producers throughout the world argue against the view that the several problems had distinct and separate causes. Equally it is implausible to claim that the deterioration in the relationship between interest rates and growth rates (called the 'fiscal terms of trade' in this book), which happened in most of the developed countries over roughly the same period, was the result of isolated forces operating independently in each of them. Instead, it should be understood as the result of a common tendency to increase budget deficits, reinforced in the early 1980s by the international impact of the large American Federal deficit in a world of increasingly free capital flows. In short, the debt problems of the 1980s are rightly interpreted as a systemic failure and not as the consequence of a large number of independent commercial and political errors of judgement. The evidence is overwhelming that the origins of this systemic failure are to be sought in the uniquely high real interest rates of recent years.

In the final section of this concluding chapter we shall ask what policy approaches might bring real interest rates to a lower and historically more normal level. There are some promising signs, but they are not enough. Real interest rates remain unacceptably high in the major currencies, while on most of the recognized measures – the ratio of public debt to national income in the more prodigal industrial nations, the ratio of external debt to exports in the leading indebted developing nations and the domestic debt/income ratio in the USA – the global debt problem is still worsening. But there has been one strand of sanguine, even hopeful, comment. Its gist is that the debt crisis has been around for over five years, some of the worst horrors are now out into the open and yet the world economy carries on somehow. There is particular relief that decisions by large international banks to make provisions against part of their Third World debt in the middle of 1987 have been received calmly. Citicorp was the first to take this step, announcing on 19 May that it would bolster its loan loss reserves by $2.5b against anticipated problems with $15b of loans to less-developed countries. Contrary to some doom-laden prognoses, the banks' provisioning has not been followed by global financial collapse or, indeed, by anything more notable than a surge in the price of bank shares. It is very important, as an antidote to premature complacency, to understand the limits of this apparent easing of the world's debt worries.

The illusion of improvement arises because the term 'the debt crisis' has been used – interchangeably and confusingly – for two distinct problems. The first is the excessive growth in the amount of money owed by ultimate borrowers (individuals, companies, governments); the second is the threat to financial institutions who may be forced out of business by the defaults of these ultimate borrowers. It is true that the second problem would disappear if a solution were found to the first. But it is not true that the first problem would disappear if a solution were found to the second. As the first problem is by far the more serious, no one should be misled by the continued soundness of large international banks into thinking that the debt crisis is over. Nevertheless, the ability of the banking system to withstand the costs of substantial bad debt provisions is impressive. Although it is far from being the end of the war, it is undoubtedly a notable victory in the plan of campaign pursued by private sector financial institutions to manage and survive the debt problems of the 1980s. The banks' broader strategy, and the role of securitization in it, deserve a section of their own.

II

Securitization is best understood as a response to the lack of capital in banks and other deposit-taking institutions. In 1981 and 1982, with the onset of a whole range of new financial uncertainties, banks realized that the assumptions of the immediate post-war decades were no longer valid. The deterioration in loan loss experience obliged them, on grounds of simple business prudence, to reverse the thinning of their equity cushions which had been continuous since the 1960s. Instead they had to fatten up capital/asset ratios as insulation against the colder business environment. Steps in this direction would have been necessary anyway because regulators had become alarmed at the erosion of capital. In December 1981 the three federal banking agencies in the USA – the Federal Deposit Insurance Corporation, the Federal Reserve and the Office of the Comptroller of the Currency – introduced precise guidelines on bank capital for the first time. The minimum capital/asset ratio was set at 5 per cent, but the 17 largest banks had to be exempted for the time being. Their capital/asset ratio of 3.6 per cent could not have been quickly raised to a healthy level without serious disruption of their activities.[1] Although the capital problem was most visible in the USA, in other countries also banks and regulators agreed that capital/asset ratios had to be strengthened.

Just as the need to rebuild the old balance sheet fortifications was perceived as urgent, the task of reconstruction became more difficult. The straightforward way to increase equity would have been to withhold profits from shareholders and retain them within the business. But, now that loan losses were being recorded on a larger scale, there were fewer profits to retain. The dilemma facing bank managements could be resolved in only one way. Since access to new capital was restricted, capital/asset ratios had to be increased by action to trim assets. If it proved difficult to achieve an actual cut in balance sheet size because the addition of interest charges tended constantly to expand the assets total, banks should at least try to moderate the growth in lending.

This involved a complete and abrupt change in management philosophy. As we saw in chapter 4, throughout the 1960s and 1970s it had been common practice to maximize profits growth by the aggressive marketing of loans. A shift towards a more conservative policy on asset growth would have been at odds with the expansionist ethos inherited from the boom years. It would undoubtedly have been unpopular in most banks. (Apart from anything else, the jets, first-class hotels and exotic places had been quite good fun.) Fortunately, a new kind of business opportunity emerged. The banks' withdrawal from traditional lending did not mean that the scope for new credit business had disappeared. On the contrary, some companies and governments still wanted to borrow money, and other companies and governments still wanted to lend it. The solution was for banks to arrange for borrowers and lenders to get together, have transactions between them registered as negotiable instruments ('securities') and take a fee for the work. Ideally, securities would come to be held by non-bank organizations, where they were off banks' balance sheets and so had no impact on capital/asset ratios. The beauty of securitization was therefore that it allowed banks to continue to earn profits from the same customer base as before, but to avoid any deterioration in balance sheet ratios. Banks could reconcile their continued eagerness to expand with the need to protect their fragile equity position.

The main arena of securitization has been the Euro-markets. They had been the principal channel for the sovereign lending boom of the 1970s, but – following the revision of expectations about the credit-worthiness of Third World borrowers in 1981 and 1982 – they had to find new outlets for the available funds. The ensuing fierce competition and constant product innovation made the Euro-markets the cheapest source of funds for many multinational companies and agencies, and even for some governments in the developed world. By the mid-1980s these highly regarded borrowers dominated Euro-market borrowing. This change in the markets' users, like the switch to off-balance-sheet business, has greatly improved the international financial system's ability to endure shocks. There are now better quality claims on more trustworthy entities than before, while it matters less if investors (who have diversified portfolios and other resources) lose money on securities than if banks (who have only their limited equity base) lose money on loans.

Indeed, the extent of the move towards securitization is a remarkable demonstration of the international financial system's adaptability. The Organization for Economic Cooperation and Development (OECD) has estimated that in 1981 the international markets raised $200.5b, with $147.7b in the form of loans, mostly syndicated credits to sovereign borrowers. In contrast, in 1985, out of the $256.5b raised by the international markets, syndicated credits accounted for only $42.0b or 16.4 per cent, while securities in one form or another represented 79.5 per cent.[2] Instrumental in this transformation have been the activities of American (and, to a lesser extent, Japanese and European) securities houses. Unlike banks they do not lend money in their own name and keep it on their balance sheets. Instead they specialize in securities business, both organizing new issues and trading existing ones. One of their great advantages over the banks has been that they do not have to keep large amounts of capital as a protective reserve against potential losses on old loans. In this respect the debt crisis – which, of course, largely explains why those old loans have gone bad – has been an important catalyst behind the process of securitization.[3]

Similar forces have been behind the securitization of American housing finance. Although the ability of savings and loan associations to lend was increasingly constrained in the 1980s by balance sheet worries and capital inadequacy, the American public still had an appetite for new mortgage credit. In the same way that the international banks now promote off-balance-sheet business in the Euro-markets, the thrifts no longer satisfy all of this appetite directly, but instead arrange mortgages and sell them in 'pools' to investors. The pools of mortgage liabilities are packaged in the form of securities and guaranteed by one of three government-sponsored institutions, the Federal National Mortgage Association, the Federal Home Loan Mortgage Corporation (FHLMC) and the Government National Mortgage Association. (The three are known colloquially as 'Fannie Mae', 'Freddie Mac' and 'Ginnie Mae'.) These institutions started trading mortgage-backed securities among themselves in 1949, many years before interest rate fluctuations became a serious problem for the savings and loan industry. But their role expanded swiftly in the 1980s, as interest rates became more volatile. A vital change was the introduction of 'collateralized mortgage obligations' (CMOs) by the FHLMC in 1983. As CMOs were structured more attractively for investors than previous types of mortgage security, they were more widely held and could be bought and sold more easily. More than $1,000b in new and existing mortgage securities were traded in 1985, six times the 1981 trading volume of just over $160b. Meanwhile issues of mortgage-backed securities climbed from $27b in 1981 to $145b in 1985.[4]

Securitization has considerable potential for further growth. In the USA it has spread from housing finance to car loans, computer leasing and real estate projects. One observer has gone so far as to state that, against such competition, traditional banking is doomed and 'will have a life cycle just as the steel industry did'.[5] But, despite this radical assessment, securitization must be kept in perspective. It does not end risk, but instead transfers it from banks who cannot absorb losses to investors who can. As we have argued, it alleviates only one aspect of the debt problem, the lack of sufficient capital in deposit-taking institutions. It does not eliminate the debt problem as a whole, which consists, more fundamentally, in the worsening indebtedness of a wide range of ultimate borrowers. There is one kind of debt for which securitization is not relevant at all. Securitization converts claims on future streams of interest income which are difficult to buy and sell (bank loans) into claims on streams of future interest income which are easy to buy and sell (securities). But most government debt in the developed countries is issued initially in the form of bonds which, from day one, are traded in sophisticated capital markets. So securitization has nothing extra to contribute here. It will play no part in meeting the threat of rapidly growing public debt in a number of the industrialized countries.

Moreover, as long as loans are converted into interest-bearing securities, the problem of too rapidly accumulating interest persists. For example, because second-ranking US companies now issue high-cost junk bonds instead of incurring high-cost bank debt, no bank is at risk if they cannot service the debt. But, since the companies still have to service the debt, high real interest rates are as much a menace to them as before. One way to take the sting out of high real interest rates is to convert bank loans (or interest-bearing securities) into equities. Debt/equity swaps in Third World countries ilustrate the possibilities, although – as we emphasized at the end of chapter 5 – they emphatically are not a complete solution to the debt difficulties of the Third World. Perhaps it is superfluous to add that, because governments do not make profits and so cannot have equity liabilities, debt/equity swaps are no answer to the public debt explosion in developed countries.

III

Securitization and the substitution of equity for debt can be viewed as the private sector's response to the excessively high real interest rates caused by public sector financial mismanagement over the last 30 years. They could be described, perhaps rather glibly, as market solutions to the problem of debt growth. By dispersing risk more evenly throughout the economy, they undoubtedly strengthen the financial system and reduce the vulnerability of market capitalism to financial shocks. But it would be wrong to overestimate the contribution that securitization can make in this role or to underestimate the gravity of the threat posed by runaway debt growth to free market mechanisms.

The challenge to market mechanisms is particularly serious in the USA. The constant expansion of debt in housing finance, real estate and farming has been taken to such extremes that both borrowers and lenders have sought bail-outs from government or government-backed agencies. The distressed sectors are important enough in terms of votes to be able to influence the outcome of Congressional and Presidential elections. Public money has therefore been made available to help them, sometimes on a large scale. Various farm aids urged by Congress and conceded by President Reagan in the months leading up to the 1986 Congressional elections could have a cost approaching $50b over a five-year period. On 21 August 1986 *The Financial Times* had a story under the heading 'Money no object as Washington tries to boost farm exports'.

The market economy is threatened in several ways by a crude resort to political bribery of this kind. Most obviously, too great a readiness to throw government money at private sector problems undermines the discipline of market forces. It weakens the connection between effort and reward which is one of the most basic attributes of market capitalism. If taken to extremes, companies come to resemble industrial junkies, addicted to continued injections of public money. Eventually they put more energy into persuading friendly politicians to sponsor their interests than into persuading customers to buy their products. The rigours of the market are replaced by lobbying, pressure group politics and Congressional infighting, and may terminate in graft and corruption. The USA may come to imitate the Italian model of the government as 'hidden banker', with the public sector handing out special grants and cheap loans because the private sector financial system is too hamstrung by official restrictions to compete effectively. Even worse the USA could see the beginning of a deterioration in business ethics towards the Latin American level. It may be exaggeration to draw parallels between the various frauds practised by so-called 'entrepreneurs' in the US savings and loan industry in the mid-1980s and the organized theft of sovereign loan proceeds in Latin American in the late 1970s and early 1980s. But the similiarity between 'screwy deals' in Texas real estate and the manipulation of *empresas de papel* in Argentina and Chile is too obvious to overlook.

American attempts to ease the debt problems of key producer groups by public subsidy are harmful internationally as well as domestically. Clearly, the more money that the US government provides to farmers, the cheaper are its farm products on world markets and the harsher is the competitive environment for other agricultural exporters. The countries of the European Economic Community (EEC) could respond by bolstering their expensive and misguided Common Agricultural Policy, countering extra American subsidies by supplements to their own. The result would be to penalize the world's most efficient agricultural producers, which include such traditional exporters of food as Australia and New Zealand. The financial strains associated with falling food prices then spread to these countries, adding a further dimension to the global debt problem.

Indeed, in the general elections which Australia and New Zealand held in the summer of 1987, financial stress in the farm sector was one of the most controversial themes. The grain belt of northern New South Wales exported more than 80 per cent of its wheat production, making it acutely vulnerable to US and EEC subsidies. Over half of its farms were classified as being 'at risk', which meant that they had zero or negative income (after deducting interest charges) and owed 30 per cent of the value of their equity. As one angry and bankrupt farmer remarked, very much in the vein of Steinbeck and *The Grapes of Wrath*, 'If I was going down the gurgler because I was a lousy farmer, or blew it on the horses I would be insignificant. But there are a lot of other blokes who bought land before interest rates went up, and they're also in big trouble.'[6] In the mid-1980s the plight of New Zealand's rural sector has, if anything, been even worse. The government of David Lange cut farm subsidies as part of a more general programme to eliminate distortions and inefficiencies in the economy. The removal of subsidies precipitated a slump in land prices at exactly the same time that financial liberalization and tight monetary policy caused interest rates to soar above 20 per cent.[7] The passage of events closely resembled that in the USA in the early 1980s. There should also be no doubt that American farm policy, while perhaps alleviating the debt crisis in the Midwest, has aggravated it in Australia and New Zealand.

Subsidies to agriculture are permitted by the General Agreement of Tariffs and Trade (GATT), the organization set up after the War to oversee the international trading order and to promote moves towards free trade. But they are antithetical to the ideals of open competition and limited government intervention which underlie the GATT. Indeed, they can be seen as part of a larger threat to the post-war international economic system, as some of its basic principles are being increasigly violated and ignored. The key principles – as we saw in chapter 4 – are that economic relations between countries should be conducted in a multilateral spirit and be free from discrimination. To elaborate, if countries restrain the flow of goods and capital across their frontiers, they must not apply different measures of restraint to one country (or group of countries) from those applied to others. A country can, if it wishes, be friendly or hostile to the rest of the world in its economic relations. But it must be equally friendly or equally hostile to all other nations and must not pick particular allies or make particular enemies. The aim is to prevent a recurrence of the 1930s, when the Depression caused almost universal payments difficulties and provoked (as in the German case) the formation of clearly defined and deliberately discriminatory currency blocs. (Currency blocs must be distinguished from exchange rate systems such as the European Monetary System. The hallmark of a currency bloc is that payments between members are reasonably free but payments between members and non-members are subject to restrictions which may be severe.)

Tension over farm subsidies between the USA, the EEC and rich nations such as Australia and New Zealand is important, but it is a sideshow compared with the challenge to the international economic order posed by the Third World debt crisis; and while the USA, EEC, Australia and New Zealand are too well-established members of the rich man's club to question the principles of multilateralism, the countries of Latin America have no such automatic loyalties. For example, Argentina must be even angrier than the Australasian countries about the USA's decision to increase agricultural support. With its debt/export ratio at nearly 10, it must also be less prepared than them to respect international financial etiquette. Suppose that Argentina frankly and aggressively repudiates its debts to the USA, Europe and Japan, and invites sanctions of the kind (sequestration of foreign assets, seizure of exports) threatened by Mr McNamar in October 1983. Suppose also that it simultaneously informs its two neighbours, Brazil and Uruguay, that it intends to maintain regular payments to them and that Brazil and Uruguay are up-to-date with their payments to the industrialized West.

Then it is difficult to see how – unless the Western nations, presumably led by the USA, widen the dispute – the sanctions could be made to work. If Argentina transfers its foreign exchange reserves from the US Federal Reserve to the Brazilian central bank before it repudiates, the American government cannot lay its hands on them. Equally, it would be futile for the USA to warn that it might impound products marked 'Made in Argentina' and prevent payment to Argentine exporters. Argentine exporters would merely ship their products through Uruguay and Brazil, where they would be given labels saying 'Made in Uruguay' or 'Made in Brazil', and the US authorities would be obliged to let them pass without hindrance. More generally, trade and financial sanctions against any one nation are ineffective unless they are enforced by every other nation. If the USA has unrestricted financial relations with Uruguay, and Uruguay has unrestricted financial relations with Argentina, citizens of the USA can make payments to citizens of Argentina with relatively little inconvenience. All that is required is to set up an appropriate series of intermediaries. It is simple enough for an Argentine company to establish a subsidiary in Montevideo and open a bank account into which money from the USA can be credited. For the American government's policy to succeed, the USA has to persuade Uruguay to introduce sanctions as well. But Uruguay has no reason to join in if payments between it and Argentina are regular and normal.

There is an obvious risk of regionalized financial tension, with accompanying pressure for the formation of a currency bloc. If Argentina, Brazil and Uruguay recognize debts between themselves, and are determined to continue doing so, the industrial nations can enforce financial sanctions against any one only by enforcing sanctions against all three. The USA, Europe and Japan may not have a specific quarrel with Uruguay and Brazil, but Uruguay and Brazil are inevitably drawn into the dispute with Argentina against their will. They may stop making payments to the industrial nations not because of inability or unwillingness to pay, but because they value good political links with Argentina more highly than orderly financial relations with the industrial world. Argentina, Brazil and Uruguay may decide to establish a currency bloc, not subject to International Monetary Fund (IMF) rules and in open defiance of the West's attempts since 1945 to forge a truly multilateral payments system.

Although this discussion of currency blocs has been to a degree hypothetical, it is certainly not remote from practical realities. In particular, it helps explain why the Presidents of Argentina and Brazil signed 12 commercial protocols on 29 July 1986 to encourage regional economic integration. There are already extensive trade agreements between Uruguay and Brazil, while the last few years have seen much economic diplomacy between the three countries and the rest of Latin

America to further the cause of a meaningful Latin American common market.[8]

The boom in sovereign lending was intended, at least in part, to bind the Third World closer to the developed industrial nations. But, with regional currency blocs and common markets likely to become an increasingly attractive option to countries in Latin America, Africa and parts of Asia, the bust in sovereign lending will ultimately have quite the opposite result. Instead of being nearer to the First World, the Third World will be more separate, and perhaps more resentful, than before. The multilateral payments mechanism promoted by the USA and its allies, which is unquestionably one of the greatest achievements of the post-war period, will be worn away by a process of attrition, as an ever-rising number of developing countries indicate that they cannot meet their debt obligations. At the end of 1986 57 countries, equivalent to two-fifths of the IMF's developing country membership, had arrears outstanding on their external debt. By contrast, a decade earlier there had been fewer than 20 such countries.[9] Although the situation today does not have the same sombre military and political overtones as in the 1930s, the fragmentation of international payments will disturb trade flows, undermine the international division of labour and reduce living standards. Third World debtors will suffer much more from this process than developed creditor nations. If nothing is done to stop it, trade disruption between developed and developing countries will be one of the most destructive results of the debt crisis.

IV

High real interest rates undermine market capitalism by necessitating the injection of public money to bail out highly borrowed producer groups; they also weaken, by distancing over-indebted Third World nations from their richer trading partners, the liberal and non-discriminatory international economic order which has been basic to post-war prosperity. In other words, they not only cause debt – in all the various contexts we have considered – to continue to grow faster than incomes, exports, assets or, indeed, whatever the relevant measure of ability to pay may be, they also, and most critically, represent a threat to the continued success of market economies. The 1930s were the greatest setback ever inflicted to the ideals of market freedom and liberal internationalism. Widespread defaults on private debt in the USA and elsewhere provoked governments to introduce regulations, controls and bureaucracies which had never previously been thought necessary. Roosevelt's New Deal was the largest example of this trend, but all the industrial nations saw a new enthusiasm for planning and state control. Meanwhile at the international level debt moratoria by major trading nations were accompanied by protectionism, exchange controls and economic isolationism. It should be emphasized that, at root, the financial problems of the 1930s stemmed from falling prices and the resulting sharp increases in real interest rates. Could the 1990s – again under the impact of high real interest rates – be equally disastrous for market capitalism?

Merely to ask this question is to demonstrate the importance of neutralizing the potential damage from high real interest rates. The dangers are serious enough that policy-makers may legitimately consider allowing other economic problems to worsen if, by so doing, they can mitigate the debt trap. There are certain trade-offs of this kind for them to consider. In particular, as was suggested in chapter 5, a deliberate policy of commodity inflation could be a solution. If commodity inflation of 20 to 25 per cent a year were accompanied by low nominal interest rates, heavily indebted commodity producers in both the Third World and the USA would enjoy a radical improvement in their financial position.

To embrace inflation as an answer to the world's economic ills would, of course, be a pathetic sequel to Volcker's long campaign against inflation from 1979 to 1987. The justification – that inflation is disagreeable, but mass insolvency and the disintegration of the post-war international payments system are intolerable – would in any case not be altogether convincing. Rapid inflation, like mounting debt, poses threats to the efficiency and integrity of market capitalism. Moreover, another episode of inflation at a pace similar to that in the late 1970s might have to be followed by another phase of very high real interest rates similar to those of the early and mid-1980s. The reason should be familiar from the argument in the early chapters of this book. Savers, notably in government bond markets, would suffer from another lurch to high inflation and would become yet more mistrustful of the political process. They would want another jump in nominal interest rates, similar to that between 1979 to 1981, to give protection against both the current inflation and possible even sharper inflation surges in future. In short, rapid inflation in the late 1980s might liberate over-indebted commodity producers from debt burdens dating back to the 1970s. But it would set the scene for a new tyranny of high real interest rates at some stage in the 1990s.

When relations between borrowers and lenders have once been poisoned by inflation, a long period of financial stability is needed to remove the toxin of inflation expectations. To engineer sharp rises in the inflation rate might cut real interest rates in the short run, but the aggravation of tensions between borrowers and lenders would necessitate high real interest rates over the long run. Indeed, for the USA, or any other developed country, to use inflation as an instrument for redistributing debt burdens would be an unforgivable act of financial hooliganism. As the plight of many Latin American countries today illustrates only too well, it could wreck established patterns of savings and investment, and permanently reduce the sustainable long-term growth rate of the US economy. It would also disqualify the dollar from the reserve currency role it has held for almost 50 years.

Frank advocacy of inflation is unusual. However, there are many arguments with a latent inflation bias which are presented with more subtlety and appear attractive in public debate. One of the most popular proposals for relieving the debt crisis is that large countries with low budget deficits should enact programmes of fiscal reflation. The objective would be to boost demand, raise the growth rate of the world economy and stimulate higher commodity prices. This proposal, virtually always addressed to the governments of Japan and West Germany, has been advocated most prominently by the Reagan administration, but it has had many other supporters. Perhaps the most surprising was the IMF in its April 1986 publication on the *World Economic Outlook*. Chapter 4 contained a section on the effect of postponing fiscal consolidation in Japan and Europe and suggested that an increase in budget deficits amounting to 1 per cent of GDP 'might increase the developing countries' export revenue by 1–1½ per cent after a period of two or three years'. (This increase was relative to a baseline scenario which included a move towards budget balance in the USA.)[10] As the IMF rarely favours a relaxation of fiscal policy in any circumstances, its argument for larger budget deficits in this instance needs to be examined carefully.

The main objection to fiscal reflation outside the USA is the same as that to large budget deficits within the USA. Prospective investors in government debt, and indeed savers of all kinds, are worried by the long-run inflationary potential of increased deficits. They require higher real interest rates on new bond issues and other savings vehicles. The increase in real interest rates spreads to all financial transactions in the currency concerned, including external debts. Of course, this effect is less serious if the relevant debts are denominated in dollars, while the increase in real interest rates occurs in yen and deutschmarks. But the fact is that – in a world of considerable capital mobility between countries – real interest rates in dollars, yen and deutschmarks are related. Fiscal reflation outside the USA will keep real dollar interest rates higher than would otherwise have been necessary. More specifically, although a 1 or 1½ per cent rise in the ratio of budget deficits to

GDP causes higher commodity prices, it also causes higher interest rates. There may not be any net benefit to Third World debtors.

Indeed, there is a general argument to suggest that the debtors will be worse off. Fiscal reflation, when it takes the form of a permanent increase in the ratio of the budget deficit to GDP, may be followed by a once and for all increase in the price of commodities. But it will not lead to persistently rising commodity prices. In other words, its effect will be on the *level*, not on the *rate of change*, of commodity prices. In contrast, higher budget deficits have an enduring impact on investor attitudes and will therefore be associated with permanently higher real interest rates. Of course, if fiscal reflation is accompanied (except in the short run when commodity prices are moving to their new higher level) by an unchanged rate of commodity price inflation and increased real interest rates, its long-run consequences will be unfavourable for debtors. Interestingly, the IMF retracted the argument for fiscal reflation in its 1987 *World Economic Outlook*. 'It has to be acknowledged . . . that the scope for easing fiscal policy is limited if, as the staff believes appropriate, the goal of medium-term budgetary strengthening is to be adhered to.'[11]

Fiscal reflation is not the answer to the debt problems of the Third World, while it would plainly aggravate the difficulties of public debt management in the industrialized nations. There is an air of unreality about its constant advocacy by many politicians and economists who ought to know better. But there is also an air of unreality about another widely favoured approach, the plan proposed by US Treasury Secretary Baker at the annual IMF–World Bank meeting in September 1985. One of the difficulties about discussing it today is to know whether to refer to it in the present or past tense. Leading Western governments, the World Bank and the IMF talk about it in the present tense as if it were a living reality, whereas the press and Third World governments mention it in the past tense as if it had been a dead letter almost from the outset. For the sake of wishing the Plan well, the present tense will be used here.

The Baker Plan makes more money available to over-borrowed developing countries on condition that they introduce policies which strengthen the free market and promote economic efficiency. This is a great merit since, as we saw in chapter 5, the deterioration in internal productive efficiency in many Third World countries may prove to be the most harmful consequence of the external shock inflicted by the debt crisis. Long-run structural reforms are now as necessary to the successful resolution of the debt problem as short-run balance-of-payments adjustment. However, the Baker Plan also has a great weakness. Although the essence of the debt crisis is that debt is growing too rapidly, the Baker Plan does nothing to stop debt from growing. On the contrary, it explicitly establishes institutional arrangements to facilitate new lending. This cannot be right in the long run. A problem which arose because there was too much lending cannot be solved by lending more. Perhaps it is unnecessary to add that the Baker Plan relates solely to Third World debt. It does not have anything to contribute to easing the pressures on public finances in the industrial nations or to alleviating the difficulties of private sector debtors in the USA or other advanced nations such as Australia and New Zealand.

V

Indeed, to assign the Baker Plan to the Third World debt problem is misjudged in another respect, in that it is based on a false compartmentalization of the debt difficulties of the 1980s. As we have emphasized throughout this book, the three aspects of the global debt problem need to be viewed as an integrated whole. If it is accepted that they have a common cause in high real interest rates and that they will worsen continually while real interest rates remain too onerous, a reduction in real interest rates is a necessary and sufficient answer to all three. Heavy emphasis should be placed on the need for any move to lower real interest rates to be durable and authentic. It should reflect progress on the underlying structural causes of dear money, not a hasty resort to artificial solutions involving administrative controls on maximum interest rates or other government-imposed regulations.

The main parts of a programme to tackle the structural causes of high real interest rates are easy enough to specify as a logical exercise, but may be difficult to implement in practice. The first element must be that the governments of the main industrial nations pursue responsible budgetary policies. True enough, Japan and most countries in Western Europe have already accomplished 'fiscal consolidation', to use to IMF's term. But too often the governments concerned have been diffident and apologetic about their budgetary achievements, perhaps because they do not want to offend the many American supporters of fiscal reflation.

Indeed, the constant hectoring of Japan and West Germany for their cautious fiscal policies is one of most unhealthy features of the contemporary debate about international economic policy. Instead of berating them, international organizations should uphold them as models for the rest of the world to follow; and instead of trying to camouflage the soundness of their budgetary positions, the two countries should be articulate and propagandist about the virtues of small budget deficits. A move towards lower real interest rates will be easier to achieve if savers can be persuaded that governments are in earnest about fiscal discipline. It is altogether misguided for governments which are good fiscal disciplinarians to pretend that they are not. By so doing, they lose potentially substantial benefits in terms of more favourable financial psychology. Savers, instead of being converted into governments' financial allies, remain suspicious about officialdom's intentions and real interest rates stay higher than is necessary.

The argument can be taken further. To restore confidence in their financial reliability the governments of the major industrial nations should consider running budget surpluses on a systematic basis. Although this suggestion may seem heretical to academic Keynesian economists in the English-speaking countries, it is not, by historical standards, a particularly daring proposal. We saw in chapter 1 that the USA has repaid its national debt twice in its two centuries of existence and in chapter 2 that West Germany and Japan had budget surpluses for much of the 1950s and 1960s. The rise of the USA to world economic pre-eminence while it was practising traditional fiscal conservatism and the spectacular growth enjoyed by West Germany and Japan in the first 20 years after the Second World War suggest that budget surpluses can be good for economies. No doubt many Keynesian economists in the USA and the UK will protest that a move from deficit to surplus on public sector finances in the large countries would lead to a substantial withdrawal of demand from the world economy. They might even start squealing about a possible international recession, the consequent risk of collapse in commodity prices and the dangers of an intensification of Third World debt anxieties. These warnings have some cogency, but they are far from being a decisive objection to fiscal restraint. It should be a sufficient answer that, if monetary policy is simultaneously managed to encourage lower real interest rates, a cutback in spending by governments creates an opportunity for extra spending by the private sector. More fundamentally, whatever the short-run and essentially cyclical problems of adjustment to budget surpluses, policy-makers should in present circumstances concentrate on ensuring an appropriate structure of financial flows, and in particular viable patterns of debt growth, over the medium term. A tendency to focus exclusively on transient demand-management issues has become the bane of economic policy formation in the large Western countries.

A world-wide return to the old-time fiscal religion has to be the main item in a programme to reduce real interest rates. Also important, although less noticed in public debate, is the need for tax systems to become more neutral in their treatment of savings, investment and consumption, and so less supportive of the credit demands which keep interest rates high and drive the growth of debt. The virtues of neutral, non-discriminatory tax regimes have tended to be undervalued in the post-war period because of a universal belief that investment has special properties as an engine of economic growth and should therefore be favoured by the tax system. Until the 1980s the enthusiasm for investment and the associated drift in tax policy towards ever stronger incentives for expenditure on capital goods were most pronounced in the nations with the worst inferiority complexes about their slow rates of economic growth. The UK was the outstanding example, but it was joined by the USA in the late 1970s. As companies and individuals frequently had to borrow to exploit the incentives, the promotion of investment by the tax system tended to stimulate credit. Moreover, the granting of new reliefs for capital expenditure, like the offer of more direct industrial assistance in the form of subsidies and cheap loans, had a revenue cost which had to be recouped by higher tax rates. By increasing the value of the interest deductions from taxable income which had long been part of most countries' fiscal arrangements, these higher rates again increased the appeal of borrowing.

Chapter 3 discussed these trends in the USA. It was explained how, during the 1970s, borrowing became steadily more advantageous because of 'bracket creep' and the proliferation of tax shelters. The 1981 Economic Recovery Tax Act crowned the process, by adding invest-ment tax credits to existing investment incentives. This piece of legislation therefore had an unfavourable influence on real interest rates not only because of its disastrous effect on the budget deficit, but also because it reduced the post-tax cost of investment and so encouraged credit growth. Fortunately, in the mid-1980s governments began to reappraise the wisdom of meddling with tax systems in the pursuit of growth objectives. A precedent was set by the British government in 1984 when it announced a comprehensive reform of company taxation which cut the standard rate of tax on profits and went far to end fiscal discrimination in favour of investment. But much more important, because of the wide international use of the dollar, was the tax reform package passed by the US Congress in the summer of 1986.

It was described in chapter 3 as 'the most promising development in American economic policy in the 1980s'. This may seem fulsome, but the praise is logically compelled by the argument of this book. By ending a host of credit-inducing features of the previous tax system, tax reform could lead to a reversal of some of the most worrying behaviour patterns of the American public in the 1970s and early 1980s. It was tempting for individual Americans to believe in the 1970s, with low real interest rates and soaring prices for hard assets, that they could become rich by borrowing. There was always and obviously a fallacy in thinking that the nation as a whole could become rich in the same way, as it could only borrow from itself. However, it was not misguided to believe that the private sector as a whole could make itself better off by borrowing, because higher indebtedness increased the value of the tax deductibility of interest. The evil went further. By eroding the tax base, the growth of private debt widened the budget deficit and so caused faster growth of public debt. In this way the problem of runaway private debt interacted with the problem of deteriorating public sector finances.

As we saw in chapter 3, tax reform cuts into this problem like a pair of scissors. One blade is the removal of the tax deductions; the other is the reduction, because of lower tax rates, in the value of those deductions that remain. Already in 1987 several of the expected changes in private sector spending and borrowing patterns have occurred. The growth of consumer credit has been very slow by the standards of recent years; sales of cars have been depressed, largely because interest on loans for car purchase is no longer fully tax-deductible; and the debt/income ratio did not rise in the first half of the year. But these are only the first-round effects. Tax reform is to be phased in over five years. When the full impact on behaviour is registered in the late 1980s, the growth of credit and money may decelerate so drastically that the Federal Reserve is obliged to reduce interest rates in order to prevent a recession. Real interest rates should be permanently lower because one of the structural reasons for the excessive borrowing of the 1970s and early 1980s will have been removed.

Excessive private credit growth, however, has often been motivated by cruder considerations than the tax advantages. A recurrent feature of capitalist economies is the business cycle, with phases of above-trend growth being followed by others of below-trend growth, and their alternation being accompanied by large fluctuations in investor expectations. In the period when investors are most optimistic about the prospects for output and profits, which normally coincides with an acceleration in output growth as the upturn becomes well defined, asset prices may be rising more rapidly than is sustainable in the long run. The explanation may be that people, finding it difficult to distinguish between cycles and trends, are apt to assume that a high rate of increase in asset prices enjoyed in the last two or three years will continue indefinitely. As long as this expected rate of asset price appreciation is above the rate of interest, they increase their borrowings in order to acquire more assets. If the extra borrowing is from the banking system, more money is created and the addition of extra liquidity gives a new stimulus to the economy. The whole process, described with particular clarity by the Swedish economist Wicksell in his famous 1898 work *Geldzins und Güterpreise* is cumulative. To stop it running out of control a sharp increase in interest rates – to a level above the expected rate of asset price increases – is needed.

If central banks refrain from putting up interest rates at an early stage of speculative excitement, the interest rate increase ultimately needed to curb a cumulative process may have to be disproportionately large. With rampant expectations of ever-rising asset prices, a central bank may have no alternative to setting the rate of interest much above the trend rate of increase in incomes. But that clearly establishes the conditions for the debt trap. There is a consequent danger that, in the aftermath of a frenzied surge in asset prices driven by too much credit, debts cannot be paid and financial institutions go bust.

Central banks have a responsibility for preventing such cyclical swings in asset prices from becoming so violent that unsustainable expectations are fostered. In this book we have come across at least three examples of misjudged booms in private sector credit. In the 1920s banks in the USA lent too much to stockbrokers and financiers who used the money to drive up share prices; in the late 1970s they lent too much to investors in hard assets, which caused the prices of these assets to rise to a level unjustified by economic fundamentals; and in the mid-1980s they have, arguably, been too willing to provide financial support for the share price manipulations of men like Ivan Boesky. The mistakes of the 1920s and the late 1970s were followed by several years of damagingly high real interest rates. The mistakes of the mid-1980s, if such they prove to be, have been committed while real interest rates are already too high. The potential disturbance to the financial system is therefore even greater. It could prove embarrassing that some of the risk arbitrageurs, leveraged buy-out specialists and kindred operators so active in recent years have had close and well-publicized banking associations.

There is nothing new about the task of private sector credit management facing leading central banks today. Ever since their foundation central banks have had to worry about certain instabilities which seem to be inherent in the extension of credit and the business of banking. What is new is that investor expectations are, in some respects, more topsy-turvey now than ever before. The degeneration of the dollar on the foreign exchanges has undermined a key fixed point of reference for international investment, while the very high valuation now placed on corporate equity suggests a profound and unhealthy disillusionment with other savings vehicles such as bonds. The mood of innovation in financial markets has proliferated trading instruments in the form of options, futures and other products, and made it worthwhile to carry out unfamiliar strategies of risk management.[12] In this volatile environment there are new uncertainties about what constitutes excessive leverage and unsound lending. In the early nineteenth century Henry Thornton, one of the earliest writers on monetary theory, understood that the Bank of England had to keep the growth of private credit in line with the growth of the economy. In his 1802 *Inquiry into Paper Credit* he advised the Bank to 'limit the amount of paper issued, and to resort for this purpose, whenever the temptation to borrow is strong, to some effectual principle of restriction; in no case, however, materially to diminish the sum in circulation, but to let it vibrate only within certain limits' and 'to afford a slow and cautious extension of it, as the general trade of the kingdom enlarges itself'.[13] These maxims remain as relevant to central banks now as they were almost 200 years ago. The difference is that they are more difficult to apply.

Hopefully, a new fiscal rigour in North America, reinforced budgetary restraint in Europe and Japan, a world-wide move towards more neutral tax systems and greater care by central banks in the management of private sector credit may enable real interest rates to decline to about the same level as – or perhaps even to somewhat beneath – the trend growth rate of the world economy. This trend growth rate is at most 3–4 per cent a year. Indeed, if the argument of this book is accepted, it would be impossible for interest rates to exceed the growth rate of world income for several decades because of the accompanying unsustainable build-up of debt. It is not an accident that there has in the past been an observed tendency for real interest rates to gravitate towards a band of 2–4 per cent over very long periods. (De Gaulle called the 50 years of financial stability before 1914 the *epoque de trois pour cent*.[14]) A closer alignment between interest rates and the world growth rate is therefore almost a logical necessity over coming decades. But there are still many doubts about how and when policy-makers in the leading industrial nations will make the decisions needed to achieve the passage to lower real interest rates. Much is at stake, since the institutions of market capitalism cannot be reconciled with a prolonged period of real interest rates at present levels. Unless real interest rates fall back to the long-run historical average of 2–4 per cent, the debt dilemmas of the 1980s will worsen inexorably and uncontrollably into the 1990s and beyond.

Appendix: The Algebra of Debt Growth*

Let us call debt D. The change in debt has two parts, interest charges, which are equal to the rate of interest i multiplied by the debt D, and the primary financial balance, which may be denoted by B. Then

$$\mathrm{d}D = B + iD \tag{1}$$

where $\mathrm{d}D$ is the change in debt.

The growth rate of debt is

$$\frac{\mathrm{d}D}{D} = \frac{B}{D} + i \tag{2}$$

So the growth rate of debt exceeds the growth rate of income, which may be denoted by Y, if

$$\frac{B}{D} + i > \frac{\mathrm{d}Y}{Y} \tag{3}$$

In words, the relevant condition is that the growth rate of debt exceeds the growth rate of income if the sum of the ratio of the primary financial balance to debt and the rate of interest exceeds the growth rate of income. If the primary financial position is balanced, debt growth is unsustainable if the rate of interest exceeds the growth rate of income. These ideas apply to any debtor, whether it be a company, person, government or country. B serves the same role in the above algebra as the concept of primary fiscal balance in chapters 1, 2 and 3, the idea of net resource transfers in chapters 4 and 5, and the excess of rent over non-interest expenditure for the real estate developer in chapter 6.

---

* This appendix is loosely based on the author's 1986 evidence to the House of Commons Treasury and Civil Service Committee.

1. THE TAX OPTIONS FACING A GOVERNMENT WHEN INTEREST RATES ARE ABOVE GROWTH RATES

The algebraic argument behind the statement on p. 72 in chapter 2 is developed in this section. The primary fiscal deficit can be denoted by F. Then the change in public debt is

$$dD = F + iD \tag{4}$$

The ratio of public debt to income can be denoted by a. It is stable if

$$dD = a \, dY \tag{5}$$

Combining (4) and (5) we have

$$a \, dY = F + iD$$

So

$$a \, \frac{dY}{Y} \, Y = F + iD$$

Now dY/Y is the growth rate of income, which can be called g. Then

$$ag = \frac{F}{Y} + i \, \frac{D}{Y}$$

or

$$a \, (g - i) = \frac{F}{Y} \tag{6}$$

Equation (6) states the condition for stability of the ratio of public debt to income. It says that, when the rate of interest exceeds the growth rate, a government must run a primary fiscal surplus (i.e. a negative deficit) in order to stabilize the debt/income ratio. The surplus must be larger, the higher is the debt/income ratio. In other words, by allowing the public debt to grow in a high interest rate environment, a government condemns its citizens to having to run a high primary fiscal surplus at some future date when the debt situation is brought under control. At that future date, for any given ratio of non-interest public expenditure to national income, taxes must be higher as a share of national income. Alternatively, for any given ratio of tax to national income, non-interest public expenditure must be lower as a share of national income.

2. THE DEBT TRAP FACING DEVELOPING COUNTRIES: THE NEED FOR NEGATIVE RESOURCE TRANSFERS IN A WORLD OF HIGH REAL INTEREST RATES

The same argument as set out in the above section can be applied to a developing country. If we denote its exports by E and its non-interest current account balance (i.e trade balance or 'negative resource transfer', roughly) by T, condition (6) becomes

$$a\,(g - i) = \frac{T}{E}$$

This condition says that, when the growth rate of exports exceeds the rate of interest, a country can run a trade deficit (i.e. T is positive, there is debt incurral apart from interest payments) without its debt situation running out of control. But, when the rate of interest exceeds the rate of growth of exports, it must run a trade surplus to achieve the same end.

The condition also show how large the trade deficits and surpluses must be for particular values of the relevant variables. The algebra is expressed in terms of the debt/export ratio, but it is readily extended to include the debt/income ratio if the export/income ratio is assumed constant. If the debt/export ratio is 4 and the export/income ratio is 12.5 per cent (i.e. the debt/income ratio is 0.5), the growth rate of exports is 15 per cent and the rate of interest 5 per cent, the trade deficit can be 5 per cent of national income while the debt/income ratio remains stable. If, in contrast, the growth rate of exports is 5 per cent and the rate of interest 15 per cent, there has to be a trade surplus of the same size. In other words, the change in the growth/interest differential requires a resource shift equivalent to 10 per cent of national income to keep the debt position under control.

Notes

Notes to Introduction, pages 1–24

1 Michael Grant, *From Cleopatra to Alexander*, 1982, pp. 44–5.
2 Raymond W. Goldsmith, *Financial Structure and Development*, 1969, p. 40.
3 R. H. Campbell and A. S. Skinner (eds), *The Glasgow Edition of the Works and Correspondence of Adam Smith II. An Enquiry into the Nature and Causes of the Wealth of Nations*, 1976, vol. 1, p. 297.
4 Raymond W. Goldsmith, *Comparative National Balance Sheets, A Study of Twenty Countries, 1688–1978*, 1985, p. 43.
5 It should be emphasized that the strong conclusions reached here about the FIR are the author's own and not Goldsmith's. Goldsmith is careful not to derive grand generalizations from his work. In his view, FIRs reflect 'the complex interplay of numerous financial and non-financial factors' and 'A simple explanation of the level and movements of the FIRs is . . . hardly to be expected.' (*Comparative National Balance Sheets*, p. 61.).
6 David Hume, *Essays, Literary, Moral, and Political*, p. 213.
7 This notion surfaces repeatedly later in the book. It is the general concept of which the 'primary fiscal surplus' in chapters 1, 2 and 3, and the 'negative resource transfer' in chapters 4 and 5 are particular examples.
8 Donald Moggridge and Elizabeth Johnson (eds), *The Collected Writings of John Maynard Keynes*, 1972, vol. 9, pp. 153, 157.
9 Ibid., p. 158.
10 Hume, *Essays*, pp. 215–6.
11 B. V. Ratchford, in *Readings in Fiscal Policy*, eds Arthur Smithies and J. Keith Butters, 1955, pp. 463–4.
12 This is not to say that in the real world borrowers' and lenders' incomes grow at the same rate.
13 Prime rate is usually above inter-bank rate and the margin between them has widened since the beginning of the debt crisis. But they normally move together, if not necessarily by the same amount.

Notes to Chapter 1, pages 27–49

1 James M. Buchanan and Richard E. Wagner, *Democracy in Deficit*, 1977, pp. 9–10.
2 John Stuart Mill, in *Collected Works of John Stuart Mill*, 1965, vol. 3, p. 873.
3 C. F. Bastable, *Public Finance*, 1903, p. 611.
4 Ibid., p. 698.
5 Buchanan and Wagner, *Democracy in Deficit*, pp. 12–3.

6 Jacob E. Cooke, *Alexander Hamilton*, 1982, p. 154.
7 John W. Kearny, *Sketch of American Finances*, 1887, quoted in Buchanan and Wagner, *Democracy in Deficit*, pp. 12–13.
8 In fact, the USA's GNP rose rapidly by 36.6 per cent between 1932 and 1937 and exceeded the 1929 peak in 1939. (Thelma Leisner, *Economic Statistics 1900–1983*, 1985, p. 42.)
9 John Hicks, *The Crisis in Keynesian Economics*, 1974, p. 1.
10 Moggridge and Johnson reproduce the 1929 pamphlet *Can Lloyd George Do It?* and the 1983 essay on 'The means to prosperity' which contains a popular version of the multiplier analysis (Moggridge and Johnson, *The Collected Writings of John Maynard Keynes*, 1972, vol. 9).
11 Moggridge and Johnson, *The Collected Writings of John Maynard Keynes*, vol. 9, pp. 125, 146.
12 Ibid., pp. 128–9.
13 David Colander, 'Was Keynes a Keynesian or a Lernerian?', *Journal of Economic Literature*, 22 (1984), pp. 1572–5.
14 Herbert Stein, *The Fiscal Revolution in America*, 1969, p. 162.
15 Ibid., pp. 324–5. The previous quotation is from p. 298.
16 Stein, in his scholarly *The Fiscal Revolution in America*, inclines towards the view that the Eisenhower Government was different from its predecessors in the early twentieth century in that it did accept responsibility for the level of economic activity and employment. But Buchanan and Wagner argue, in *Democracy in Deficit*, that 'the label "pre-Keynesian" fits the Eisenhower politicians better than does its opposite' (p. 45).
17 Stein, *The Fiscal Revolution*, p. 432.
18 Ibid., p. 420.
19 Sir Herbert Brittain, *The British Budgetary System*, 1959, p. 53.
20 The phrase was used by Rowan in an article in the 1975 *Banca Nazionale del Lavoro Review*.
21 According to a Treasury press release of 21 November 1975 on 'Public Expenditure in 1974/75', debt interest payments were £800m more, in constant prices, in 1974–75 than was estimated in 1971. The release includes the extraordinary remark, 'There is no practical way of ensuring that an estimate of the future level of debt interest will be fulfilled.'
22 See, for example, Christopher Allsopp, *Oxford Review of Economic Policy*, 1 (Spring 1985), pp. 1–20.
23 Alfred Grosser, *Germany in Our Time*, 1974, p. 276. See also Nevil Johnson, *Government in the Federal Republic of Germany*, 1973, which mentions on p. 194 that 'the regulation of the money supply, a vital factor in post-war economic policy, has rested with the Federal Bank (later re-named the Bundesbank), whilst until the later sixties deficit spending by the state was firmly prohibted by both budgetary law and the powers of the Bank itself'.
24 Paul Johnson, *A History of the Modern World*, 1983, p. 596. According to Jack Hayward, *The One and Indivisible French Republic*, 1973, the mid-1960s saw a restoration of the finance ministry's traditional power due in part to 'the revival of the pre-Keynesian principle of the balanced budget. This aim was inspired by Jacques Rueff, an economist who had the ear of President de Gaulle.' One of Rueff's ideas – that public expenditure should not increase faster than GNP – was 'the prelude to the 1964 application of the aim of a balanced budget in the preparation of the 1965 budget' (p. 156).

25 Shepard B. Clough, *The Economic History of Modern Italy*, 1964, pp. 344–5.
26 Henry Kaufman, *Interest Rates, the Markets, and the New Financial World*, 1986, p. 29.
27 Paul Craig Roberts, *The Supply-Side Revolution*, 1984, pp. 80, 141.
28 Ibid., p. 87.
29 Ibid., pp. 48–56. Roberts identifies the Senate Republicans (of the 'Republican establishment') as among the main opponents of supply-side ideas.
30 Moggridge and Johnson, *The Collected Writings of John Maynard Keynes*, vol. 10, pp. 446–7.
31 Quoted in R. Shepherd, 'Lawson's words for eating', *Investors Chronicle*, 9 March 1984.
32 Samuel Brittan, 'No magic rule for setting budget deficits', *The Financial Times*, 28 November 1985.
33 This statement is not formally correct, because governments could run higher inflation rates and so reduce the real value of past debts. It is nevertheless a reasonable remark to make, particularly as the deliberate use of inflation for this purpose is not sustainable for ever.
34 This should not be taken as a recommendation that governments fix artificially low interest rates on their debt and then force financial institutions to hold it. It is instead an approval of attempts to influence investor expectations favourably and so help debt sales.
35 Again quoted by Shepherd, *Investor's Chronicle*, 9 March 1984.
36 David Stockman, *The Triumph of Politics*, 1986, p. 99.

Notes to Chapter 2, pages 50–79

1 James O'Connor, *The Fiscal Crisis of the State*, 1973, p.2, quoted in Daniel Bell, *The Cultural Contradictions of Capitalism*, 1976, pp. 221–2.
2 The phrase comes from Bell, *Cultural Contradictions of Capitalism*, p. 220, where it is said to have originated, rather ominously, from 'German and Austrian sociological economists in the 1920s'.
3 Samuel Brittan, *The Role and Limits of Government*, 1983, p. 4.
4 D. Lascelles, 'The $100b. a day market', *The Financial Times*, 4 August 1986.
5 The facts and figures here, and in the next few paragraphs, are taken from *Economic Report of the President 1986*.
6 Benjamin Friedman, in *The American Economy in Transition*, ed. Martin Feldstein, 1980, p. 18. This article also has a good discussion of the stability of the overall debt/income ratio in the USA.
7 The primary balance was in deficit in calendar 1967, but fiscal 1968.
8 These figures, and many more in the next few paragraphs, are taken from Chouraqui, Jones and Montador, *OECD Working Paper no. 30*, 1986. The information on gross and net public debt is given on pp. 9–10.
9 Bell, *Cultural Contradictions of Capitalism*, p. 235. The idea is, of course, a commonplace. For a good discussion of an aspect of excessive expectations, namely the irreconcilability of full employment with both inflation control and free collective bargaining, see the first essay in Peter Jay, *The Crisis for Western Political Economy*, 1984.
10 Deepak Lal and Martin Wolf, *Stagflation, Savings and the State*, 1986, p. 245.

11 See Gavyn Davies, 'Debt pessimists should not scare Lawson', *Financial Weekly*, 12–18 July 1985, and the reply, Tim Congdon, 'Heresy of worshipping the national debt', *Financial Weekly*, 26 July–1 August 1985. The debate followed an earlier exchange in *The Times*, with Davies, 'The jobs debt we can afford' of 1 August 1985, responding to Congdon, 'Jobs: avoiding the spending trap' of 19 June. The issue was clarified by Congdon in an L. Messel & Co. paper, *The Debt Trap: A Sequel*, of 15 August 1985. The root of the problem is that the primary fiscal balance can be defined inclusive or exclusive of tax on debt interest. The appropriateness of the post- or pre-tax rate of interest depends on which definition is used.

12 Even modern governments indulge in fiscal expedients of this kind. In July 1986 the Brazilian government introduced a system of 'compulsory loans', applied at a rate of 30 per cent on new cars and 28 per cent on car fuels. The loans were to be 'repaid' three years later with shares, not cash. A dispute arose about whether the 'loans' should be fully inflation-adjusted. They are evidently a tax, but with extra administrative hassle. ('Inflation row splits Sarney advisers', *The Financial Times*, 6 August 1986.)

13 The point is developed in more detail in Congdon, 'A new approach to the balance of payments', *Lloyds Bank Review*, October 1982.

14 It is interesting to note that, even after the doubling of the price level, the government remains in the debt trap if the increase in money GNP falls back to less than 10 per cent. However, it can escape by running a primary surplus. Because the public debt ratio has been halved, the needed primary surplus is smaller than would have been the case before the doubling of the price level.

   The example may seem extreme, but there is one such case known to the author. In July/August 1982 the Argentine government (apparently under the influence of something called the 'MIT–Dornbusch model') doubled the price level in order to halve the real value of debts, both public and private.

15 Leonard Hakim and Christine Wallich, 'Deficits, debt and savings structure and trends, 1965–81', in *Stagflation, Savings and the State*, p. 323.

16 The only comparable country is Switzerland.

17 Ford Madox Ford, *Some Do Not*, from the quartet *Parade's End*, 1982, p. 3.

18 Henry Neuberger, 'Turning the clock back?', in *The Economy and the 1983 Budget*, ed. John Kay, 1983, p. 46. Neuberger was developing ideas expressed in Marcus Miller, 'Inflation-adjusting the public sector financial deficit', in *The Economy and the 1982 Budget*, ed. John Kay, 1982, pp. 48–74.

19 For a rather different, but equally trenchant, rebuttal of the idea of inflation adjustment to nominal budget deficits, see Sir Alan Walters, *Britain's Economic Renaissance*, 1986, pp. 66–73.

20 This paragraph is a synopsis of Congdon, 'A challenge to public sector net worth', *The Times*, 1 March 1984. The article was written in response to John Hills, 'Public assets and liabilities', in Mark Ashworth, John Hills and Nick Morris, *Public Finances in Perspective*, 1984.

21 Robert Eisner and Paul J. Pieper, 'A new view of Federal debt and budget deficits', *American Economic Review*, (74) 1984, p. 23.

22 Mario Deaglio, 'Craxi's Italy', *The Banker*, October 1983, p. 36.

23 David Lane, 'Public borrowing weighs heavily', *The Banker*, August 1986, p. 99.

24 The point is explained in the algebraic appendix.

25 J. C. Chouraqui, Brian Jones and Robert Bruce Montador, *OECD Working Paper no. 30* p. 18.

26 Ibid., p. 18. The figures may be misleading because more industries are in public hands in Japan than in the USA and much of the borrowing may have been to finance their investment.

27 The projections turned out to be too optimistic. The Government's estimates of net debt interest for the 1986–7 financial year were £2b higher in the 1985 Expenditure White Paper than in the 1984 Expenditure White Paper. See Congdon, 'Does Mr. Lawson really believe in the medium-term financial strategy?', in *The Economy and the 1985 Budget*, ed. M. J. Keen, 1985, pp. 6–9.

28 US insurance companies subject to New York state rules are permitted to hold a large proportion of their assets in Canadian government debt, which is not deemed to be a 'foreign' investment.

29 Organization of Economic Cooperation and Development (OECD), *Economic Outlook*, December 1984, p. 33.

30 Chouraqui, Jones and Montador, *OECD Working Paper no. 30*, p. 14.

31 The point is developed in the algebraic appendix.

32 David Housego, 'National debt threat to France', *The Financial Times*, 18 June 1985.

33 David Stockman, *The Triumph of Politics*, 1986, pp. 130–1.

34 Ibid., p. 11.

35 Council of Economic Advisers, *Economic Report of the President 1986*, p. 339, table B–73.

36 Chouraqui, Jones and Montador, *OECD Working Paper no. 30*, p. 14. Their 'threshold level' of the primary budget balance depends on the public debt ratio and the size of the gap between interest rates on public debt and the economy's growth rate.

37 Most attempts to prove rigorously a connection between budget deficits and real interest rates are unsuccessful. See, for example, Paul Evans, 'Do large deficits produce high interest rates?', *American Economic Review*, 75 (1985), and John Tatom, 'Two views on the effects of government budget deficits in the 1980s', *Review of the Federal Reserve Bank of St. Louis*, October 1985. But this sceptical conclusion should not be accepted uncritically. So many factors influence interest rates that it may be impossible, in any case, to identify the independent effect of each.

Notes to Chapter 3, pages 80–103

1 Herbert Stein, *The Fiscal Revolution in America*, 1969, p. 368.

2 Robert J. Barro, 'Are government bonds net wealth?', *Journal of Political Economy*, 82 (1974).

3 The point is recognized by Paul Evans, 'Do large deficits produce high interest rates?', *American Economic Review*, 75 (1985), p. 86.

4 James Tobin, 'The monetary–fiscal mix: long-run implications', *American Economic Review: Papers and Proceedings of the American Economic Association*, 76 (1986), p. 213.

5 Ibid., p. 217.

6 See above, p. 00.

7 Milton Friedman, 'Letters to the Editor: monetarist as supply-sider', *The Wall Street Journal*, 4 September 1984.

8 M. Monti and B. Siracusano, *The Public Sector's Financial Intermediation, the Composition of Credit and the Allocation of Resources*, 1980, p. 15.
9 Organization of Economic Cooperation and Development (OECD), *Economic Outlook*, December 1985, p. 29.
10 OECD, *Economic Outlook*, May 1986, p. 176.
11 Leonard Hakim and Christine Wallich, 'Deficits, debt and savings structure', in *Stagflation, Savings and the State*, eds Deepak Lal and Martin Wolf, 1986, p. 348.
12 Michael T. Belongia and R. Alton Gilbert, 'The farm credit crisis', *Review of Federal Reserve Bank of St. Louis*, December 1985.
13 These figures are taken from Council of Economic Advisers, *Economic Report of the President 1982*, pp. 310–11.
14 Volcker's predecessor as Chairman of the Federal Reserve was G. William Miller of whom it has been said that he 'decided that independence of the Fed was something to describe in textbooks but had no meaning in the real world' and who has been described as 'a tool of the Carter administration'. Michael K. Evans, *The Truth about Supply-Side Economics*, 1983, p. 65.
15 Michael K. Evans, *The Truth about Supply-Side Economics*, pp. 102–3.
16 'Trying to bring the Fed to heel', *Business Week*, 4 August 1986.
17 See, for example, Allen Sinai, 'The US budget: progress, but not enough', *Amex Bank Review*, June 1987.
18 'Reagan hails plan on tax and hints cuts for military', *The New York Times*, 8 December 1984.
19 Figures are derived from *Federal Reserve Bulletin*, various issues.
20 Internation Monetary Fund, *World Economic Outlook*, 1986, p. 115.
21 Morgan Guaranty, 'Exchange markets and the US external deficit', *World Financial Markets*, January 1986, p. 10.
23 OECD, *Economic Outlook*, May 1986, p. 42.
23 Ibid., p. 42. See also, J. C. Chouraqui, Brian Jones and Robert Bruce Montador, 'Public debt in a medium-term perspective', *OECD Economic Studies*, 5 (Autumn 1986).
24 R. H. Campbell and A. S. Skinner (eds), *The Glasgow Edition of the Works and Correspondence of Adam Smith II. An Inquiry into the Nature and Causes of the Wealth of Nations*, 1976, vol. 2, p. 928.
25 See Thomas J. Sargent, 'The ends of four big inflations', in *Inflation: Causes and Effects*, ed. Robert E. Hall, 1982, pp. 41–97, for some examples of rapid recovery from financial chaos.
26 The gap between the average deposit rate and the average borrowing rate in the Italian banking system was 6.31 per cent in 1986, one of the highest in the industrial world. See David Lane, 'No room for complacency', *The Banker*, August 1987, pp. 34–9.

Notes to Chapter 4, pages 107–130

1 See, for example, Harold Lever and Christopher Huhne, *Debt and Danger*, 1985, p. 11. Lever and Huhne's book can be regarded as an extended critique of resource transfers from developing countries to developed.
2 World Bank, *World Development Report*, 1985, p. 22.
3 Brian Kettell and George Magnus, *The International Debt Game*, 1986, p. 53.

4 World Bank, *World Development Report*, p. 24.
5 Clifford Dammers, 'A brief history of sovereign defaults and rescheduling', in *Default and Rescheduling*, ed. David Suratgar, 1984, p. 77.
6 Norman St. John-Stevas (ed.), *The Collected Works of Walter Bagehot*, 1978, vol. 10, p. 423.
7 Dammers, 'A brief history of sovereign defaults and rescheduling', p. 81.
8 World Bank, *World Development Report*, p. 16.
9 Charles P. Kindleberger, *A Financial History of Western Europe*, 1984, p. 390.
10 David Lomax, *The Developing Country Debt Crisis*, 1986, p. 31, based on OECD, *Development Co-operation, 1983 Review*.
11 Kettell and Magnus, *The International Debt Game*, p. 53.
12 Lomax, *The Developing Country Debt Crisis*, p. 31.
13 The term 'spread banking' seems to have been invented by Henry Kaufman. See, for example, Henry Kaufman, *Interest Rates, the Markets, and the New Financial World*, 1986, p. 43.
14 Quoted in Lever and Huhne, *Debt and Danger*, p. 53.
15 World Bank, *World Development Report*, pp. 46–7.
16 Jonathan Hakim, 'Latin America's financial crisis: causes and cures', in *Latin America and the World Recession*, ed. Esperanza Duran, 1985, p. 22.
17 It should be said that there are difficulties reconciling the figure of $106b net transfer to Latin America with the official data on the Latin American balance of payments. The cumulative trade deficit between 1976 and 1981 was much less than $106b. As we shall see later, capital outflows are part of the explanation for the discrepancy.
18 Morgan Guaranty, 'Global debt: assessment and long-term strategy', June 1983, p. 3.
19 Ibid., p. 3.
20 Morgan Guaranty, 'Global debt: assessment and prescriptions', *World Financial Markets*, February 1983, pp. 3–4.
21 International Monetary Fund (IMF), *World Economic Outlook*, 1985, p. 239.
22 David Lomax, 'The recycling folly', *The Banker*, August 1982, p. 89.
23 Lever and Huhne, *Debt and Danger*, p. 62.
24 Inter-American Development Bank (IDB), *Economic and Social Progress in Latin America: The External Sector*, 1982, p. 74.
25 Deepak Lal and Martin Wolf (eds), *Stagflation, Savings and the State*, 1986, p. 252.
26 Quoted in Lever and Huhne, *Debt and Danger*, p. 57.
27 Lomax, *The Developing Country Debt Crisis*, p. 59.
28 World Bank, *World Development Report*, pp. 46–7.
29 IDB, *The External Sector*, p. 40.
30 IDB, *Economic and Social Progress in Latin America: Economic Integration*, 1984, p. 30.
31 Alan Gelb, in *Stagflation, Savings and the State*, p. 123.
32 Lomax, *The Developing Country Debt Crisis*, p. 59.
33 IDB, *Economic Integration*, p. 30.
34 IDB, *The External Sector*, p. 44.
35 IDB, *Economic and Social Progress in Latin America: External Debt Crisis and Adjustment*, 1985, p. 66.
36 World Bank, *World Development Report*, p. 64.

37 An exception is the Chilean government's refusal in 1980 and 1981 to give guarantees on foreign loans to its financial institutions. However, when these institutions were unable to service their debts properly in late 1982, the state was forced – by the international banks – to assume responsibility for them. (The banks even tried, for a time, to make the Chilean government assume responsibility for foreign loans to non-financial companies.) As the potential sanctions against a small country with an internationally much disliked military government would have been difficult to resist, the Chilean government did accept responsibility, even though this was contrary to the original terms of the contracts. This is perhaps one of the most dishonourable episodes in modern banking.

38 T. G. Congdon, *Economic Liberalism in the Cone of Latin America*, 1985, p. 91.

39 Joseph Conrad, *Nostromo*, 1982, p. 199.

40 Octavio Paz, 'After the cultural delirium', *Encounter*, July/August 1986, pp. 63–4.

41 Morgan Guaranty, 'LDC prospects and the role of the IMF', *World Financial Markets*, September 1980, p.6.

Notes to Chapter 5, pages 131–161

1 Quoted by Philip O'Brien, 'The debt cannot be paid: Castro and the Latin American debt', *Bulletin of Latin American Research*, 5 (1986), p. 48.

2 American Express Bank, *International Debt: Banks and the LDCs*, 1984, pp. 17, 52–3, 58–9, 119.

3 Ibid., p. 14.

4 IDB, *Economic and Social Progress in Latin America: External Debt Crisis and Adjustment*, 1985, p. 22.

5 Data supplied to the author by Mr Hector Luisi, IDB Representative in London.

6 IDB, *External Debt Crisis and Adjustment*, p. 39.

7 IDB, *Economic and Social Progress in Latin America: Economic Integration*, 1984, p. 28.

8 Morgan Guaranty, 'Strengthening the LDC debt strategy', *World Financial Markets*, September/October 1985, p. 7.

9 Morgan Guaranty, 'Growth and financial market reform in Latin America', *World Financial Markets*, April/May 1986, p. 3.

10 R. Nazario, 'When inflation rate is 116,000%, prices change by the hour', *The Wall Street Journal*, European edition, 8 February 1985.

11 IDB, *External Debt Crisis and Adjustment*, p. 43.

12 These subjects are discussed in T. G. Congdon, *Economic Liberalism in the Cone of Latin America*, 1985, particularly in chapter 4.

13 Ronald I. McKinnon, *Money and Capital in Economic Development*, 1973, is the fullest development of his views.

14 Morgan Guaranty, 'Brazil: beyond the Cruzado Plan', *World Financial Markets*, August 1986, p. 1.

15 G. A. D. Emerson, 'Can Argentina turn the corner?', *The Banker*, August, 1986, p. 40.

16 *Latin American Economic Report*, 30 April 1987, p.2.

17 R. Coone, 'Argentine debt "needs different approach" ', *The Financial Times*, 18 August 1987.

18 Eduardo Cué, 'Argentine bankers in £78m. scandal', *The Times*, 30 September 1986.
19 Daniel Cohen, 'How to evaluate the solvency of an indebted nation', *Economic Policy*, November 1985, pp. 139–56.
20 Oliver Jean Blanchard, in *Financial Policies and the World Capital Market: the Problem of the Latin American Countries*, eds Petro Aspe Armella et al., 1983, pp. 187–97.
21 Chapter 4 in William R. Cline, *International Debt: Systemic Risk and Policy Response*, 1984, is recognized as the best discussion of this issue.
22 Quoted by Rudiger Dornbusch in 'On the consequences of muddling through the debt crisis', *The World Economy*, 7 (1984), pp. 147–8.
23 Anatole Kaletsky, *The Costs of Default*, 1985, p. 19.
24 *Latin American Economic Report*, 30 November 1986, p. 12.
25 *Latin American Economic Report*, 31 August 1986, p.3.
26 Mentioned by Stephany Griffith-Jones in 'Ways forward from the debt crisis', *Oxford Review of Economic Policy* 2 (Spring 1986), p. 49.
27 This is a theme of Kenneth W. Clements and Larry A. Sjaastad, *How Protection Taxes Exporters*, 1984.
28 Richard A. Debs et al., *Finance for Developing Countries*, 1987, p. 21. This publication also distinguishes between debt/debt swaps, debt/equity swaps and debt/peso swaps.
29 Morgan Guaranty, 'LDC debt: debt relief or market solutions?', *World Financial Markets*, September 1986, p. 11.

Notes to Chapter 6, pages 165–177

1 Citicorp Economic Services, 'Financial markets outlook – the leveraging of America', *US Economic and Financial Outlook*, 9 April 1986.
2 Caroline Bird, *The Invisible Scar*, 1966.
3 Council of Economic Advisers, Economic Report of the President 1974, p. 304.
4 John Steinbeck, *The Grapes of Wrath*, 1986, p. 41.
5 Margaret G. Myers, *A Financial History of the United States*, 1970, p. 313.
6 Milton Friedman and Anna Schwartz, *A Monetary History of the United States, 1867–1960*, 1963, p. 351.
7 Ray B. Westerfield, *Money Credit and Banking*, 1938, p. 707.
8 Benjamin M. Friedman, 'Postwar changes in the American financial markets', in *The American Economy in Transition*, ed. Martin Feldstein, 1980, p. 20.
9 Henry Kaufman, *Interest Rates, the Markets, and the New Financial World*, 1986, p. 186.
10 John Hughes, 'An industry in transition', in *US Thrifts and Housing Finance: Winds of Change*, supplement to *Euromoney*, June 1986, p. 2.
11 US Bureau of Census, Series C–25.
12 B. Friedman, in The American Economy in Transition, p. 18.
13 Michael T. Belongia and R. Alton Gilbert, 'The farm credit crisis: will it hurt the whole economy?', *Review of the Federal Reserve Bank of St. Louis*, December 1985, pp. 6–7.
14 Council of Economic Advisers, *Economic Report of the President 1985*, p. 343.
15 Michael T. Belongia and Kenneth C. Carraro, 'The status of farm lenders:

an assessment of Eighth District and national trends', *Review of the Federal Reserve Bank of St. Louis*, October 1985, p. 21.

Notes to Chapter 7, pages 178–192

1 Edward J. Kane, *The Gathering Crisis in Federal Deposit Insurance*, 1985, p. 91.
2 Jeffrey Tuchman, 'Living on borrowed time', *US Thrifts and Housing Finance* (supplement to *Euromoney*), June 1986, p. 21.
3 Henry Kaufman, *Interest Rates, the Markets, and the New Financial World*, 1986, p. 21.
4 Christopher Farrell with Gary Weiss, 'Credit card wars: profits are taking a direct hit', *Business Week*, 17 November 1986.
5 'FSLIC: Down but not out', *The Banker*, April 1987.
6 'Investing in US real estate 1986', advertising supplement to *The Wall Street Journal*, 7 April 1986, p. 8.
7 Ibid., pp. 13–14.
8 Cynthia Williams, 'End of the Texan mystique', *The Banker*, May 1987, p. 54.
9 Michael T. Belongia, 'The farm sector in the 1980s: sudden collapse or steady down-turn?', *Review of the Federal Reserve Bank of St. Louis*, November 1986, pp. 17–25, argues that underlying farm profitability has been in long-term decline since 1950. The apparent 'boom' of the 1970s was due to farmers' capital gains on land and was therefore principally a by-product of financial conditions. Equally, the 'bust' of the 1980s was due to the jump in interest rates and the disappearance of the capital gains, not a sudden change in the market for farm produce.
10 M. Kolbenschlag, 'The case for farm aid', *Euromoney*, November 1985, p. 105.
11 'US Farm Credit System posts loss of \$115m.', *The Wall Street Journal*, 6 May 1987; 'Farmers, FmHA discuss ways to ease debt burden', *USA Today*, 19 May 1986.
12 'The Feds to the rescue', *American Farming* (supplement to *The Economist*), 1 December 1984, p. 52.
13 'In the farm belt, the worst is over', *Business Week*, 18 May 1987.
14 Henry Kaufman, *Interest Rates, the Markets, and the New Financial World*, p. 102.
15 John D. Paulus, 'Corporate restructuring, "junk" and leverage: too much or too little?' in Morgan Stanley, *Economic Perspectives*, 12 March 1986; 'Corporate debt–equity ratios' in *Federal Reserve Bank of New York Quarterly Review*, Summer 1985.
16 'Coupon' refers to the interest payment on a bond.
17 'A recession might hit junk-bond issuers between the eyes', *Business Week*, 20 July 1987.
18 Bank Credit Analyst, *Investment and Business Forecast*, April 1986, p. 33.
19 Ibid., p. 36.
20 D. J. Danker and M. M. McLaughlin, 'Profitability of insured commercial banks in 1984', *Federal Reserve Bulletin*, November 1985.
21 'An S & L whodunit where everyone's a suspect', *Business Week*, 13 July 1987.

Notes to Chapter 8, pages 195–215

1 R. A. Gilbert, C. C. Stone and M. E. Trebling, 'The new bank capital adequacy standards', *Review of Federal Reserve Bank of St. Louis*, May 1985, p. 15.

2 OECD, 'International capital markets: historical series', *Financial Market Trends*, March 1984, p. 141, and OECD, 'Highlights', *Financial Market Trends*, June 1986, p. 5.

3 Tim Congdon, 'Securitisation: its meaning, causes and significance', to be published in *Securitisation in International Debt Markets*, ed. Michael P. Lee, 1988.

4 *US Thrifts and Housing Finance: Winds of Change*, supplement to Euromoney, June 1986, p. 25.

5 J. Walmsley, 'Risk and reward on Wall Street', *The Banker*, January 1986, p. 36, citing the views of the First Manhattan Consulting Group.

6 Stephen Taylor, 'Australia's debt-ridden grain farmers reap a bitter harvest', *The Times*, 11 May 1987.

7 Richard Long, 'Lange caught in rural crossfire', *The Times*, 13 August 1987.

8 *Latin American Economic Report*, 31 August 1986, p. 1.

9 'Exchange and trade liberalization predominated in developing countries in '86', *IMF Survey*, 27 July 1987, p. 231.

10 International Monetary Fund, *World Economic Outlook*, April 1986, p. 83.

11 IMF, *World Economic Outlook*, April 1987, p. 21.

12 Katharine Campbell, 'A skeptic's guide to derivative products', *Intermarket*, October 1987.

13 Henry Thornton, *An Equiry into the Nature and Effects of the Paper Credit of Great Britain*, 1978, p. 259.

14 Harold James, *The German Slump: Politics and Economies 1924–36*, 1986, p. 2.

List of Sources

Introduction

Campbell, R. H. and Skinner, A. S. (eds) 1976: *The Glasgow Edition of the Works and Correspondence of Adam Smith II. An Inquiry into the Nature and Causes of the Wealth of Nations* (originally published 1776). Oxford: Clarendon Press.

Goldsmith, Raymond W. 1969: *Financial Structure and Development*. New Haven and London: Yale University Press.

Goldsmith, Raymond W. 1985: *Comparative National Balance Sheets. A Study of Twenty Countries, 1688–1978*. Chicago and London: University of Chicago Press.

Grant, Michael 1982: *From Cleopatra to Alexander*. London: Weidenfeld and Nicholson.

Hume, David: *Essays, Literary, Moral, and Political*. London: Ward, Lock & Co.

Moggridge, Donald and Johnson, Elizabeth (eds) 1972: *The Collected Writings of John Maynard Keynes:* Vol. VIII, *The General Theory* (originally published 1936), vol. IX, *Essays in Persuasion* (1931), and vol. X, *Essays in Biography* (1933). London and Basingstoke: Macmillan.

Ratchford, B. V. 'The burden of a domestic debt', *American Economic Review*, 1942. Reprinted in Arthur Smithies and J. Keith Butters (eds) 1955: *Readings in Fiscal Policy*. London: Allen and Unwin, pp. 451–67.

The Debt Threat in the Industrial Economies

Allsopp, Christopher 'Assessment: monetary and fiscal policy in the 1980s', *Oxford Review of Economic Policy*, 1 (Spring 1985), pp. 1–19.

Ashworth, Mark, Hills, John and Morris, Nick 1984: *Public Finances in Perspective*. London: Institute for Fiscal Studies.

Barro, Robert J. 'Are government bonds net wealth?', *Journal of Political Economy*, 82 (1974), 1095–117.

Bastable, C. F. 1903: *Public Finance* (3rd edn). London: Macmillan.

Bell, Daniel 1976: *The Cultural Contradictions of Capitalism*. New York: Basic Books.

Belongia, Michael T. and Gilbert, R. Alton 'The farm credit crisis: will it hurt the whole economy?', *Review of the Federal Reserve Bank of St. Louis* (December 1985), pp. 5–15.

Brittain, Sir Herbert 1959: *The British Budgetary System*. London: Allen and Unwin.

Brittan, Samuel 1983: *The Role and Limits of Government*. London: Temple Smith.

Brittan, Samuel 'No magic rule for setting budget deficits', *The Financial Times*, 28 November 1985.

Buchanan, James M. and Wagner, Richard E. 1977: *Democracy in Deficit*. New York, San Francisco and London: Academic Press.

Chouraqui, J. C., Jones, Brian and Montador, Robert Bruce 1986: 'Public debt in a medium-term context and its implications for policy, *OECD Working Paper no. 30*. Paris: Organization for Economic Cooperation and Development.

Chouraqui, J. C., Jones, B. and Montador, Robert Bruce 'Public debt in a medium-term perspective', *OECD Economic Studies*, 5 (1986), pp. 103–53.

Clough, Shepard B. 1964: *The Economic History of Modern Italy*. New York and London: Columbia University Press.

Colander, David 'Was Keynes a Keynesian or a Lernerian?', *Journal of Economic Literature* 22 (1984), pp. 1572–5.

Congdon, Tim 'A new approach to the balance of payments', *Lloyds Bank Review* 146 (1982), pp. 1–14.

Congdon, Tim 'A challenge to public sector net worth', *The Times*, 1 March 1984.

Congdon, Tim 'Jobs: avoiding the spending trap', *The Times*, 19 June 1985.

Congdon, Tim 'Heresy of worshipping the national debt', *The Financial Weekly*, 26 July–1 August 1985.

Congdon, Tim 'Does Mr. Lawson really believe in the medium-term financial strategy?', in M. J. Keen (ed.) 1985 *The Economy and the 1985 Budget*. Oxford: Basil Blackwell.

Congdon, Tim 1985: *The Debt Trap: a Sequel*. London: L. Messel & Co.

Cooke, Jacob E. 1982: *Alexander Hamilton*. New York: Charles Scribner's Sons.

Council of Economic Advisers 1982: *Economic Report of the President*. Washington: US Government Printing Office.

Council of Economic Advisers 1986: *Economic Report of the President*. Washington: US Government Printing Office.

Davies, Gavyn 'Debt pessimists should not scare Lawson', *The Financial Weekly*, 12–18 July 1985.

Davies, Gavyn 'The jobs debt we can afford', *The Times*, 1 August 1985.

Deaglio, Mario 'Craxi's Italy', *The Banker*, October 1983, pp. 35–9.

Eisner, Robert and Pieper, Paul J. 'A new view of the Federal debt and the budget deficits, *American Economic Review*, 74 (1984), pp. 11–29.

Evans, Michael K. 1983: *The Truth about Supply-Side Economies*. New York: Basic Books.

Evans, Paul 'Do large deficits produce high interest rates?', *American Economic Review*, 75 (1985), pp. 68–87.

Ford, Ford Madox 1982: *Some Do Not*, from the quartet *Parade's End*. Harmondsowrth: Penguin Books (originally published 1924).

Friedman, Benjamin M. 'Postwar changes in the American financial markets', in Martin Feldstein (ed.) 1980: *The American Economy in Transition*. Chicago and London: University of Chicago Press.

Friedman, Milton 'Letters to the Editor, monetarist as supply-sider', *The Wall Street Journal*, 4 September 1984.

Grosser, Alfred 1974: *Germany in Our Time*. Harmondsworth: Pelican Books.

Hakim, Leonard and Wallich, Christine 'OECD deficits, debt and savings structure and trends 1965–81: a survey of the evidence', in Deepak Lal and Martin Wolf (eds) 1986: *Stagflation, Savings and the State*. New York and Oxford: Oxford University Press for the World Bank, pp. 292–360.

Hayward, Jack 1973: *The One and Indivisible French Republic*. London: Weidenfeld and Nicholson.

Hicks, John 1974: *The Crisis in Keynesian Economics*. Oxford: Basil Blackwell.

Housego, David 'National debt threat to France', *The Financial Times*, 18 June 1985.

International Monetary Fund 1986: *World Economic Outlook*. Washington: IMF.

Jay, Peter 1984: *The Crisis for Western Political Economy*. London: Andre Deutsch.

Johnson, Nevil 1973: *Government in the Federal Republic of Germany*. Oxford: Pergamon Press.

Johnson, Paul 1983: *A History of the Modern World*. London: Weidenfeld and Nicholson.

Kaufman, Henry 1986: *Interest Rates, the Markets, and the New Financial World*. New York: Times Books.

Kearny, John W. 1887: *Sketch of American Finances, 1789–1835*. New York: Greenwood Press.

Lal, Deepak and Wolf, Martin 'Debt, deficits distortions', in Deepak Lal and Martin Wolf (eds) 1986: *Stagflation, Savings and the State*. New York and Oxford: Oxford University Press for the World Bank, pp. 239–91.

Lane, David 'Public borrowing weighs heavily', *The Banker*, August 1986, pp. 97–103.

Lane, David 'No room for complacency', *The Banker*, August 1987, pp. 34–9.

Lascelles, D. 'The $100b. a day market', *The Financial Times*, 4 August 1986.

Liesner, Thelma 1985: *Economic Statistics 1900–1983*. London: The Economist Publications.

Mill, John Stuart 1965: *Principles of Political Economy* (originally published 1848), vol. 3 in *Collected Works of John Stuart Mill*. Toronto and London: University of Toronto Press and Routledge and Kegan Paul.

Miller, Marcus 'Inflation-adjusting the public sector deficit', in John Kay (ed.) 1982: *The 1982 Budget*. Oxford: Basil Blackwell, pp. 48–74.

Moggridge, Donald and Johnson, Elizabeth (eds) 1972: *The Collected Writings of John Maynard Keynes*: vol. VIII, *The General Theory* (originally published 1936), vol. IX, *Essays in Persuasion* (1931) and vol. X, *Essays in Biography* (1933), London and Basingstoke: Macmillan.

Monti, M. and Siracusano, B. 1980: *The Public Sector's Financial Intermediation, the Composition of Credit and the Allocation of Resources*. Tilburg: Société Universitaire Européenne de Réchèrches Financières.

Morgan Guaranty Trust Company of New York 'Exchange markets and the US external deficit', *World Financial Markets*, January 1986.

Neuberger, Henry 'Turning the clock back?' in John Kay (ed.) 1983: *The Economy and the 1983 Budget*. Oxford: Basil Blackwell, pp. 43–53.

O'Connor, James 1973: *The Fiscal Crisis of the State*. New York: St Martin's Press.

Organization of Economic Cooperation and Development, *Economic Outlook*, December 1984, Paris: OECD.

Organization of Economic Cooperation and Development, *Economic Outlook*, December 1985, Paris: OECD.

Organization of Economic Cooperation and Development, *Economic Outlook*, May 1986, Paris: OECD.

Roberts, Paul Craig 1984: *The Supply-Side Revolution*. Cambridge, Massachusetts, and London: Harvard University Press.

Sargent, Thomas J. 'The end of four big inflations', in Robert E. Hall (ed.) 1982. *Inflation: Causes and Effects*. Chicago and London: University of Chicago Press, for National Bureau of Economic Research.

Shepherd, R. 'Lawson's words for eating', *Investor's Chronicle*, 9 March 1984.

Sinai, Allen 'The US budget: progress, but not enough', *Amex Bank Review*, June 1987.

Stein, Herbert 1969: *The Fiscal Revolution in America*. Chicago and London: University of Chicago Press.

Stockman, David 1986: *The Triumph of Politics*. New York: Harper and Row.

Tatom, John 'Two views of the effects of government budget deficits in the 1980s', *Review of the Federal Reserve Bank of St. Louis*, October 1985, pp. 5–16.

Tobin, James 'The monetary–fiscal mix: long-run implications', *American Economic Review: Papers and Proceedings of the American Economic Association*, 76 (1986), pp. 213–18.

Walters, Sir Alan 1986: *Britain's Economic Renaissance*. Oxford: Oxford University Press.

The Debt Threat to the Third World

American Express Bank 1984: *International Debt: Banks and the LDCs*. London: American Express Bank.

Blanchard, Olivier Jean 'Debt and the current account deficit in Brazil', in Petro Aspe Armella et al. (eds) 1983: *Financial Policies and the World Capital Market: the Problem of the Latin American Countries*. Chicago and London: University of Chicago Press.

Clements, Kenneth W. and Sjaastad, Larry A. 1984: *How Protection Taxes Exporters*. London: Trade Policy Research Centre.

Cline, William R. 1984: *International Debt: Systemic Risk and Policy Response*. Cambridge, Massachusetts, and London: MIT Press, for the Institute for International Economics.

Cohen, Daniel 'How to evaluate the solvency of an indebted nation', *Economic Policy*, November 1985, pp. 139–156.

Congdon, T. G. 1985: *Economic Liberalism in the Cone of Latin America*. London: Trade Policy Research Centre.

Conrad, Joseph 1982: *Nostromo*. Harmondsworth: Penguin Books (originally published 1904).

Coone, R. 'Argentine debt needs different approach', *The Financial Times*, 18 August 1987.

Cué, Eduardo 'Argentine bankers in £78m. scandal', *The Times*, 30 September 1986.

Dammers, Clifford 'A brief history of sovereign defaults and rescheduling', in David Suratgar (ed.) 1984: *Default and Rescheduling*. London: Euromoney Publications.

Debs, Richard A., Roberts, David L. and Remonola, Eli M. 1987: *Finance for Developing Countries*. New York and London: Group of Thirty.

Dornbusch, Rudiger 'On the consequences of muddling through the debt crisis', *The World Economy*, 7 (1984), pp. 145–61.

Emerson, G. A. D. 'Can Argentina turn the corner?', *The Banker*, August 1986, pp. 39–41.

Gelb, Alan 'The oil syndrome: adjustment to windfall gains in developing countries', in D. Lal and M. Wolf (eds): *Stagflation, Savings and the State*, pp. 115–30.

Griffith-Jones, Stephany 'Ways forward from the debt crisis', *Oxford Review of Economic Policy*, 2 (Spring 1986), pp. 39–61.

Hakim, Jonathan 'Latin America's financial crisis: causes and cures', in Esperanza Duran (ed.) 1985: *Latin American and the World Recession*. Cambridge: Cambridge University Press.

Inter-American Development Bank 1982: *Economic and Social Progress in Latin America: The External Sector*. Washington: IDB.

Inter-American Development Bank 1984: *Economic and Social Progress in Latin America: Economic Integration*. Washington: IDB.

Inter-American Development Bank 1985: *Economic and Social Progress in Latin America: External Debt Crisis and Adjustment*. Washington: IDB.

Inter-American Development Bank 1986: *Economic and Social Progress in Latin America: Agricultural Development*. Washington: IDB.

International Monetary Fund 1985: *World Economic Outlook*. Washington: IMF.

Kaletsky, Anatole 1985. *The Costs of Default*. New York: Priority Press, for Twentieth Century Fund.

Kaufman, Henry 1986: *Interest Rates, the Markets, and the New Financial World*. New York: Times Books.

Kettell, Brian and Magnus, George 1986: *The International Debt Game*. London: Graham & Trotman.

Kindleberger, Charles P. 1984: *A Financial History of Western Europe*. London: Allen and Unwin.

Lal, Deepak and Wolf, Martin 'Debts, deficits and distortions', in Deepak Lal and Martin Wolf (eds) 1986: *Stagflation, Savings and the State*. New York and Oxford: Oxford University Press, for the World Bank, pp. 239–91.

Latin American Economic Report, several issues, dates as referenced. London: Latin American Newsletters.

Lever, Harold and Huhne, Christopher 1985: *Debt and Danger*. Harmondsworth: Penguin Books.

Lomax, David 'The recycling folly', *The Banker*, August 1982, pp. 81–9.

Lomax, David 1986: *The Developing Country Debt Crisis*. Basingstoke and London: Macmillan.

McKinnon, Ronald I. 1973: *Money and Capital in Economic Development*. Washington, DC: Brookings Institution.

Morgan Guaranty Trust Company of New York 'LDC prospects and the role of the IMF', *World Financial Markets*, September 1980.

Morgan Guaranty Trust Company of New York 'Global debt: assessment and prescriptions', *World Financial Markets*, February 1983.

Morgan Guaranty Trust Company of New York 'Global debt, assessment and long term strategy', *World Financial Markets*, June 1983.

Morgan Guaranty Trust Company of New York 'Global debt: assessment and long-term strategy', *World Financial Markets*, September/October 1985.

Morgan Guaranty Trust Company of New York 'Strengthening the LDC debt strategy', *World Financial Markets*, September/October 1985.

Morgan Guaranty Trust Company of New York 'Growth and financial market reform in Latin America', *World Financial Markets*, April/May 1986.

Morgan Guaranty Trust Company of New York 'Brazil: beyond the Cruzado Plan', *World Financial Markets*, August 1986.

Morgan Guaranty Trust Company of New York 'LDC debt: debt relief or market solutions?', *World Financial Markets*, September 1986.

Nazario, R. 'When inflation rate is 116,000%, prices change by the hour', *The Wall Street Journal*, European edition, 8 February 1985.

O'Brien, Philip 'The debt cannot be paid: Castro and the Latin American debt', *Bulletin of Latin American Research*, 5 (1986), pp. 41–63.

Paz, Octavio, conversation with Jean-François Revel, 'After the cultural delirium', *Encounter*, July/August 1986, pp. 63–7.

St. John-Stevas, Norman 1978: *The Collected Works of Walter Bagehot*: vol. X, *The Economic Essays*. London: The Economist.

World Bank 1985: *World Development Report*. Washington: Oxford University Press, for the World Bank.

The Debt Threat to the American Private Sector

'An S & L whodunit where everyone's a suspect', *Business Week*, 13 July 1987.

Bank Credit Analyst, *Investment and Business Forecast*, April 1986.

Belongia, Michael T. and Carraro, Kenneth C. 'The status of farm lenders: an assessment of Eighth District and national trends', *Review of the Federal Reserve Bank of St. Louis*, October 1985, pp. 17–27.

Belongia, Michael T. and Gilbert, R. Alton 'The farm credit crisis: will it hurt the whole economy?', *Review of the Federal Reserve Bank of St. Louis*, December 1985, pp. 5–15.

Belongia, Michael T. 'The farm sector in the 1980s: sudden collapse or steady down-turn?', *Review of the Federal Reserve Bank of St. Louis*, November 1986, pp. 17–25.

Bird, Caroline 1966: *The Invisible Scar*. New York: David McKay Company.

Citicorp Economic Services 'Financial markets outlook – the leveraging of America', *US Economic and Financial Outlook*, 9 April 1986. New York: Citicorp Investment Bank, pp. 9–11.

Council of Economic Advisers 1974: *Economic Report of the President*. Washington: US Government Printing Office.

Council of Economic Advisers 1985: *Economic Report of the President*. Washington: US Government Printing Office.

Danker, D. J. and McLaughlin, M. M. 1985: 'Profitability of insured commercial banks in 1984', *Federal Reserve Bulletin* 71, 836–49.

Farrell, Christopher with Weiss, Gary, 'Credit-card wards: profits are taking a direct hit', *Business Week*, 17 November 1986.

Friedman, Benjamin M. 'Postwar changes in the American financial markets', in Martin Feldstein (ed.) 1980: *The American Economy in Transition.* Chicago and London: University of Chicago Press.

Friedman, Milton and Schwartz, Anna 1963: *A Monetary History of the United States, 1867–1960.* Princeton: Princeton University Press, for the National Bureau of Economic Research.

Hughes, John 'An industry in transition', in *US Thrifts and Housing Finance* (supplement to *Euromoney*), June 1986. London: Euromoney Publications, pp. 1–2.

Investing in US Real Estate '86, advertising supplement to *The Wall Street Journal*, 7 April 1986, pp. 5–16. Several authors, but no editor mentioned.

Kane, Edward J. 1985: *The Gathering Crisis in Federal Deposit Insurance.* Cambridge, Massachusetts, and London: MIT Press.

Kaufman, Henry 1986: *Interest Rates, the Markets, and the New Financial World.* New York: Times Books.

Kolbenschlag, M. 'The case for farm aid', *Euromoney*, November 1985, pp. 105–9.

Myers, Margaret G. 1970: *A Financial History of the United States.* New York and London: Columbia University Press.

Paulus, John 'D. 'Corporate restructuring, "junk" and leverage: too much or too little?', in Morgan Stanley, *Economic Perspectives*, 12 March 1986.

Steinbeck, John 1986: *The Grapes of Wrath* (originally published 1939). New York and Harmondsworth: Viking Penguin and Penguin.

'The Feds to the rescue', *American Farming* (supplement to *The Economist*), 1 December, 1984, pp. 47–52. No author mentioned.

Tuchman, Jeffrey 'Living on borrowed time', *US Thrifts and Housing Finance*, Euromoney Publications, pp. 21–3.

Westerfield, Ray B. 1938: *Money, Credit and Banking.* New York: Ronald Press Company.

Williams, Cynthia 'End of the Texan mystique', *The Banker*, May 1987, pp. 51–4.

The Debt Dilemma: a Global Perspective

Campbell, Katharine 'A skeptic's guide to derivative products', *Intermarket*, October 1987, pp. 13–19, 38.

Congdon, Tim 'Securitisation: its meaning, causes and significance', to be published in Michael P. Lee (ed.) 1988: *Securitisation in International Debt Markets.* London: Butterworth.

'Exchange and trade liberalization predominated in developing countries in '86', *IMF Survey*, 27 July 1987. Washington, DC: IMF.

Gilbert, R. A., Stone, C. C. and Trebling, M. E. 'The new bank capital adequacy standards', *Review of the Federal Reserve Bank of St. Louis*, May 1985, pp. 12–20.

'Highlights', in *Financial Market Trends*, June 1986. Paris: Organization of Economic Cooperation and Development, pp. 3–9. No author mentioned.

'International capital markets: historical series', in *Financial Market Trends*, March 1984. Paris: Organization of Economic Cooperation and Development, pp. 137–65. No author mentioned.

International Monetary Fund 1986: *World Economic Outlook.* Washington: IMF.

International Monetary Fund 1987: *World Economic Outlook*. Washington: IMF.

James, Harold 1986: *The German Slump: Politics and Economics 1924–36*. Oxford: Oxford University Press.

Long, Richard 'Lange caught in rural crossfire', *The Times*, 13 August 1987.

Taylor, Stephen 'Australia's debt-ridden grain farmers reap a bitter harvest', *The Times*, 11 May 1987.

Thornton, Henry 1978: *An Enquiry into the Nature and Effects of the Paper Credit of Great Britain* (originally published 1802). Fairfield, New Jersey: Augustus M. Kelley.

Walmsley, J. 'Risk and reward on Wall Street', *The Banker*, January 1986, citing the views of the First Manhattan Consulting Group.

Index

Index by Geoffrey C. Jones